THE NEW
brazil

THE NEW brazil

REGIONAL IMPERIALISM AND THE NEW DEMOCRACY

Raúl Zibechi

Translated by Ramor Ryan

The New Brazil: Regional Imperialism and the New Democracy
By Raúl Zibechi
Translation © 2014 Ramor Ryan
This edition © 2014 AK Press (Edinburgh, Oakland, Baltimore)

ISBN: 978-1-84935-168-3
e-ISBN: 978-1-84935-169-0
Library of Congress Control Number: 2013952051

AK Press	AK Press UK
674-A 23rd Street	PO Box 12766
Oakland, CA 94612	Edinburgh EH8 9YE
USA	Scotland
www.akpress.org	www.akuk.com
akpress@akpress.org	ak@akedin.demon.co.uk

The above addresses would be delighted to provide you with the latest AK Press
distribution catalog, which features several thousand books, pamphlets, zines,
audio and video recordings, and gear, all published or distributed by AK Press.
Alternately, visit our websites to browse the catalog and find out
the latest news from the world of anarchist publishing:
www.akpress.org | www.akuk.com
revolutionbythebook.akpress.org

Printed in the United States on recycled, acid-free paper.
Interior & Cover by Kate Khatib | www.manifestor.org/design
Based on the Editora Nacional Quimantú edition of the book,
designed by Fabian Flores.

Translator Ramor Ryan wishes to thank copyeditors Charles Weigl and Chuck
Morse, and Raúl Zibechi who offered assistance throughout. Additional thanks
goes to the following—Zach Blue, Luigi Alberto Carlos Celentano, Nancy
Lucita Serrano, Don Tomás de San Ramón, Shane O'Curry, James Mary Davis,
Ali Tonak, El Médico Lothar, Muireann de Barra, Harold Cudmore, Lauren,
Linda and Bobby.
Gracias compañer@s. And of course, ¡Visca Ixim13!

Contents

Introduction

The center-periphery relationship is a prison that was constructed with the bars of colonialism and reinforced by the rigid division of labor established by the capitalist world system. The jailers are the northern countries and multinational companies that, for five centuries, have enriched themselves with the expropriated labor and commons of the South. It would seem that the only way to break free from this oppressive and exploitative system is through an uninterrupted series of conflicts that shatter the locks and chains keeping people and peoples subjected.

Brazil is one of the few countries in the world that is escaping from the periphery. It has many things going for it: size, wealth, population, and above all, the political will necessary to turn capacities into deeds. It's not even enough to be the sixth largest economy in the world, or to be among the world's leaders in resources like hydropower, hydrocarbons, fresh water, biodiversity, biofuels, uranium, iron ore, and more. It's not enough because abundance, in itself, does not guarantee a nation's independence and sovereignty.

It will take great historical processes—and the removal of the center-periphery relationship is one of them—to change the way the system works. It's likely that capitalism cannot survive the breakup of the center-periphery structural link, which for 500 years has been the basis for the accumulation of capital and power by the ruling classes of the North, that 1 percent of humanity controlling the planet. However, deep changes like the reconfiguration of North-South relations involve diverse stakeholders with conflicting interests. It is likely that a handful of nations will emerge from the peripheries to become global powers, standing on the shoulders of the popular sectors of these countries themselves as well as their neighbors, which tend to become peripheries of the new powers.

If the center-periphery relationship was forged with the hot iron of colonialism, then it is possible that none of the emerging countries can escape their peripheral status without violent interstate conflict, even though the United States superpower is in no condition to unleash the kind of wars that made it a hegemonic power. Nevertheless, even in a period of acute economic decline, the United States still maintains significant military supremacy, which guarantees it at least the ability to blackmail its competitors, as it is doing indirectly with China and openly with Russia.

I think Brazil's rise to the status of a global power is an irreversible and conflictual process. First, because internal conditions have been maturing slowly since the 1930s, when the Getúlio Vargas regime began the industrialization process, promoting the formation of an industrial bourgeoisie and weakening the old agro-export oligarchy. Seven decades later, under the Lula government, this process may have reached the point of no return. With the expansion and strengthening of the ruling elites, the adoption of a strategy to make the country a global power, the solid alliance between the internationalized Brazilian bourgeoisie and the state apparatus (including the armed forces and state managers), and the maturity of the process of capital accumulation in Brazil, those ruling elites can take advantage of the relative decline of the United States and occupy spaces that intensify their hegemony in the country and the region. This allows a move on "empty" spaces like the Amazon, on other countries in South America and West Africa, regions recently opened up for "Brazilian" capital, its private and state banking system, its armed forces, and its civil bureaucracy.

It will be a contentious process because Latin America has always been the key region for United States global hegemony. In other words: the superpower cannot maintain its leading place in the world without reinforcing its dominance in the region, where the Caribbean, Mexico, and Central America are vital, as is South America. Washington faces its greatest challenges in South America, particularly in the Andean region as it becomes the hub of interstate social conflict. We cannot know how this conflict will develop, but the reactivation of the US Fourth Fleet by the Pentagon to operate around Central and South America, as well as the deployment of new military bases in Colombia and Panama, appear to anticipate the worsening of regional tensions. For US elites, it is clear that the only country capable of matching its hegemonic position is Brazil. For the Brazilian elites, it is increasingly clear that their main adversary is the superpower in the North.

Although this work shares a world-systems analytical perspective, it attempts to address the reality of Latin America from the viewpoint of social and antisystemic movements. It tries to understand Brazil's rise to the rank of global power as a process fraught with risks and opportunities for the popular sectors facing a reality in which both old alliances and the composition of the ruling classes are changing rapidly.

Understanding this process involves becoming acquainted with the new balance of power, the alliances the elite are weaving from above, the sectors they are incorporating into the power bloc and those that are marginalized in the new political and social scenario. The region is experiencing its third hegemonic transition to completely reconfigure regional dynamics and its relationship with the world beyond. The first hegemonic shift began around the first decade of the nineteenth century and lasted until the middle of the century, approximately between the 1804 Haitian Revolution and 1850. Or perhaps it can be dated earlier to 1780 and the revolutions led by Tupac Amaru and Tupac Katari. British domination followed that of the Spanish and Portuguese. Those variegated decades saw the rise of nation-states, the republics with which settlers brought local elites to power, and condemned the popular sectors—particularly Indians and blacks—to an even more miserable social position than in the colonial era.

Conservative and liberal parties were also formed during this era, political groupings that took turns administrating the new republics, creating new state bureaucracies, both civil and military, that were responsible for keeping those from below at bay, especially rural dwellers on the large estates, where power was exercised brutally. These landed oligarchies ruled by blood and fire for more than a century.

With the second hegemonic transition, which began in the early twentieth century and lasted until the end of the Second World War, the new power of the United States dethroned the British Empire. The industrial bourgeoisie displaced oligarchies by means of drastic measures (such as in Argentina or Bolivia) or more smoothly through the state (such as in Brazil), or sometimes by negotiation and agreement to safeguard the interests of all the ruling classes.

If during the first hegemonic transition popular sectors—Creole, mestizo, indigenous, or black—participated in the revolt, as *montoneras* or through other irregular forms of collective action, generally in the service of local chieftains, in the second transition, the emergence of organized workers in unions allowed the working class to make its mark on the new power configuration. During the same period, left-wing parties formed alongside various expressions of popular and revolutionary nationalism. Industrial development through import substitution—uneven across countries and regions—was lubricated by agreements between employers and unions, often with the support of the governments that created local and shoddy welfare states. Universal suffrage and the rights of free expression, assembly, demonstration, and elections replaced the dictatorial authoritarianism that characterized the oligarchic period.

In the previous two hegemonic transitions, which provide our only clues about what to expect in the transition currently under way, there were profound changes in the classes in power, in the system of alliances and government, in the political regime, and in the economic system. The position occupied by those from below until the imposition of the neoliberal model, ushered in by the military dictatorships of the 1960s and 1970s, was incomparably more solid than in the previous period. From a historical perspective, we see that the emergence of popular sectors was particularly intense during the period of independence, in the 1920s and 1940s, and during periods of hegemonic transitions.

Based on these considerations, I would like to highlight five aspects of the current period in which US hegemony in South America tends towards being displaced by Brazil.

1. *The current hegemonic transition is a tremendous opportunity to change the balance of power in favor of the popular sectors.* Transitions are brief periods where social movements set the tone, when ebullience, transformations, and rearrangements reconfigure reality, so that after a certain time, nothing remains in its original place.[1]

In the two previous hegemonic transitions there were two types of movements during the period of independence: in the first period, the Creoles, on the one hand, and the Indians and blacks on the other, with mestizos oscillating between two poles but definitely leaning towards the ruling classes; and in the second, the industrial bourgeoisie along with the middle classes and the working classes in the first half of the twentieth century. In the first period of transition, the lower classes (Indians and blacks) were crushed everywhere except in Haiti, whose triumphant revolution was ignored and isolated. In the second period of transition, the industrial workers, sometimes allied with the peasants, achieved notable successes in several countries, but the victories were then appropriated by other sectors that disfigured their revolutionary objectives. Everywhere, those from below converted themselves into a class conscious of their goals and organized to achieve them.

Despite fierce repression from dictatorships, the exploited and oppressed in Latin America have been able to delegitimize the neoliberal model and open cracks deep enough to form governments that oppose the Washington Consensus in most South American countries. Despite attempts by these progressive governments to co-opt and bewilder antisystemic movements, the cycle of struggles against the neoliberal model remains strong. It appears that in the coming years, up until the end of this hegemonic transition, movements from below will remain important players in shaping the new emerging powers.

Two major risks threaten the popular classes. In the long term, there is the risk of losing sight of their own independent project if they embrace the developmentalist project advocated by the bourgeoisie and ruling elites, a project that grants the oppressed a subordinate role, in exchange for less repression, and meager and conditional material gains. And in the short term, the popular classes run the risk of social and political isolation in the face of the powerful capitalist expansion and their own lack of clarity around how to relate to governments that proclaim themselves progressive and revolutionary.

2. *The birth of an intraregional hegemon for the first time in the history of Latin America represents an unprecedented challenge* because of the kind of relationships that the ruling classes tend to establish with the elites of other countries and peoples of the entire region. All hegemonic powers over five centuries have been extracontinental and were unable to conceal how their interests differed from those of the region. When the hegemon comes from the region itself, things are more complex.

First of all, cultural similarities tend to dilute the consciousness of oppression. Colonialism is by definition something from outside, alien to the colonized society. The difference and strangeness facilitates a quick perception of oppression. By contrast, the relative cultural proximity of the leaders and the popular sectors of the region's countries, alongside the prevalence of integration projects (such as Mercosur, UNASUR and CELAC) tend to limit the potential for conflict, or even an awareness that there are new elites and alliances in power. Many social movements in the region, and almost all of their bases, still have difficulty visualizing the historical leaders of the Workers' Party—such as Lula, and the leaders of the CUT—as part of the new oppressive and exploitative power elite.

Secondly, this presents a particularly difficult scenario for small South American countries, as their very survival as relatively autonomous states will be challenged in the coming decades. Vast swaths of Paraguayan, Bolivian, and Uruguayan borderlands have already been colonized by Brazilian entrepreneurs and migrants. In designing a regional integration project, Brazilian strategists have tried to avoid establishing bonds of domination with their neighbors. However, the logic of capital is not the same as the logic of government, as I hope to demonstrate in this book, and one transparent example of this dilemma is the tension between the Ecuadoran government and the Brazilian construction company Odebrecht.

Thirdly, it seems apparent that the popular sectors in the region will have fewer allies than in other periods when the enemies were distant empires. The new power structure establishes an extensive network of alliances between governments and businesses across the political spectrum, from the left of Evo Morales to the right of Juan Manuel Santos. It is necessary to understand the new global and regional geopolitics taking shape as the old power relationships are breaking apart. In some smaller South American countries, Brazil controls the economy, banking, business, part of the state through taxes paid by their companies, and even some social movements through the funding of social forums that never speak of Brazilian expansionism.

3. We still do not know if Brazilian power will manifest itself as a new imperialism. *There is no deterministic element that predetermines emerging countries to repeat the history of the European colonial powers.* There is the possibility, as Giovanni Arrighi points out in the case of China, for a peaceful rise to global power that opens a space among other countries for building a community of civilizations respectful of different cultures.[2]

But China is very different from Brazil. In China, a revolution led to extensive land reform, consolidating the unification of agricultural producers and the means of production, allowing for what has been referred to "accumulation without dispossession."[3] Nothing similar has happened elsewhere in the world, certainly not in Latin America, the most unequal region in world, or in Brazil, the world champion of inequality.

There are three tendencies that may prevent Brazil from becoming a new power center surrounded by peripheries. The most important is that a multipolar world, which appears to be in formation, imposes limits on any hegemony, thus creating a multiplicity of relatively equal power centers. This is a very unstable equilibrium that can induce concessions from large countries, and even smaller ones. The search for allies and the need to shield oneself from rivals forms part of the game of multiple equilibria. On the other hand, the United States will remain a great power in any future scenario, which means that Brazil must make major concessions. It will also have to deal with China as a counterweight and a competitor.

The second is that other countries in the region can limit the ambitions of the new power, as happened with Ecuador, which broke with Brazil and turned to China. Several other countries, such as Venezuela, Argentina, Chile, and Colombia, for different reasons, have the ability to resist Brazil's rise and to force negotiations. For now a tendency toward consensus reigns in intraregional relations, with the Brazilian Foreign Ministry assuming a role that oscillates between firmness and moderation. However, when dealing with vital interests like energy, Brazil may threaten to use force, as demonstrated by its military exercises on the Paraguayan border.

Thirdly, social movements also have the capacity to deter the new power. The most transparent example of this occurred in Bolivia in 2011, when a significant part of the local population mobilized against the construction of a road crossing the Isiboro Secure National Park and Indigenous Territory (TIPNIS)[4]. The construction of the highway is in Brazil's commercial and geopolitical interests, but negatively affects Bolivian indigenous peoples who, through mobilization and political action, won its temporary suspension. Something similar is occurring in Peru, where the energy agreement to construct several hydroelectric dams, signed by Alan Garcia and Lula, has been seriously questioned.

4. *There need to be alliances between the Brazilian popular classes and other Latin American peoples displaced and hurt by the Brazilian expansion.* The reasons for the popular rejection of the Belo Monte Dam in Brazil are the same as those at Inambari in Peru. The Brazilian state company Eletrobras aims to build eleven dams in Argentina, Peru, Bolivia, Colombia, and Uruguay with a total installed capacity of 26,000 MW, almost double that supplied by Itaipu in Brazil, which itself supplies 17 percent of Brazil's total energy consumption.[5]

In 2011, Brazilian multinationals repatriated $21.2 billion to Brazil, equivalent to the annual GDP of Paraguay.[6] A substantial portion of this was returned from Latin American countries, where the multinationals have their largest investments. These figures show that Brazilian capital is exploiting not just Brazilian people, but other Latin Americans too. They have, therefore, common interests that should lead to a coordinated struggle.

At this point, there are also new challenges. Large unions like CUT and Força Sindical are allies of domestic capital and will not act in solidarity with the oppressed of the region, as evidenced by the union's attitude during the construction workers' rebellions at various dams and toward the plight of the Indians affected by dams. In any case, the direction taken by the social and political struggles in Brazil will be crucial for the region, but ominously, social movements have noticeably declined in the last few years.

5. *The movements in the region are subject to multiple pressures and find themselves organizing in more complex and contradictory scenarios.* Social movement campaigns are accused of favoring the United States and the right-wing because their struggles weaken the left-wing governments. In turn, the same governments are responsible for co-opting and weakening the movements through the criminalization of their leadership and the implementation of extensive social policies to cushion the impact of the current extractive model. There are clear contradictions between the short and long term, between governments and movements, between economic growth and *buen vivir* (living life well).

The movements are attempting to confront these contradictions, but are not always successful. Nevertheless, one can point to a new cycle of struggle with a series of actions like the march in defense of TIPNIS in Bolivia in 2011, the struggle for water and against mining in Peru and Ecuador in 2012, the popular resistance against the Belo Monte dam, citizens' assemblies in Argentina, and the uprising in southern Chile against Hidroaysén. These new antisystemic movements are perhaps even more radically anticapitalist than previous struggles, inasmuch as they now question the developmentalist model and embrace the concept of *buen vivir* as their main ethical and political framework.

In the last two centuries, capitalism has appropriated the demands and desires of those from below in order to restore new and more refined forms of oppression, which, more recently, has come in the form of sophisticated goods and gadgets that capture the aspirations and inspirations of ordinary people. Movements need to address these issues, as well as other internal challenges. Inertia from below coupled with the cleverness of the ruling classes often pushes a dynamic social movement to establish itself as a formal organization, which inevitably softens its antisystemic edge and leads to an accommodation with the situation it was organizing against.

For this reason, each new cycle of protest and mobilization is a response to the legacies of the previous cycle. Old forms of resistance are rendered useless and are absorbed by the system. It is the cycle of life. What were once new shoots sprouting into fruits fall into decay and, over time, must be trimmed to renew growth. Time is cyclical, and so are antisystemic and emancipatory struggles. Nevertheless, the world of rebellions and revolutions has been so infiltrated by the culture of progress that it falls for political parties and organizations guided by a linear concept of time that preys upon life.

This book is dedicated to the new forces emerging in Latin America, to all the movements and acts of rebellion against current forms of oppression in mining, monoculture, large dams—and against the new imperialism. I started researching materials for this work twelve years ago, when compañer@s from the Uruguayan newspaper *Brecha* suggested I take charge of the weekly's international section. The seven years I spent on this task were key to perceiving all that was still unknown about Brazil's trajectory, and the need to understand it better. I became convinced that it was important for movements and militants to understand the implications of Brazil's rise to the global power as part of the changes happening in the world system. With that conviction, I wrote this book.

I thank the Uruguayan sociologist Gustavo Cabrera, of Londrina University, for his literary support for several years. For more than a decade, many people have contributed in various ways, sometimes unknowingly, to bring this book to completion, and I am deeply grateful to them all. Augustine was born the same year I started working on it and has been an attentive companion; Pola has played a gentle and decisive role.

Raúl Zibechi
Montevideo, March 2012

1
The Return of Sub-Imperialism

"The evolution of Latin American social science in recent years—despite the frequent recurrence of old errors—has progressed enough to invalidate one of the theses that I have tried to combat here: that the Brazilian military regime was a simple effect of the *deus ex machina* of US imperialism."
—*Ruy Mauro Marini*

On May 16, 2008, landless farmers from the militant San Pedro department, northern Paraguay, gathered outside the *hacienda* of a Brazilian settler who cultivated 30,000 hectares of genetically modified (GM) soy. They performed a ceremony that they called "second independence," and which included the governor-elect of San Pedro, José "Pakova" Ledesma, a deputy from the Authentic Radical Liberal Party (ally of newly elected President Fernando Lugo), and members of the Communist Party and the Homeless Movement. They read a manifesto calling for "an end to the destruction of forests, burning and extraction of trees, and the withdrawal of the security forces who create fear in the communities." They directed their denunciations towards President Lula, protesting the invasion of Brazilian companies "that have destroyed 75 percent of the native forest, and have expelled, uprooted, and killed peasants." The leader, Elvio Benitez, said: "We will maintain a full-on struggle against the Brazilians." The event concluded with the burning of the Brazilian flag.[1]

This seems strange. Thousands of United States flags have been burned in Latin America, to the point that it is no longer news because such actions have become commonplace in political and social struggles. But burning a Brazilian flag is something new. In Paraguay, the sense of undergoing a Brazilian invasion goes back a long way. It's a general and diffuse feeling, because the invasion is subtle rather than traditional, a matter of an incremental presence of Brazilians crossing the border, buying land, cultivating soy or raising cattle. Furthermore, the Itaipu Dam exports almost all the energy it produces to Brazil at prices below market value, something Paraguayans consider an affront.

The notion that a powerful country is taking over space in its smaller, and even medium-sized, neighbors has been growing steadily as Brazil becomes a power with global reach. In southern Peru, there have been protests in recent years against the construction of the Inambari hydroelectric project. In December 2009, hundreds of protesters blocked the Inambari River bridge linking the regions of Cusco, Puno, and Madre de Dios for two days. In the ensuing repression, three protesters were shot while *ronderos* captured and beat a security guard.[2]

The Puno Defense Coalition held a two-day strike against the hydroelectric project in March 2010, with the participation of much of the city, including all of the unions. Students took control of the university, hurled stones at the Puno government headquarters and a police patrol, and during the ensuing repression, protesters attempted to occupy the police precinct in order to free the detained.[3] The protest was so significant that the merchants and people of Puno, Ayaviri, Juli, and Yunguyo joined in—even the municipal authorities and regional president. A document released by the organizations that called the protest revealed that the Empresa de Generación Eléctrica Amazonas Sur (EGASUR)—comprised of the Brazilian OAS, Eletrobras, and Furnas companies—would invest $4 billion in the construction of a power plant on the Inambari river to produce 2,000 MW. The project includes the construction of a dam that will force the migration of some 15,000 people. It also puts the Bahuaja-Sonene National Park at serious risk.

On June 16, 2010, the governments of Peru and Brazil signed an agreement to supply electricity to Peru and export the surplus to Brazil.[4] The total potential of the five hydroelectric projects to be developed by Eletrobras will be 6,673 MW (at the present moment Peru consumes 5,000 MW), of which 90% will be exported to Brazil. The projects were developed by Eletrobras, whose investments benefit other Brazilian companies responsible for the construction work, such as Odebrecht, OAS, and Andrade Gutierrez. Peruvian companies like Electroperú are not involved in the process. In short, these are mega projects unnecessary for Peru, benefiting the Brazilian state and its private corporations, and in the process will cause serious environmental and social problems for Peru, particularly its indigenous people.[5]

In Bolivia, during the indigenous marches in defense of the Isiboro Secure National Park and Indigenous Territory (TIPNIS) between August 15 and October 19, 2011, slogans against Brazil and Brazilian companies could be heard. In major cities there were marches and blockades in response to the harsh police repression of September 25, triggering a political crisis with the resignation of ministers and senior officials. During the September 28 strike—culminating in a large rally descending from the city of El Alto to the Plaza Murillo in La Paz—a new slogan was heard: "Evo, lackey of Brazilian companies."[6] The Brazilian construction company OAS designed the controversial road to be built with a BNDES (Brazilian Development Bank) loan that was frozen during the protests.

In light of this dual offensive of capital and the Brazilian State in the region, it is not surprising that the concept of "sub-imperialism" has reappeared in political discussions and academic studies. Three decades after the publication of Ruy Mauro Marini's famous "World Capitalist Accumulation and Sub-imperialism," the concept is once again rigorously relevant.[7] In recent years, several studies have addressed the issue, and the media have picked up the notions of "sub-imperialism" and even "imperialism" in relation to Brazil's ascent. Conflicts generated by large Brazilian companies in small neighboring countries (Petrobras in Bolivia, Odebrecht in Ecuador, among others), have put Brazil's role in the region under the microscope.

In the following pages, I discuss the concept of "sub-imperialism" in light of Marini's original text and related papers published in recent years: *O subimperialismo brasileiro revisitado: a politica de Integração regional do governo Lula (2003–2007)* by Mathias Seibel Luce; *A teoria do subimperialismo brasileiro: notes para uma (re) discussão contemporânea,* by Fabio Bueno and Raphael Seabra; *O imperialismo brasileiro nos séculos XX e XXI: uma discussão teórica,* by Pedro Enrique Pedreira Campos; and *O Brasil e o capital imperialismo,* by Virginia Fontes.[8]

The political climate in Brazil during the 1970s

When Marini addressed Brazilian expansionism using the term "sub-imperialism," the country was under a military dictatorship that sought to turn it into a regional power allied to the United States. Marini was part of the Politica Operária (POLOP) revolutionary group. Formed in 1961, it was a pioneer organization of the Brazilian Marxist left, differentiating itself from the Brazilian Communist Party (PCB), which defended parliamentary legalism and collaborated with what they called a "national bourgeoisie." Various important revolutionary organizations later emerged from the POLOP nucleus, as did notable political and theoretical work.

Following the 1964 coup, Marini was forced into exile in Mexico and returned to Brazil twenty years later. His most important theoretical production, in which he develops his reflection on sub-imperialism, was written in exile: *Underdevelopment and Revolution* was published in Mexico in 1967, his most widely available work, with numerous editions including an expanded 1974 edition. In 1972, he published *Dialectics of Dependency* in Chile, where he played a militant role in the Revolutionary

Left Movement (MIR), and lived until the 1973 coup; in 1977, he wrote the article "World Capitalist Accumulation and Sub-Imperialism," again published in Mexico.

In those years of intense theoretical creativity and militant activity, the climate surrounding Latin American revolutionary thinkers is defined by the class struggle as well as the imperialist offensive by the United States and its close alliance with local elites to quell the Left and popular movements. In a brief autobiographical text, Marini pointed out that the theoretical production of activists of his generation would bear fruit only after the military coup of 1964, "when, their militancy curbed, the young Brazilian intellectuals would find time and conditions to devote themselves fully to academic work, which the situation in Latin America, ravaged by counterrevolution, in fact demanded."[9]

His efforts to differentiate his work from the PCB analysis, which asserted that the 1964 coup installed a "puppet" regime of the Pentagon and US State Department, led him to study the internal causes of the coup, related to some degree to the development of dependency capitalism. Marini thought that the explanation for a political phenomenon "is decidedly bad if it assumed that a key factor comes from outside."[10] He observed the peculiarities of the new regime, which he considered distinct from those installed by previous coups, emphasizing the merger between military leadership and the bourgeoisie, the export of manufactured goods and capital, and the direct intervention in surrounding countries, always in line with US imperialism, pursuing a massive project of national and regional reorganization.

Three decades later, the theoretical originality, political audacity, and serious analysis of Marini's work still shines. It seems necessary to stop for a moment and consider the concept of "sub-imperialism" to evaluate whether the passage of time—and changes in the world-system—has even partially modified his analysis.

Firstly, Marini considers the 1964 coup as "a response to the economic crisis that affected the Brazilian economy between 1962 and 1967, and the resulting intensification of the class struggle."[11]

It is not, however, a mechanical or economistic analysis because he always emphasizes—in line with Marx—class struggle, and uses it as an epistemological key to unlock reality. For this reason, he argues that the military elite leading the coup was intervening in the ongoing class struggle, merging their interests with those of big capital. Consequently, sub-imperialism is "the form taken by dependency capitalism in order to reach the stage of monopoly and finance capital."[12]

Secondly, this alliance between big capital and the military has somewhat different interests than those of empire, which is why he uses the term "antagonistic cooperation" to describe the relationship between Washington and Brasilia.[13] That alliance was created to unlock specific problems of dependency capitalism in Brazil. He explains that the core of the sub-imperialist solution implemented since 1964 is to solve a problem of the market that creates difficulties for the accumulation of capital in industry, Brazil's most dynamic sector. Indeed, because of the concentration of land ownership and the nature of social relations in the *latifundista* monoculture, the domestic market is unable to absorb industrial production, a difficulty that could only be resolved through land reform. That is the crux of the political crisis that caused the 1964 coup.

The contradictions between industry and the *latifundist* system were compounded by the external sector crisis that involved falling coffee prices in the 1950s, Brazil's main export product. The resulting trade deficit revealed one of the bottlenecks in the Brazilian economy and society. As Marini noted, the complementarity between the agricultural export sector and industry was shattered for two reasons: first, the redistribution that might have overcome the impasse had affected the surplus value of a section of the bourgeoisie; and secondly, the emergence of popular sectors (farmers, workers, students) took away all the maneuvering room for implementing reforms. "The depletion of the market for industrial products (...) can only be augmented through the reform of the agrarian structure."[14] The political radicalization of the social movement, which included the rebellion of sergeants and sailors, threatened the disintegration of the repressive apparatus, and was answered with the radicalization of the oligarchy, the bourgeoisie and its armed forces.

The coup was a reaction of that sector, and shows that the claim by the PCB that the "current military regime in Brazil is a result of external forces"[15] is wrong. The regime born of the coup resolves the structural problem by facing outward and toward foreign capital: through the export of manufactured goods and by means of state intervention via major infrastructure projects in transport, electrification, and militarization.

> The solution, typical of a dependent country that converts its imperialism to a sub-imperialism, was to offer foreign monopolies a part in the exploitation of the Brazilian worker and the profits derived from trade expansion, which is to say, to realize this policy by means of an unrestricted alliance with foreign capital.[16]

In subsequent years, the country would grow at formidable rates, as much as 12 percent annually during the early 1970s, while industry grew at a yearly rate of 18 percent. US investment grew sharply, and real wages fell over 20 percent between 1965 and 1974, but exports of manufactured goods tripled in the same period.[17] Subsidiaries of foreign companies accounted for the bulk of those exports. In just a few years, Brazil became the world's eighth largest industrial power. Under the military regime, the Brazilian industrial bourgeoisie "attempts to offset their inability to expand the domestic market through the extensive incorporation of already formed markets such as Uruguay."[18] Incidentally, that "inability" reflects, on the one hand, the weakness of a bourgeoisie unable to stand up to the large *latifundist* landowners, and on the other hand, it also reflects the power of the social movement and a fear of the masses that led the bourgeoisie into the arms of the landed oligarchy and the military.

But that expansion into regional foreign markets could not happen without a close alliance with US monopoly capital, because the Brazilian industrial bourgeoisie's capacity for domestic savings was still very weak, impeding the constant technological renewal of industry. For a long time, these weaknesses prevented the bourgeoisie from building a relatively autonomous political and economic strategy.

The "economic miracle," with very high growth rates and the establishment of large multinationals in Brazil, complemented an active expansionism that realized US interests in the region. This is the third aspect Marini addresses: the militarization of Brazilian capitalism, something neither accidental nor incidental, but structural. As can be seen, this was something different from the depleted process of import substitution and the role attributed to any previous or subsequent coups in the region. It was a different reality requiring a new analysis. Hence the theory of sub-imperialism as a way to break the repetition of old clichés that have been exhausted by the new reality:

> Sub-imperialism involves two basic components: on one side, an average organic composition in the global scale of national manufacturing apparatus and, on the other side, the exercise of a relatively autonomous expansionist policy, which is not only accompanied by increased integration into the imperialist productive system but also remains under the hegemony of imperialism on an international level. Put in these terms, it seems that regardless of the efforts of Argentina and other countries for access to the sub-imperialist rank, a phenomenon of this nature is only fully expressed in Latin America by Brazil.[19]

But sub-imperialism is not only an economic phenomenon. It not only exports manufactured goods but also capital and, more importantly from this point of view, it plunders natural resources, raw materials, and energy sources. Some of the more prominent acts of this policy of expansion include the threat of invading Uruguay in the early 1970s, participation in the coup of Hugo Banzer in Bolivia in 1971, and the signing of the Treaty of Itaipu with Paraguay in 1973.

This expansionist policy is a central characteristic of sub-imperialism, touted by members of the Superior War School like Colonel Golbery do Couto e Silva. His biography is a kind of synthesis of the alliance between big business and the military elite: he completed his military training in the US and then joined the Brazilian Expeditionary Force, part of the US Fifth Army that fought in World War II in Italy. He joined the Armed Forces Command, participated in the Brazilian military mission in Paraguay for three years, and in 1952 was appointed deputy of the Research Department of the Superior War School. The government that emerged from the 1964 coup made him chief of the National Intelligence Service, where he, as one of the *strong men* of the regime, remained organizer and primary head of the new intelligence service until the end of the Humberto Castelo Branco government in 1967. He then returned to the private sector, contracted by the US multinational Dow Chemical as head of its Latin American division.[20] Under do Couto e Silva, the multinational has become one of the largest petrochemical companies in Brazil.

His proposal was as simple as it was straightforward: to ally with the US against communism, for internal expansion into the Amazon to occupy that "empty space," and external expansion towards the Pacific to fulfill Brazil's "manifest destiny." Finally, to take control of the South Atlantic. He said Brazil should make a "fair deal" with the empire, which meant "negotiating a bilateral partnership" in which resources and geostrategic positions were exchanged for "the necessary resources for us to participate in the security of the South Atlantic," which would be considered a "Brazilian monopoly."[21] He thought the South Atlantic could play a role similar to that played by the Caribbean in the expansion of the United States.

After consolidating that alliance, and in the tradition of the Brazilian armed forces, he argued that the main likelihood of conflict was not in the Amazonian arc, which he considered "dead frontiers," but in the south, where the challenge of Argentina remained. In his opinion, Paraguay and Bolivia were economically subordinate to Argentina, "geopolitical prisoners"; they were "external friction zones where Brazilian and Argentine interests may collide." However, "the place that defines the maximum tension in the South American theatre" is the border of Uruguay, "due to the greater proximity of potential enemies."[22] These were the "live borders" that needed to be addressed.

It is no coincidence, therefore, that the Brazilian regime took steps to expand in that direction. The goal was "to become the center from which imperialist expansion radiated in Latin America, including becoming a military power."[23] In the early 1970s, a military intervention plan was drawn up for Uruguay called "Operation Thirty Hours," which would be launched if political instability threatened or overwhelmed the Uruguayan state, or if the newly created opposition, Frente Amplio, won the Presidency in the 1972 elections.

Political instability on the borders troubled the Brazilian military. The Argentinian military learned of the existence of Operation Thirty Hours (at that time the country was ruled by General Alejandro Agustín Lanusse) and they were alarmed by the possibility of Brazil reaching the Rio de La Plata.[24] During this period, both countries distributed their military forces based upon the possibility of a conflict to control the great estuary of La Plata, an inheritance of the rivalry between Spain and Portugal. In the 1970s, Brazil conducted military exercises in the southern region, built roads in that direction, and in October 1971, unveiled "the largest air base in South America in Santa Maria."[25]

Brazilian intervention during the August 1971 Bolivian coup of General Hugo Banzer against the government of Juan José Torres is well documented, and was publicly defended by military spokesmen. Intervention in Bolivia was based on two arguments then in vogue among the Brazilian military: the "doctrine of the perimeter," which claimed that Brazil was surrounded by hostile regimes, and the "preventive ideological war" to neutralize that situation.[26] The coup originated in Santa Cruz, which had been turned into a territorial bastion for the rebellion by a group of powerful Brazilian businessmen based there.

In the days before and after the Banzer uprising, aircraft landed at Santa Cruz airport bearing ammunition and weapons for the rebels. A large number of machine guns were distributed during those few days, when miners and students armed themselves to resist members of the right-wing Bolivian Socialist Falange, who had adopted the name Christian Nationalist Army.[27] On August 15, four days before the coup, Brazil announced a mobilization of troops along the Bolivian border; the planes carrying weapons to military and civilian participants in the coup sported the Brazilian flag. So deep was the direct involvement with the coup that the Brazilian consul in Santa Cruz, Mario Amorío, was wounded during combat.[28]

The rewards came soon afterward. In the following years, a series of agreements were signed giving preferential prices to Brazil for Bolivian oil, gas, manganese, and iron ore.[29] Not content with just controlling natural resources, Brazil also designed plans for the communication routes to reach the Pacific, most notably "the construction of the Cochabamba–Santa Cruz railway, connecting with rail systems that lead to Santos in the Atlantic, and Arica in the Pacific."[30] Much later, these same objectives assumed other names, such as the IIRSA initiative.

There were also territorial concessions. In 1974, Bolivia ceded 12,000 square kilometers to Brazil, including the towns of San Ignacio and Palmarito; in 1976, over 27,000 square kilometers more were ceded, always under the guise of border revisions. Brazil also occupied the island of Suarez in Beni.[31] As in countries like Paraguay, Brazilian citizens undertook a steady colonization process, buying up land that was much cheaper than in Brazil, until they began to form the majority in these territories.

The third case is that of Paraguay, where Brazil was granted huge concessions with the signing of the "Treaty of Itaipu" in 1973. Thirty-seven years later, Marco Aurelio Garcia, President Lula's Foreign Policy Adviser, would write that the Brazilian military regime's decision to build Itaipu while assuming all the construction costs of the dam, "rather than being an energy policy, had a clear geopolitical significance."[32] It was an attempt to lure

Paraguay into the Brazilian sphere and thus isolate Argentina. The events surrounding the construction of Itaipu give a clear picture of what Marini considered sub-imperialism.

It was the world's largest hydroelectric dam for three decades, until it was surpassed by the Three Gorges Dam in China. The signing of the Itaipu Agreement between Brazil and Paraguay generated a lot of controversy at the time, and created a deep malaise in Argentina. Brazil had long intended to take advantage of the Sete Quedas Falls or Guairá Falls to build a large hydroelectric dam on the Paraná River, which marked the border with Paraguay according to a peace treaty signed between the two countries in 1872, after the Triple Alliance War. However, the demarcation of a stretch about twenty miles upstream of the falls was a matter of dispute between the authorities of both countries.

To resolve the dispute, the Ibarra-Mangabeira treaty was signed in 1927 ratifying that the Paraguay River constitutes the border between the Apa and Bahia rivers. In 1963, under the presidency of João Goulart, the Minister of Energy and Mines for Brazil visited Paraguay and assured its president that Brazil would not go forward in the construction of the Sete Quedas dam without the total consent of Paraguay.[33] In January 1964, the Joint Brazilian-Paraguayan Commission was established to study all aspects of the project, which could have a capacity of between twelve and fifteen million MW, equal or greater than the capacity Itaipu would eventually have.[34]

With the advent of the military regime, everything changed. On March 31, 1964, Goulart was overthrown, and in June 1965, a military detachment composed of one sergeant and seven soldiers occupied Puerto Renato in the disputed and yet-to-be-defined area. On October 21, the Paraguayan Border Commission, consisting of Deputy Foreign Minister Peter Godinot and five other officials, arrived on location to verify the border violation and were detained by the Brazilian sergeant.[35] Another version of the story says that Brazilian Foreign Minister Juracy Magalhães threatened Paraguay with war—this according to his own memoirs.[36] This is how the military dictatorship consolidated a new encroachment on Paraguayan territory, now with the objective of constructing a huge hydroelectric dam.

However, the regime decided not to construct the Sete Quedas dam and instead constructed one at Itaipu. The Schilling analysis concluded that the change, since they had been making progress in terms of getting international funding, was a geopolitical decision:

> Why, from one moment to another, did the Brazilians change plans and decide instead to construct at Itaipu, 160 kilometers further south, on the same Paraná river?
>
> The only explanation for that change, which had no apparent technical or economic advantages, could be found in a purely geopolitical technicality. The construction of Itaipu would—due to the proximity of the two dams and the consequent decrease in the force of the current—interfere with the construction of Corpus dam by Argentina. Technicians affirmed that, the way they were planned, the two hydropower dams would be mutually exclusive. The only way to make the Corpus dam viable would be for the Brazilians to increase the height of Itaipu from its planned 100 meters above sea level to 125. The Brazilian government was unlikely to even consider such a scenario, because it would mean reducing the potential of their project.
>
> The geopolitical maneuver seems to have completely succeeded: Brazil secured 12.6 million kw of power, they practically annexed Paraguay, and damaged the largest hydroelectric project in Argentina, leaving them, unlike Brazil, without any exclusively national alternatives.[37]

But by accepting the Brazilian project, Paraguay broke the neutrality it had maintained since the war of 1870, a hundred years previous, incorporating itself as a subordinate country within Brazil's sphere of influence. Authorities of the military regime, like Minister of Mines and Energy Antonio Dias Leite, confirmed this assessment by noting that the Itaipu decision was political rather than energy related. For this reason, the Ministry of Mines and Energy had to cede control to the Chancellor's Office.[38]

Itaipu and the Banzer coup in Bolivia both reveal the pressure Brazil exerted against much weaker neighbors. The role that Brazil took on was something new in the South American region, and Marini goes to considerable lengths to understand it, based on a concept of great theoretical and political value. The export of capital—which businesses based in Brazil began to do around the region during this same period—was the economic face of this expansionist policy.

The political and ideological environment in which Marini thinks and writes was overshadowed by an exaltation of Brazilian nationalism and a strong alliance with the United States. In the regional political context inaugurated by the 1964 coup, Brazil became a threat to its neighbors, particularly for smaller and weaker countries like Paraguay, Bolivia, and Uruguay. That was of little concern to one of the main ideologists of the regime, do Couto e Silva:

> Small nations see themselves reduced overnight to the condition of a pygmy state and can already envisage their own melancholic end, inevitable under the regional integration plans; the power equation in the world is reduced to a small number of factors, and only a few feudal constellations—baron states—are visible, surrounded by satellite states and vassals…. There is no alternative for us [the vassal states] but to accept them [the integration plans of the empire] and accept them consciously…[39]

The idea that Brazil should "expand or perish," born in the Superior War School, was also spreading amongst the Brazilian bourgeoisie and large sectors of society. In this climate of national expansion, Marini seeks to explain the reasons for the coup and the sense of hegemony growing within the country by going beyond established categories and thus forging new ideas. Within this endeavor lies both his theoretical creativity and relevance for today.

Marini and the theory of sub-imperialism

Like most of the Latin American revolutionary left, Marini was developing a theoretical assault on orthodox Marxism, represented by communist parties that emphasized the "pre-capitalist" character of Latin American economies.[40] On the contrary, he argues, it is "*sui generis* capitalism, which only makes sense if looked at from the perspective of the whole system, both nationally and, principally, internationally."[41] This theoretical battle was part of an ambitious revolutionary project that proposed an anti-capitalist revolution, without going through a bourgeois revolution or bourgeois democracy led by the "national" bourgeoisie, which is what the communist parties advocated. This issue not only affected alliances, but also the question of the form—legal or illegal, electoral or insurrectionary/armed—taken by the struggle. Marini was convinced of the need for an urgent critique of communist postulates in the wake of the 1964 coup, which had demonstrated that the supposed "national" bourgeoisie was a firm ally of imperialism and seamlessly supported the military regime. In the face of such a critical political situation, Marini's theoretical analyses assume a more profound character.

Ruy Mauro Marini's thesis of sub-imperialism is articulated around three axes. First, the absolute global hegemony of the United States. Second, the existence of medium-sized centers of accumulation, dependent on the center, which maintain relationships of antagonistic cooperation with the United States and at the same time practice forms of regional expansionism. And third, the existence of a sub-imperialist political project that in some manner is embodied by the military dictatorship. Each of these three axes has changed substantially in the three decades since the text was written.

• *Invincible US hegemony.* This assertion is found throughout Marini's work and is one of the pillars that shapes the concept of sub-imperialism. Marini employs these statistics to support his thesis: in 1948, 72 percent of the world's gold reserves were in the United States, and 61 percent of direct global investment was US capital, which had been able to "reorganize the world capitalist economy for its own benefit."[42] To economic hegemony must be added absolute military superiority and an overwhelming presence in the bodies established by the 1944 Bretton Woods Conference, such as the World Bank and the International Monetary Fund.

Marini accurately established the peculiarities of US dominance, and asserted that, just as British hegemony had created and consolidated the global market, "the period of U.S. hegemony would be that of the imperialist integration of production systems."[43] In 1968, US capital controlled the major multinationals responsible for 25 percent of global gross national product. The export of capital and the weight of finance capital are central features of capitalism at this stage. The other is the strict hierarchy of the various links to the US capital system, so that peripheral countries are necessarily *dependent* and *subordinate* to the United States. Although Marini registered a tendency towards "the decline of monopolarity in the capitalist world," he recognized the existence of a "hierarchical integration of the centers of accumulation" with US capital at the apex.[44]

• *Medium-sized centers of accumulation.* Capitalist development itself encourages "the emergence of medium-sized centers of accumulation," which are also medium-sized capitalist powers: "The time of the simple model of center-periphery, characterized by the exchange of manufactured goods for food and raw materials, has passed."[45] Marini captures the complexity of the international division of labor. It's not about the conquest of markets through trade, but above all, it is capital accumulation by means of production across borders, with the installation of factories in "third world" countries.

This is a fundamental aspect of his thesis on sub-imperialism: the existence of intermediate centers where a sector of large companies has crystallized. "Now it's a process of linking foreign capital to a sector of the national productive structure, which is denationalized in terms of ownership, but remains part of the national economy."[46] Marini emphasizes the dependency of this trade sector, most notably on US capital—which during the years he analyzed was a beyond doubt the main investor in the region, attracted by low wages, a growing internal market, and the possibility of export to nearby countries.

He detects a double dynamic for intermediate centers of accumulation. On the one hand, economic dependency, and on the other, a need to turn to exports due to the narrowness of the domestic market and the structural difficulties for expansion. This is due to the bourgeoisie's inability to carry out any land reform that might deal with the latifundist landowners dominating the economy and the state apparatus. Fundamentally, it is a struggle for markets. But he immediately points out that exporting manufactured goods is not sufficient to indicate whether a country is sub-imperialist. He concludes that sub-imperialism is "the form taken by the dependent economy to reach the stage of monopoly and finance capital."[47]

• *A policy of sub-power.* Marini says that Brazil is the only country that expresses this phenomenon in Latin America. Being fully integrated into the framework of imperialist hegemony, the "technocratic-military" regime that took power after the 1964 coup had a "political project" that was in fact a response to the rise of social struggles in Latin America after the Cuban revolution. The existence of such a project, which involves building a sphere of influence within the region, is an important point in Marini's argument. But this regional role is performed in close cooperation with the global hegemon, with the sub-power assuming a role akin to gendarme, defending the interests of the empire.

Marini's analysis rejects the idea that the military regime is "a mere puppet of the Pentagon and State Department," but emphasizes that the Brazilian bourgeoisie "accepted the role of junior partner in its alliance with foreign capital" and that the foreign policy of the dictatorship sought "a careful balance between national interests and United States global hegemony."[48] Understanding this duality is one of the great merits of Marini's theory. But it goes further, because it doesn't separate theory from political action, and concludes that this new sub-imperialist reality has political implications.

Marini employs the concept of "antagonistic cooperation" to describe the relationship between the hegemonic superpower and a moderately developed dependent country. The term was coined by the German Marxist August Talheimer, who used it in the postwar period to understand the relationships between the United States and industrialized countries receiving investments but which became, in turn, exporters of capital. Marini says that "antagonistic cooperation" reflects tensions between the various centers in the process of imperialist integration, which "open fissures in the structure of the imperialist world and operate strongly in favor of that which tends to destroy its very foundations: revolutionary movements in underdeveloped countries."[49]

The development of a military-industrial complex and a capital goods industry not only sought to turn Brazil into an industrial power but was also a necessary condition for international expansion. Thus it was possible to create "a symbiosis between the interests of big business and the hegemonic dreams of the military elite."[50] Indeed, this expansion does not contradict imperialism but rather becomes key to the spreading influence of the hegemonic power.

The main political consequence of the new reality involves "the internationalization of Latin American revolution," which becomes "the inevitable consequence of the imperialist integration process" that converts Brazil into a sub-imperialist and a sub-power.[51]

In the three decades following the publication of Marini's work on sub-imperialism, significant changes have occurred in the world, in the South American region, and in Brazil. The US position has undergone significant changes to the point that there is a general consensus regarding the decline of the former superpower, although it maintains a significant superiority in the military terrain—which still does not allow it to win wars—and in some advanced technologies. In South America, the United States is no longer the sole player; it now contends with a strong Chinese, Spanish, and especially Brazilian presence. Although this is the most obvious and commented-upon change, it is not the only variable modifying Marini analysis.

In the following pages, I hope to expound upon a number of notable changes in Brazil: the expansion of the elite in power, which integrates new players in the alliance between the military and the Brazilian bourgeoisie; that this new elite has constructed a power strategy that should lead Brazil to becoming a world power (it is already the main regional power); that the country has become an autonomous center of capital accumulation with large multinational companies that—with state support—are among the most important in the world in several areas; that it is designing a political, economic, and infrastructural architecture for South America that will convert it into its own "backyard," based on highly asymmetrical relations with some neighboring countries. Finally, the strengthening of Brazil's military, taking on the UN military mission in Haiti, and drawing up strategies to intervene, directly or indirectly, in regional trouble spots should also be added to the above list.

Certainly, these changing policies modify the relevance of the concept of sub-imperialism to describe Brazil's role. In any case, more important than the concept (I think, with some reservations, that we could simply use the term "imperialism") are the political consequences that stem from understanding the new reality for Latin American peoples, and particularly for the collective form of action embodied by the social movements.

2
Broadening the Ruling Elite

The leaders of the old proletariat became, in part, what Robert Reich called "symbolic analysts": they are pension-fund managers, natives of former state enterprises (like Previ, the most powerful), and officials of the Bank of Brazil (still state-run); they make up the administrative boards (as in the BNDES), assuming the role of representing the workers.
—*Francisco de Oliveira*

As the lights went out on the October 30, 2010 presidential elections that announced Dilma Rousseff as the successor to President Luiz Inácio Lula da Silva, statistics confirming the new composition of power in Brazil were revealed. The Workers' Party (PT) elected eighty-eight deputies, the largest bloc in the chamber. The majority, 60 percent of PT deputies, came from the trade union sector. In the parliament chamber, sixty-two elected deputies hailed from a union background, with six more in the Senate. Of these, forty-nine belonged to the PT, seven to the Communist Party of Brazil (PC do B), two to the Democratic Workers Party (PDT), two to the Green Party (PV), one each to the Party of Socialism and Liberty (PSOL) and the Popular Socialist Party (PPS). In the Senate, four of the six trade union senators were from the PT, and the other two from the PC do B.

Taking into account the major areas of decision making, the PT is primarily a party of trade unionists, although it should be noted that seven of its elected deputies are entrepreneurs. Furthermore, the PT virtually monopolizes union representation because 80 percent of elected union members belong to that party, as do 78 percent of the total elected parliamentarians.[1] The growth of the unionist bloc has been significant in the past twenty years: in 1991 there were only twenty-five trade unionists in Congress. It is true that the business caucus is much greater than that of the trade unionists—now totaling 169 parliamentarians (previously 120)—thirty-two belonging to the Brazilian Democratic Movement Party (PMDB), a government ally, and twenty-eight to the right-wing Democrats (DEM). Unlike the trade union bloc, with most affiliated to the PT, the business bloc is distributed across almost all parliamentary parties. Finally, the rural caucus (linked to big farmers and agribusiness) is declining sharply: falling from 117 elected parliamentarians to sixty-one. The first conclusion: the old latifundista electoral force is declining while business and trade union representation is increasing.

A second statistic worth analyzing is related to the financing of political parties, and particularly the funds received by the PT. Of note is the important role of entrepreneurs in party financing, especially construction companies. The business sector contributed $470 million to elected candidates. Fifty four percent of elected parliamentarians received some support from the construction sector, some 264 deputies and forty-two senators.[2]

The party that received the most money from the construction sector was the PT ($15 million) followed by the PSDB ($11 million).[3] These are construction companies that benefit directly from the large infrastructure projects of the Initiative for the Integration of the Regional Infrastructure of South America (IIRSA) and the Growth Acceleration Program (PAC), and who now expect to increase their profits with projects for the 2014 World Cup and the Olympic Games in Rio de Janeiro in 2016. The companies leading in donations were Camargo Corrêa, Queiroz Galvão, Andrade Gutierrez, OAS, and Odebrecht, names that the reader will see repeated throughout this book. It is estimated that the construction companies are responsible for a quarter of all electoral donations.[4] The companies linked to agribusiness made their principal donations to candidates from the central-west region, and for the most part opted to contribute to DEM party members, a group that has excelled in defending the interests of this sector via the *bancada ruralista* (interest group representing the big rural landowners). In the 2006 elections, the thousand largest private companies were responsible for 30 percent of the total revenue for the campaigns of the presidential candidates, which certainly shows the importance of this kind of financing.[5]

Given all this, we can say that we have the paradox of a business sector partially financing the election of trade unionists, supposedly their biggest enemies, if you believe the political rhetoric of both sectors. More concretely, it is a case of construction companies funding the party of trade unions. However, if we look closely at who exactly these unionists-turned-parliamentarians really are, we find a somewhat different profile than we might expect. Two-thirds have college degrees. Among them, we find economists, lawyers, and teachers. Most of them hail from state enterprises and the banking sector. The vast majority—two-thirds—were re-elected incumbents.[6] In other words, they were specialized professionals as parliamentarians.

It seems necessary to inquire more into the history of trade unionism in Brazil, since this sector now makes up—alongside entrepreneurs and senior state bureaucrats—the heart of the new Brazilian elite.

The union trajectory

On January 6, 2003, just days after Lula began his first term as president, the PT treasurer for the 2002 election campaign, Delúbio Soares, hosted a party in his hometown Buriti Alegre in the interior of Goiás. Between fifteen and eighteen executive aircraft arrived on the small town's runway, a town of only 12,000 inhabitants. Guests included the governors of Goiás and Mato Grosso do Sul, and Duda Mendonça, the publicist who had designed Lula's campaign.[7] Two years later Delúbio Soares was accused of corruption. On March 30, 2006, the state judiciary brought charges against him as part of a "criminal organization" responsible for buying parliamentarians' votes in what became known as the *mensalão* scandal.[8] Soares resigned, a path soon followed by other PT leaders and members of the Lula government.

Soares was a trade unionist and served as national treasurer for the Unified Workers' Central union (CUT), joined the Worker's Support Fund (FAT) as a union delegate, and was coordinator of Lula's presidential campaigns in 1989 and 1998.[9] These details allow us to map some trajectories of union officials linked to the leadership of a party like the PT, as well as senior officials of the FAT, defined by Francisco de Oliveira as "the largest long-term capital financer in the country."[10] In his opinion, the "hardcore" of the PT is composed of workers converted into pension fund operators, allowing them access to public funds and the ability to liaise with finance capital, whereupon they become co-managers. In just two decades, the CUT and PT have experienced a rapid process of transformation.

1. The neoliberal decade of the 1990s brought enormous changes in Brazil's social and political life, influencing not only the behavior of the elites but also large sections of the popular sector. Armando Boito Jr. argues that the conversion of the Workers' Party into its role as manager of a new bourgeois hegemony "was neither superficial nor sudden," but part of a larger process that cuts across all social classes, including the working class.[11] He started by observing the changes in the daily lives of workers in auto plants, and in the banking and oil sectors, and then began to understand the reasons that led the CUT—the biggest trade union on the continent, with 20 million members—to take its current path.

A 2003 survey of employees at four companies (Ford, Mercedes Benz, Scania, and Volkswagen) in São Bernardo do Campo allows us to construct a profile of these workers: 90 percent owned homes in neighborhoods with water, electricity, sanitation, and asphalt roads; 70 percent had completed high school; 75 percent had more than eleven years on the job, earned high salaries, and most had computers and access to the Internet.[12] Such workers, with an undeniable urban, middle-class culture and consumer access, controlled the ABC metallurgy union movement, cradle of the new Brazilian labor movement, from the beginning.[13] Three quarters of the workers at the four plants were union members and eighty-one declared their sympathy for the PT.

Workers in the auto, banking, and oil industries are the driving force within the CUT mainstream, known as the Union Articulation, which is also hegemonic in the leadership of the PT. That same force held five ministries in the first Lula government: Labor, Social Security, Finance, Social Communication, and Cities—and the president's office itself. Militants from the Articulation faction also occupy important positions in state enterprises and pension funds, leading Boito Jr. to argue that a "class" has taken control of the state apparatus. Since the birth of "new unionism" in the late 1970s, during the latter part of the military dictatorship, the union practice of this key sector of the movement suffered symptoms of corporatism, craved economic growth to raise family consumption, and aspired to build a welfare state in Brazil.[14]

The changes that occurred in the early 1990s, especially the transformations in the car industry where the São Paulo ABC operated, were a blow to the unions.[15] The adoption of Toyotism, alongside technological changes that introduced computers and robots, created a new type of worker, highly qualified and schooled, ready to partner with company management. So within a few short years, a mutation occurred in the profile of the working class: politically, it was more willing to negotiate than to struggle, while in workplace culture, the multipurpose workers were no longer focused on one profession or task, but were committed to increasing productivity. In parallel, the number of strikes decreased: from 4,000 in 1989, to only 557 in 1992 and 653 in 1993, with a peak of 1,258 in 1995. There were an average of about 600 strikes per year from then until the end of the decade.[16]

2. At the same time, and partly as a result of these changes in the profile of the working class, other changes occurred in the unions and in the political arena, leading analysts to speak of

the "defeat" of the working class or, more precisely, of a set of failures: the political defeat of failing to elect Lula in the 1989 presidential elections, to which they added the economic and cultural loss represented by neoliberal hegemony since 1990. In the union field, the 1988 Constitution—which established democracy and the end of military rule—left the old corporatist union practices intact, including the so-called "union tax" or mandatory deduction of union dues from all workers. The new unionism represented by the CUT could not impose a break with the old *pelego* (collaborationist) model of unionism in the Constituent Assembly.[17]

These failures, along with corporate restructuring at the dawn of neoliberalism, accelerated the "corporate corralling" of the main unions of the CUT, which henceforth devoted all its efforts toward the upkeep of members' standard of living through increased consumerism.[18] The National Plenary of the CUT, held in September 1990 in Belo Horizonte, was the turning point, replacing confrontational unionism with propositive unionism (willing to negotiate). During the 1990s, banking, oil, petrochemical, and automobile unions chose to struggle for collective bargaining agreements rather than protective rules about the right to work, an about-face that led them to ignore most other workers, now precarious, outsourced, unemployed, or informal. In parallel, in the course of negotiations in the Sectorial Chamber of the Automotive Industry, the unions came closer to the bourgeoisie, particularly to the business leaders union, the Federation of Industries of the State of São Paulo (FIESP).

According to Boito Jr., this reconfiguration of industrial action began at the base and spread to the upper echelons, and he concludes that the experience in the Sectoral Chamber was a kind of rehearsal for a more ambitious policy of cooperation. Thus, "assembly operators, through the ABC Metalworkers Union, tried to establish an economic front for growth in conjunction with a segment of the Brazilian bourgeoisie, believing that the FIESP might be a reliable ally in the struggle against the recessionary policies overseen by financial sector interests."[19]

3. Amid the neoliberal restructuring of production—which led to massive layoffs in all sectors, including automotive, state oil, banking, and all industry—in the late 1990s, the unions were integrated into government schemes through the FAT funds, which ensured a multimillion dollar income for CUT, much more than earned through union dues.

Lacking the strength it had in the previous decade—their candidate defeated in the presidential election, and capital fully on the offensive—the CUT decided to insert itself into the official professional retraining programs, via the National Professional Qualification Plan, a scheme implemented by FAT in 1995, which united unions and employers.

This proposal was in line with the analysis of entrepreneurs and the Fernando Henrique Cardoso government that unemployment was due to workers' lack of professional qualifications.[20] In 1998, the CUT grossed $17 million, of which $2 million, from the FAT, was earmarked for professional training. In 1999, the CUT earned nearly $32 million: $12 million from the FAT, a figure that rises to $20 million in 2000. Since 1999, 70 percent of the CUT's costs are linked to the FAT Professional Qualification Programs, which is to say, to state and business bodies.[21]

On one hand, CUT loses financial autonomy as it depends increasingly on income unrelated to the contributions of its members. And on the other hand, "the union culture that generates this structure encourages the emergence of leaders more concerned with staying at the head of these apparatuses, and developing their own union career, rather than effectively representing their bases."[22]

Finally, this institutionalization of the CUT, and its state-dependent professionalism, could not fail to influence its leadership organs as well as its affiliated masses. At the 1988 Congress, 50.8 percent of the delegates came from the union base, while 49.2 percent were leaders. At the 1991 Congress, there is a phenomenal turnaround: 83 percent were leaders and only 17 percent from the base.[23]

4. Under the Lula government the unions naturally became more entangled in the state. Sociologist Rudá Ricci, who advised

the CUT Department of Rural Workers in 1990, summarizes this process:

> Since the 1980s, people's organizations have conquered many co-management posts. Today there are some 30,000 public management positions [...] throughout Brazil. So, social leaders, including trade unionists, are changing their profile: from leaders of mobilizations to leaders with the technical capacity to govern. One could perceive a change in the profile of the leaders from the big unions: from charismatic personalities with oratorical skills towards more reflective personas. The end point of this process was their entry into government ministries. They are no longer union leaders, they are government functionaries.[24]

As we have seen, two processes converge here. The first is the decline in union mobilization. From 4,000 in 1989, the number of strikes declined to an average of between six and nine hundred per year in the 1990s, and then to an average of three hundred between 2004 and 2007.[25] This sharp decline in union activity has been interpreted in various ways: from those who believe it is a phase of recomposition in the wake of the past decade's defeats, a time when the CUT is "adapting" to the continuity of the Lula government, to those who argue that the union's ability to resist declined when the main leaders were co-opted.[26]

What is certain is that the labor movement did not mobilize their members when pension reform was approved, seriously affecting workers by lowering benefits and expanding the private or "complementary" pension system, using pension funds. How did it come to this? On the one hand, "hundreds of trade unionists and former unionists assumed positions in government ministries, public administration and on the boards of state companies."[27] But that's only the tip of the iceberg. The other is what Ricci mentioned: the 30,000 positions in which unionists co-manage services such as health, education, social assistance, and various benefits. In 2001, before Lula entered the Planalto Palace, there were 22,000 positions held by social activists and especially unionists in the municipalities alone.[28] Ricci also cites the participation of unionists in ministerial posts, in bodies like the Council of Economic and Social Development and the National Labor Forum, places where state policies and reform are debated.

A second issue relates to the specific Brazilian union style, which is known as *citizen unionism*, heir to the *propositive unionism* of the 1990s, which provides services to the employee, such as the aforementioned professional training, bringing the union a sizable income. Under the Lula government, unions negotiated bank loans for their members, which could be deducted from their salary. This benefited both the banks (by reducing the risk of default) and the workers (because they'd pay less interest than they would for other loans, such as credit cards). It also benefits the unions, who make 0.5 percent profit on each loan.[29] These sorts of actions, overseen by citizen unionism, are presented as "victories" to their membership.

Citizen unionism prioritizes *fiestas* over protests, as witnessed with the May 1st spectaculars. In 2004, the CUT began hiring marketing specialists to organize the May 1st festival with popular stars, car and apartment giveaways, and hairdressing services. Thus, to the growing institutionalization of unions, and their loss of autonomy, we can also add depoliticization and the consolidation of neoliberal ideas, market values, and the individualization of labor problems.[30]

The Lula government promoted reforms in labor legislation to allow the direct transfer of a percentage of union dues directly to the union central, if the unions meet certain requirements such as representing at least 5 percent of the workers in the workplace and having more than a hundred affiliated union members. The union obtains legal recognition upon meeting these requirements, and thus earns 10 percent of the amount of contributions that, incidentally, are compulsory for workers to pay even if they are not affiliated to the union. This strengthens the power of the union leaders and, in parallel, is an incentive to form new unions. For some analysts the creation of the Conlutas (National

Coordination of Struggles) and the Inter-Syndical (both left-wing breakaway unions emerging from the left-wing of the CUT) and the New Trade Union of Workers, would be related in some way to these changes in labor legislation, in addition to the disagreement of the union left with the loss of CUT's autonomy.[31]

The fifth issue to consider is the participation of unionists in Lula's government, to a degree never before seen in Brazil.

Unionists in state positions

Significant changes have taken place within the federal state power elite in recent years, particularly since January 2003 when Lula took office. There are about 80,000 positions of trust (politically appointed positions) in Brazil—about 47,500 of which are positions in the administration that can be appointed at the discretion of the Executive.[32] Of these positions, those belonging to the Management and Advisory Institutions (DAS) levels 5 and 6, and those of the Special Nature Offices (NES) are defined as "management positions overseen by public officials," since they are a level immediately below ministers and secretaries of state.[33] As high-level management positions directly appointed by ministers or the president, they are regarded as the elite leadership of the government.

This echelon consists of over a thousand positions. A study by sociologist Maria Celina D'Araujo Soares sheds light on this elite. In 2009, 984 positions of trust were in the DAS 5: heads of the minister's office, department managers, legal advisors, secretaries of internal auditing, and undersecretaries of planning, budgeting, and administration. Another 212 positions were part of the DAS 6: special advisers, secretaries and undersecretaries of the executive office of the president. NES positions numbered sixty-two in 2009: Command of the Armed Forces, Central Bank management, and various legal positions and special secretariats. The study received responses from 30 percent of those 1,258 positions, which makes it the most important source of information available regarding the highest echelon of the Lula government.

First of all, in reference to the first and second Lula administrations—2003–2006 and 2007–2010—only 20 percent of this sector were women, and 84–87 percent were white. Ninety-five percent had college education or were postgraduates, predominantly in economics, engineering, and law.[34] However, their parents' educational levels were much lower, with only 45 percent of them having completed a college education, which shows that most positions of trust in Lula's administration went to operatives who came from families with lower socio-economic levels than themselves.[35]

But the most relevant data in this study of elites in the Lula government pertains to the social involvement of the people in these positions of trust: extrapolating from the survey, we can surmise that almost half the 1,200 positions in federal government are taken by trade unionists. D'Araujo Soares posits that the strong union presence in government is not a reflection of the PT's electoral victory, but of the high rate of unionization in the public sector, with most union members generally being affiliated to the PT, including almost 80 percent of public officials in the executive branch. The strong presence of trade unionists in government must be understood, according to D'Araujo Soares, as part of a project that gives greater representation to the class organizations of workers. Nevertheless, she notes:

> In a country with as many inequalities as Brazil, nothing indicates that strengthening the corporate union structure could become an instrument for greater social, economic and political equality. Because it never was. Rather, it was an instrument for the hierarchization of gains and rights in Brazilian society, based on unequal rights and restricted only to those in the formal labor market.[36]

This raises the issue of a recurrence of the old "union oligarchies" that have plagued Brazilian labor history, privileging a small part of the workforce, while the vast majority of workers exist in the informal market, without even the possibility of organizing.

To conclude this section, I will give a brief description of the importance of the state ministries held by the union sector. In the first Lula government, 26 percent of the ministers came from the unions, and during the second, 16 percent. It should be noted that in the seven post-dictatorship governments, the average percentage of union members in the cabinet was only 11.5 percent. In terms of participation in social movements, 45 percent of Lula's ministers were linked to them. Thirty-eight percent of his ministers held positions on the management board of a state company.[37]

With this data we have a rough profile of the importance of the union movement in the two Lula administrations, especially in the top echelons of power. It should be clear, however, that this is a middle-class trade unionism, composed of teachers, bankers, and other professionals with graduate and postgraduate degrees and careers as state officials. Unlike previous administrations, Lula's *Casa Civil* (Civil Cabinet) centralizes the appointment of positions in DAS 5 and 6, and NES. The Casa Civil occupies, therefore, a strategic position: in the first Lula administration it was headed by José Dirceu, who was meant to be Lula's successor until he had to resign over the *mensalão* scandal. Dilma Rousseff then took up the post and, when she assumed the presidency, she appointed Lula's former finance minister Antonio Palocci to the position. They are all key figures in the PT government.

The role of pension funds

The relationship between unions and pension funds is a central theme in this discussion. Union immersion in the financial world did not begin during the Lula era, but its consequences became visible under his rule. Because they are such important funds—not only as enormous sums of money, but also because they require a layer of unionists specializing in financial investment—pension funds deserve a closer look.

To understand the role they play, one must first go back to the formation of the Worker's Support Fund (FAT) and the National Bank for Economic and Social Development (BNDES). The bank was created in 1952 to meet the long-term financing needs of the Brazilian economy, which in those years was seeking to modernize the industrial matrix. At first, the main source of the banks revenues was income tax, but incoming monetary flows were irregular. To resolve this situation, the 1988 Constitution created the FAT and earmarked 60 percent of the revenue from the Social Integration Program and the Asset Building Program for Public Servants (PIS-PASEP) for unemployment insurance with, the remaining 40 percent going to BNDES in order to finance development programs.[38] However, because spending on unemployment insurance was less than the constitutionally determined percentage, the FAT had its surplus transferred to BNDES as special deposits, leading to an increase in the volume of contributions.

The FAT operates within the orbit of the Ministry of Labor and Employment and is governed by a Deliberative Council made up of government representatives, workers, and employers: four unionists; four entrepreneurs; representatives from the ministries of Labor, Social Welfare, and Agriculture; as well as a member of the BNDES. One of the functions of the council is to develop proposals to invest the considerable resources of the FAT. There are also union representatives on the board of the BNDES.

The FAT resources in the BNDES grew from 2 percent, in 1989, to 40 percent, in 1999, so it is considered "the largest long-term capital financier in the country."[39] By 2006, the FAT was responsible for 67 percent of BNDES disbursements, a figure that grew from $11 billion, in 1997, to over $100 billion, in 2010.[40] This figure gives an idea of the importance of the BNDES, which has become the principal development bank in the world and an institution capable of guiding Brazil's economy where the government wants. In its early years, the BNDES was a key component in building the country's infrastructure; in the 1970s "it was responsible for the maturation of the capital goods industry"; in the 1980s it played a role in saving companies in crisis; and in 1990s "it acted by facilitating and funding privatization."[41] During the first Lula administration, the bank orientated itself toward boosting exports in order to then concentrate on financing infrastructure and restructuring Brazilian capitalism.

Despite growing costs associated with unemployment insurance, the transfer of funds from the FAT to the BNDES continued to increase. It remains the BNDES's main source of income, although at this stage the bank has several other sources of funds. From 2001 to 2008, the FAT's contribution to the BNDES rose from 49 billion *reals* to 116 billion, nearly $70 billion, about half the bank's revenues.[42]

To get an idea of the material and symbolic place occupied by unionists in Brazil, note that BNDES investments represent about 7 percent of Gross Domestic Product (GDP), giving it the capacity to guide the economy. The BNDES has investments in a multitude of companies, generally as a minority partner but with the potential of seating a representative on the board of directors. It is a partner in Petrobras and Vale, two strategic Brazilian businesses: Petrobras is the second largest oil company in the world and the overseer of Brazil's energy sovereignty, and Vale is the second largest mining concern on the planet. It also has a presence in the Banco do Brasil, which is among the ten most important banks in the world. The BNDES also played an important role in the wave of privatizations during the 1990s, boosted by President Fernando Henrique Cardoso. Currently, it finances mergers between large Brazilian companies in order to deliver them to the global market to compete with global multinationals, and is the main financier of the Initiative for the Integration of the Regional Infrastructure of South America (IIRSA).

The other place where trade unionists, in particular those from the banking sector, have a predominant position is in the capitalization of pension funds. The privatization of the pension system has been partly responsible for the enormous growth of the financial sector. To get an idea of the size of the business, the 300 largest pension funds in the world gather assets of $11 trillion, similar to the GDP of the United States. In some countries, pension funds assets are higher than GDP: in the Netherlands it is 155 percent of GDP, in Switzerland 143 percent, in the United Kingdom and the United States it reaches 72 percent of GDP.[43]

In Brazil, private pension funds were created in 1977 by the military regime to encourage savings. In the 1990s, some companies went bankrupt and the funds were used to promote privatization. In 2001, under President Cardoso, Complementary Law 108 was passed, democratizing the participation of union members in the administration of funds.[44] That law was subsequently regulated in 2003 under the Lula government, which promoted the participation of workers in the management of funds—an inclusion that they believed would moralize, humanize, and domesticate capitalism.[45]

In 2010 the pension fund assets in Brazil reached $300 billion, 16 percent of GDP (equal to the GDP of Argentina), becoming the largest institutional investors in the country.[46] From this point of view, pension funds are even more important than the BNDES. Several studies agree that they have a large margin of growth, to the point that it is estimated that in just ten years they could account for 40 percent of GDP.

The optimism of the pension fund operators and their own government that promotes the funds is based on two elements. First, their evolution in recent years: the number of pension institutions grew from 323 in 2003 to 372 in 2010; public and private sponsor companies went from 1,626 to 2,250 in the same period; and participating groups (unions, cooperatives, professional associations) increased from seven in 2003 to 476 in 2010, data that reveals the steady growth of the sector.[47]

But the most encouraging data for operators and government alike, lies in the profound change in the countries' social structure. As shown in Table 1, in 2003, the absolute majority of the population was poor, having a household income of less than three minimum wages. By 2010, the middle classes (Group C) increased by 30 million people becoming 50 percent of the population, and in 2014 it is estimated to reach 56 percent, about 113 million.[48] Meanwhile the poorest would become less than one-third of the population for first time in the history of Brazil.

Table 1: Evolution of class by income 2003–2014

(percent of the population)

YEAR	A/B	C	D	E	TOTAL
2003	8	37	27	28	100
2009	11	50	24	15	100
2014	16	56	20	8	100

Source: FGV/IBGE[49]

We are talking about more than 50 million new mass consumers and a good percentage of them are potential clients of private pension funds. So we can say that the expectation that the funds reach 40 percent of GDP is realistic, which with the enthusiastic support given them by the government, implies that they will become an even greater motor for the countries' economic growth.

However, of the 372 pension funds that existed in late 2010, the majority of the resources were concentrated in only a handful. The ten largest together counted for some $175 billion, 60 percent of the total. The three largest account for 45 percent of the total assets. They are state workers' pension funds from three companies: Previ, the fund of Banco do Brasil employees, has a capital estimated at over $90 billion, 30 percent of pension funds assets in Brazil. Petros, the fund of Petrobras workers, is the second largest with $31 billion and Funcef, for employees of Caixa Economica Federal, is third with $26 billion.[50] The state has preferential access to these fabulous sums. And those best placed in the management of those funds are affiliates of the Union Bank of São Paulo.

Let's take a closer look at Previ. In August 2010, it was placed twenty-fifth in the world ranking of private pension funds.[51] It is the largest fund in Latin America and its capital exceeds the sum of the GDPs of Uruguay, Paraguay, and Bolivia. Previ chooses their management every two years. Half of the candidates for management positions are elected by the shareholders (170,000 people were involved in the May 2010 election) and the other half are elected by the Bank of Brazil.

Table 2: Top ten pension funds in 2010

ENTITY	COMPANY	INVESTMENTS*	ACTIVE MEMBERS	PASSIVE MEMBERS
PREVI	Public Fed.	$90,880,000,000	94,514	87,180
PETROS	Public Fed.	$31,171,000,000	89,388	55,631
FUNCEF	Public Fed.	$26,200,000,000	78,516	32,990
CESP	Private	$11,176,000,000	15,936	29,897
VALIA	Private	$8,241,000,000	58,295	21,292
ITAUBANCO	Private	$7,102,000,000	26,924	7,264
SISTEL	Private	$6,850,000,000	1,849	26,088
BANESPREV	Private	$5,848,000,000	4,720	22,793
FOLRUZ	Public State.	$5,370,000,000	9,258	12,030
REAL GRANDEZA	Public Fed.	$5,130,000,000	5,720	6,703

Source: Petros
*Dollars in October 2011

If we look at the five principal organs of Previ management, the importance of the banking union appears clear. The executive board is composed of five members, two of whom are from the Union Bank of São Paulo. Of the twelve members of the Deliberative Council, three hail from the banking union, as do two of eight members on the Fiscal Council. On the other two executive boards, the union has six members. Out of a total of fifty executive positions, thirteen come from the union. The domination of PT in the management of state pension funds is overwhelming because the directors are appointed by the Bank, which is controlled by the federal government.[52] I want to stress that those thirteen executives of the Previ pension fund control decisions about the allocation of millions and millions of dollars, who to lend to and on what terms, where and how to invest. And Previ is no exception. In Petros, three of the top four positions are held by unionists.

Maria Celina D'Araujo's study on the Lula government elite arrives at similar conclusions. Of the eighty-six leaders of the executive management and fiscal council of three major pension funds between 1999 and 2008, only ten were women; 50 percent of the Previ and Petros management, and 40 percent of Funcef are from unions, an even higher percentage than in DAS as detailed above.[53] It is interesting to note that in the second Cardoso government (1999–2002), 41.2 percent of the senior management of these three funds belonged to unions, but the percentage increases under the two Lula administrations: during the first (2003–2006) it rises to 51.3 percent and in the second (2007–2010) it reaches a staggering 66.6 percent, a figure that could be called absolute hegemony.[54]

It is estimated that among the various pension funds there are about 8,000 executive positions, of which half receive monthly incomes averaging between $12,000 and $18,000 dollars.[55] Of course, not all of the positions are occupied by unionists but a good portion are, perhaps 1,000 or 2,000, and they certainly have a strong presence in the state enterprise funds, which are the largest. In 2010, the PT controlled fifteen funds, including Previ, Petros, and Funcef, while the PMDB controlled eight, and the PSDB only one of the state companies.[56] Of the ten largest pension funds, the PT has control of six.[57]

Pension fund investment covers the whole economy, including private companies. Taking into account the BNDES and state pension funds, the government's influence extends to 119 large private companies.[58] Previ, for example, can nominate the president of Vale, despite being a private company, because it is the main investor in the multinational alongside Petros and Funcef. Sergio Rosa was the Previ director for eight years, and also chaired Vale's board of directors until both positions were occupied by Ricardo Flores, nominated by the PT.[59] Previ is the main investor in Brazil's capital market and has the largest shareholding companies: besides Vale, it also plays a role in Embraer, Petrobras, the Itaú-Unibanco and Bradesco banks, Ambev, Usiminas, Gerdau, Neoenergia, CPFL, and Oi telecommunications, and is moving into the real estate sector, where it has investments in fourteen shopping centers.[60] Petros, meanwhile, entered into Itaú-Unibanco with an investment of $1.5 billion, representing 11 percent of the voting capital, and also has shares in Petrobras, Vale, and Oi.[61]

Previ is involved in seventy companies with the power to appoint a total of 285 advisors. Some of the companies are genuine multinationals: Previ has a 15 percent ownership in Brazil Foods, the country's second largest food producer; it has 31 percent in CPFL, the energy distributor of São Paulo; and 14 percent of the shares at Embraer, the third largest aeronautical company in the world. Previ also has $18 billion invested in Vale, the second largest mining firm on the planet, and controls Valepar, the main shareholder in the company.[62] This case is the best example of the ability of funds to control even the largest private company in the country. Valepar owns 53.3 percent of the voting equity in Vale and 33.6 percent of the total capital. Valepar is controlled by pension funds, since Previ has 49 percent of the shares and the BNDES has 9 percent, thus allowing the federal government and the pension funds to make important decisions in a private multinational.

Several ministers and senior officials in the Lula administrations moved from trade unionism into the pension fund sector. Ricardo Berzoini was Minister of Social Welfare and Labor and then president of the Union of Banks of São Paulo. Luiz Gushiken occupied the Communications Ministry of the Presidency and was also president of the Union of Banks of São Paulo, as well as a pension fund consultant. José Sasseron was president of Anapar and head of the Union of Banks of São Paulo. Wagner Pinheiro was director of Petros and the banking union. Sergio Rosa was president of Previ and of the National Confederation of Bank Employees. Guilherme Lacerda was president of Funcef and founder of the CUT.[63]

The list goes on. Olivio Dutra, Minister of Cities, was also president of the Union of Banks of Rio Grande do Sul. Jacques Wagner was Minister of the Council of Economic Development and president of Sindiquímica. Miguel Rosseto was Minister for Agrarian Development and directed the Rio Grande do Sul Polo Petrochemical union. Humberto Costa was Health Minister and

Secretary of the Medical Union of Pernambuco. Luiz Dulce was General Secretary of Welfare and union president of Ensenanza de Minas Gerais. Marina Silva, Minister of Environment, was founder of the CUT in Acre. Osvaldo Barga was National Secretary of Labor and director of the Metal Union of São Bernardo do Campo. Antonio Palocci was Minister of Finance and director of the Medical Union of São Paulo.[64]

Maria Chaves Jardim's doctoral thesis is the most complete work available on the relationship between unions and pension funds. Jardim notes that "the key posts in the financial market, such as banks and pension fund leadership, were partially occupied by former unionists with experience in pension funds," revealing their capacity to approach the financial market thanks to "accumulated social and symbolic capital, a result of their previous interactions with the fund industry."[65] This confluence was not a casual process, but an intentional one, both desired and planned. The bank, electrician, telephone, oil, and some metallurgical unions were responsible for creating private pension funds for their members, and actively participated in their management. In three decades, these unions went from offering its affiliates traditional services to providing financial services in what Jardim considers an "unprecedented strategy."[66]

The union leadership had a change of attitude during the 1990s in regards to union involvement in the financial market.[67] Between 2000 and 2003, a thousand unionists participated in courses in pension fund management. Perhaps the high point of this process was the decision for a unionist to join the board of the São Paulo Stock Exchange (Bovespa), which incorporated the economic agenda of the market into unionism. The courses the CUT provided for its members emphasized that pension fund resources should be managed by the workers themselves and guided by "a culture of caution and not the aggression typical of a capitalist." The training courses advocated investing funds in social progress to benefit the workers.[68]

The formation of a union elite linked to pension funds was a process begun in the 1990s that accelerated during Lula's two administrations. Lula's electoral victory was made possible by the support of this elite-in-training. A good example is the Charter of Brasilia, a manifesto issued on October 17, 2002, by 193 elected representatives of thirty-nine pension funds who, according to the text, "managed funds to the tune of $90 billion."[69] The signatories included presidents, directors, and consultants of major state and private pension funds. The manifesto stated that "pension funds represent a sound and viable option to supplement retirement and to build long-term savings," and affirmed Lula as the candidate pledging "the full development of this system, its democratization, and the rights of the participants."

Moreover, Lula's arrival in government led to the institutionalization of pension funds as resources to accelerate growth in the economy and, as we shall see, as a strategy for social inclusion and the moralization of capitalism. The elite that arose from this dual tendency—which we can sum up as a confluence of State and financial market—has been defined in Jardim's investigation as:

> native to the São Paulo banking sector, and also part of the core decision-making process of the PT; graduates of the Getúlio Vargas Foundation business school in São Paulo, middle-class white, heterosexual males. Women, blacks or Indians do not exist in this social space, where, in the same way, the rule of "good etiquette" does not allow room for "deviant positions" such as homosexuality.[70]

The fact that members of this new elite were formed in the environment of the Getúlio Vargas Foundation and the São Paulo banking union allowed them to move in social circles that share certain assumptions about the role of pension funds. Unionists interested in pension funds began to frequent business milieus, attend lectures and courses related to the subject, and develop a different discourse from the traditional union one. São Paulo is the epicenter of this movement, as 162 of the state's 370 pension funds are based there, but it is also where the CUT emerged and the cradle of Brazil's new unionism movement.

To complete the portrait of this new elite, let us briefly look at some personal biographies. Before becoming one of Lula's ministers, *Luiz Gushiken* was a partner in the consulting firm Global Prev (formerly Gushiken and Associates), and as parliamentary deputy, he was always the PT go-to guy in the pensions area. He trained at the School of Business Administration of the Getúlio Vargas Foundation, with Ricardo Berzoini. Gushiken picked out several names for Lula's first cabinet and was responsible for the presidential nominations for the three largest funds, Previ, Petros, and Funcef: Sergio Rosa, a colleague of his from the banking union, Wagner Pinheiro, another colleague from the union, who also helped plan Lula's candidacy in 2002, and Guilherme Lacerda who was economic adviser to the PT from 1998 on.[71]

Ricardo Berzoini was a PT deputy, banking sector leader, and worked with Gushiken in campaigns, lobbying for legislation in favor of pension funds. In the first Lula government, he was Minister of Welfare and, later, Labor. Following the mensalão scandal, he left office and went on to become the general secretary of the PT.

The lawyer *Adacir Reis* completes the trio of the most influential people in pension funds. A friend of Gushiken, he headed the Secretariat of Complementary Welfare (pension funds) during the first Lula government and is known as the "guardian" of the funds. He is an influential figure in the associations of fund entities (ABRAPP) and their users (ANAPAR). Unlike the other two, Reis does not come from a union background but made his career as a key pension fund operator.

Another influential figure, *Wagner Pinheiro*, has a different profile. He worked as an economist in the private sector at Santander Bank, and was a director and chairman of the bank's pension fund, Banesprev—the seventh largest fund due to its volume of assets, which amounted to $6 billion. Under Lula, he became president of Petros, the pension fund of Petrobras.

Sergio Rosa's rise to influence is a notable rags-to-riches story. According to *Piauí* magazine, his father came from Portugal, with fourteen children, to work in a butcher shop in São Paulo. At thirteen Rosa began to work in the shop, then moved on to sell books door-to-door, joining the Internationalist Socialist Organization, a clandestine Trotskyist group, where he met Luiz Gushiken, then a member of the central committee. In 1980, he worked in the Banco do Brasil where he got to know Ricardo Berzoini. He became involved in the PT "articulation" faction, headed by Gushiken, alongside Lula and José Dirceu. From 2003 to 2010 Rosa managed the largest pension fund in Latin America and twenty-fifth largest in the world. As *Piauí* magazine explained, "Pension funds became part of the articulation faction's project to win power. As they designed their strategy in 1992, the articulation faction realized that the battle for power within the PT party or indeed beyond it, could not be won solely ideologically, and what party would not like to have access to that multi-million-dollar fund?"[72]

The unions and union headquarters had been in training, often with business professionals like Gushiken or members of centers like the Ethos Institute (dedicated to corporate social responsibility) and the Brazilian Institute of Corporate Governance. In 2003, ANAPAR organized a course with Gushiken's Global Prev, with the participation of the US trade union AFL-CIO.[73] The Union Bank of São Paulo operated a vocational training center, which eventually became the Banking School, teaching seven business management courses per year—intended, according to the union itself, to create "entrepreneurs, consultants, financial analysts, managers, investors, administrators, executives."[74]

Formed around these kind of courses, the new elite socialized in different spaces than workers did, and attended cocktail parties and weekend conferences in luxury hotels, in what Jardim calls "rituals of self-legitimization."[75]

A new class or union capitalism?

There is an ongoing debate about the emergence of this new union elite and its participation in pension funds and the top levels of government. Let's briefly review some of the arguments put forward, starting with the position of Lula's government and the union movement.

The PT platform, during the 2002 election campaign, asserted that pension funds are "a powerful tool for strengthening the internal market, and a form of long-term savings for the country's growth."[76] Beyond this classic and reasonable argument in favor of pension funds, there was another line of thinking within the PT that saw pension funds as a new strategy to control capitalism and to moralize it. It is a shift in perspective that is embraced by the PT leadership and leads them to strategize, alongside trade unionists linked to pension funds, about the country's future in terms of the market and the financial system.

In this sense, Lula began to emphasize the importance of pension funds to the country's development and, furthermore, as a key to social integration. Shortly after he took office, three of the major funds—Previ, Petros, and Funcef—convened the First International Seminar on Pension Funds, in Rio de Janeiro. In the closing speech, Lula called upon the unions to create pension funds on the grounds of their "social use."[77] "If we do not increase savings, there will be no investment resources, and if there is no investment, there will be no economic growth; without growth there will be no job creation, and if there is no job creation, there will be no income."[78]

Tasks that once were the responsibility of the state are now assumed by the financial market, which happens to be the cornerstone of the success of a leftist government. The Secretary of Complementary Welfare at the time, Adacir Reis, asserted that "pension funds are part of the strategic project of President Luiz Inácio Lula da Silva, and they have a key role in the reform process that is attempting to start a new cycle of growth in pension savings in the country."[79]

One of the most interesting interventions in this seminar—which was attended by the top brass of the Brazilian pension funds, as well as unionists and various authorities—was that of Oded Grajew, at the time special adviser to Lula. Grajew is an entrepreneur, president of the Brazilian Association of Toy Manufacturers, and founder/president of the Ethos Institute of Business and Social Responsibility. Like many of the unionists involved in pension funds, he has a postgraduate degree in management from the Getulio Vargas Foundation in São Paulo. But more importantly, he is one of the instigators of the World Social Forum, an annual global meeting of social movements.

Grajew is an advocate of "corporate responsibility," or corporate social responsibility. He is an advocate for pension funds playing a crucial role in providing capitalism with "an ethical and social vision." He argues that this can provide a turning point in the capitalist system, ensuring that the financial market is not solely guided by profitability criteria and safeguarding investments.[80] He argues that Brazil is in a unique position to become a global reference point in this regard. But the way Grajew defends "the social responsibility" of business is, to say the least, contradictory. On the one hand he defends values like respect for human rights and worker's rights, the environment, and concern for "good corporate governance practices." Likewise, he points out that corporate social responsibility is good business because it is "the only path towards the long-term sustainability of profits," because it "attracts and retains talent, motivates employees, earns consumer and community loyalty, access to markets, finance, and investments, and runs less risk of accumulating environmental, social, and ethical liabilities."[81]

On the other hand, he defends social inclusion via the market, in the same vein as pension fund managers and the PT government. He argues that a third sector has mobilized, comprised of civil society and NGOs, guided by the notion of social responsibility, and based upon the progress made in human rights, gender, race, and other social rights through "solidarity actions," and by "paying attention to the social emergency." For companies in the financial sector, their social responsibility lies in choosing the right investments. "The Banco Itaú and ABN AMRO Real are two good examples of this new market attitude," claims Grajew.[82]

Perspectives like this lead Jardim to conclude that the Lula government is overseeing a "domestication" or "moralization of capitalism," embodied in the notion of social inclusion through pension funds:

In this context, to legitimize pension funds and delegitimize "savage capitalism" is a symbolic strategy that
marks a distinction between social inclusion activities
and speculative activities; between pension funds of
the past and those of the present. As a result, pension funds gain social legitimacy through a purely economic activity.[83]

But at the same time, Jardim believes that this is a double standard, since the Brazilian pension funds are the largest buyers of
government debt: 63 percent of the investments in the funds are
placed in bonds, that is to say, public debt funds, making them
mere government speculators and "loan sharks."[84] Brazil has one
of the highest interest rates in the world, which contradicts both
the rhetoric about the prevalence of the social over the economic
and the alleged prioritization of the long term over the short. It is,
therefore, a turnabout that leads to a convergence of interests with
financial capital, something reflected in a discourse that "allowed
the PT government, unions and trade union federations to add
the concept of 'market' to its traditional social discourse."[85]

Beyond superficial accusations of co-optation or treason
thrown at the PT, there has been no thorough analysis of these
new realities from the left. The harshest critic of union involvement in the management of pension funds comes from the
sociologist Francisco de Oliveira. In his view, there is "a real, new
social class" formed out of "control of access to public funds."[86]
His controversial proposal that we are witnessing the formation
of a new class was rejected by pro-unionists. He argues that the
new class, composed of persons like Gushiken and Berzoini,
"has unity of purpose, was formed with ideological consensus
around the new role of the state, works within management of
state or semi-state pension funds, and creates the link to the
financial system."[87]

This "hard-core PT nucleus," which is to say, "workers transformed into pension fund operators" is similar to the class in
socialist countries "that took control of the productive apparatus

through bureaucratic means."[88] This PT nucleus is not out to control the profits of private enterprise, but it places itself at the source of those earnings—in pension funds. The peculiarity of the Brazilian case, argues De Oliveira, is that financial accumulation occurs mainly in the state realm.[89]

In later work, De Oliveira repeats more or less the same arguments without elaborating on the "new class." He says that taking control of the state made it easier for the PT to access public funds, which seems obvious. He sees this driven by the growing power of the bourgeoisie and the parallel weakening of labor, which had originally created the CUT and the PT itself:

> In a situation characterized by the decomposition of the class base, the symmetric growth of the power of a non-unifiable bourgeoisie class, and the preeminence within it of the "new class" of pension fund managers, the PT responded with its own "state-ization," which took the form of occupying state office and taking over the functions of government, in order to legitimately gain access to public funds. It is a strategy of replacing politics with administration.[90]

Jardim, on the contrary, considers two arguments against the idea of a "new class" based around pension funds. She recalls Gushiken's view that there are only a few unions actively involved in elections for pension fund management positions.[91] Secondly, she calls into question the actual power of those trade unionists elected to management positions and their ability to influence pension fund decisions, arguing that "in the financial realm unionists fail to definitively impose their voice" and "the trade unionists' power of negotiation at the business table is limited."[92] In contrast to De Oliveira, she believes that the involvement of unionists in pension funds is not guided by economic interests but by a political strategy focused more within the union than outside of it.[93]

Her thesis, published in 2007, collects data from previous years, and it is likely that the same process has since intensified.

However, more recently, an investigation carried out in pension funds such as Petros and Previ, conclude that the presence of trade unionists on the various deliberative councils is significant enough to influence decisions in their partnership with the federal government. The fact is, pension funds have played an important role in the economic and political line designed by the Lula government. This data is also surveyed in D'Araujo's analysis of the new government elite.

I think we need to investigate further before deciding whether a new social class is in formation, or has already been formed, around the management of pension funds. In any case, better to avoid repeating the old divisions in the revolutionary movement between those who argued that a new bourgeoisie had emerged in the Soviet Union and those who thought a bureaucracy had come to power.

Nevertheless we can say that a new elite exists in state power in Brazil, one that, as we shall see in the following chapters, manages important aspects of the economy. In that sense, the pension funds are a powerful tool in the hands of the elite, allowing them to handle as much as 16 percent of Brazil's GDP, as are the BNDES funds, which promote the restructuring of Brazilian capitalism, invest heavily in South American infrastructure, and enable Brazilian multinationals to compete globally.

Most Brazilian analysts agree that the formation of an industrial bourgeoisie during the 1950s changed the face of the country. That bourgeoisie became aware of their interests as a national class with the creation of the Superior War School (ESG) in 1949 as an institute of policy and strategy studies linked to the Ministry of Defense. Just as the industrial bourgeoisie focused on capital accumulation through industrial production, the ESG became the main powerhouse of strategic thinking, and according to Severino Cabral, "played a central role in contemporary Brazilian political culture."[94]

In principle, the bourgeoisie and the military can be considered complementary, but in actuality there was a lot of interaction because the top level of the bourgeoisie participated in ESG courses and adopted the military's perspective on Brazil's global role. Military strategist Golbery do Couto e Silva argued that the economic development of a country with the size and wealth of Brazil should naturally lead to becoming a world power and "a center of autonomous power on the world stage."[95] The marriage between developmentalism and nationalism, or, that is to say, between business and the military, was leading the country toward the construction of an independent foreign policy.[96]

Five decades after the creation of the economic class that led Brazil from building its industrial base in the 1950s to the military coup of 1964, a new economic elite has emerged during the first decade of the century. These are state managers and unionists from state enterprises who have embedded themselves in positions where economic decisions are made. They have forged relationships of trust with the old elites, the business class, and the military. I do not think we are witnessing the creation of a new class in power but the gradual expansion of the old elite, one that feels revitalized with a strong injection of fresh capital and mega projects that revive the old dream of the military caste to turn Brazil into a global power.

3
Building a Strategy

"For South America, but especially for Brazil, the current moment is decisive, but the dilemma is always the same: the challenge of realizing the potential of Brazilian society, overcoming its extraordinary disparities and vulnerabilities by means of the arduous and persistent implementation of a national project, in the context of forming a nonhegemonic South American pole, in close alliance with Argentina—or being incorporated as a subordinate into the United States political system."
— *Samuel Pinheiro Guimarães*

Speaking at the Seventh National Meeting on Strategic Affairs in November 2007, Ambassador Samuel Pinheiro Guimarães said that if one drew up lists of the ten most populated countries, the ten most productive countries, and the ten countries with the largest area, only three—the US, China, and Brazil—would be on all three lists.[1] It seems logical to assume that a country that is among the most powerful and richest in the world requires some long-term planning, at least in areas where the market does not usually intervene, such as defense and technology, in order to occupy its rightful place in the world relative to its size, population, and wealth. Brazil has a long tradition of research, strategic analysis, and planning in this area, and now within the upper echelons of state power, it has the active will to define such a path and take its place among the great global powers.

Upon taking power, Lula and the Workers Party (PT) set up the Strategic Affairs Center (NAE), an initiative operating in the orbit of the Secretariat of Government Communication and Strategic Management. At the start, Luiz Gushiken was Minister, Glauco Arbix was Coordinator (and also head of the Institute of Applied Economic Research, IPEA), and the retired Col. Oswaldo Oliva Neto was Executive Secretary. It became the Secretariat of Strategic Affairs (SAE) in 2008, staffed by some of the country's most notable intellectuals, including Roberto Unger and Samuel Pinheiro Guimarães.

Around mid-2004, just one year after its establishment, the NAE published its first paper, entitled *Project Brazil 3 Phases: 2007, 2015, 2022*, outlining the think-tank's long-term strategic plan for Brazil.[2] It was the first strategic pronouncement of a new political force that was not simply occupying the Planalto Palace but seeking to change the historical destiny of Brazil. From that moment on, the NAE (and later the SAE) became a powerhouse of ideas, proposals, and initiatives that were followed up by state actions that began to shape the project for the country. Some of the most notable projects initiated include the National Defense Strategy, which inspired the reorganization and rearmament of the armed forces with a more precise focus, as well as the consolidation of a technologically independent defense industry. *Project Brazil 3 Phases* maps the trajectory for the country to become a global power. In addition to these proposals, the NAE/SAE produced countless strategic analyses, addressing everything from nano and biotechnology to biofuels and climate change, all significant contributions to government teams, informing key, long-term decisions.

To convert Brazil into a global power requires a dual strategy in the short term. Domestically, Brazil needs to promote high rates of economic growth; overcome the extreme poverty and inequality that act as a drag on development; invest in infrastructure, education, science, and technology research to encourage large Brazilian companies to restructure and increase competitiveness with global multinationals; and build armed forces that can provide security for a country that will be the fifth largest in the world by the end of the decade.

Internationally, the strategy to become a global power requires forging a set of alliances, first regionally with other countries in South America, then with the Global South, and ultimately with the Global North. It also requires ensuring a significant Brazilian presence in international forums, in world trade, and gaining legitimacy in all fields. To achieve these ambitious goals certainly requires strategic thinking.

A history of plans and planning

Even before the developmentalist government of Juscelino Kubitschek (1956–1960), the country had experienced the need to start planning expenditures and investments, to make focused economic plans, to promote sustainable growth. The central objective of the first development plans under the *Estado Novo* (New State) of Getúlio Vargas was the industrialization of the country, beginning with the construction of the National Steel Company in 1941, whose large foundry in Volta Redonda was producing steel by 1946. Kubitschek's Target Plan (1956), however, marks a turning point because it concentrated the state's capacity to stimulate whole sectors of the economy with the Presidential Council for Development and funding from the BNDE.

The emphasis of the Target Plan was on major infrastructure works and developing the industrial base. It included thirty strategic goals organized by sector. The development of the energy sector was allocated 44 percent of total public works investment in order to generate electricity and nuclear energy, and produce and refine petroleum. Thirty percent of investments concentrated on highways, roads, railways and ports, while 20 percent was earmarked for basic industries, particularly steel, aluminum, nonferrous metals, cement, pulp, and paper. Growth averaged 7 percent (GNP) annually between 1957 and 1962, far exceeding the 5.2 percent average during previous periods, with a peak of almost 11 percent in 1958, corresponding to a 17 percent growth that year in industry.

The Plan accelerated industrial growth but did not initiate comprehensive overall development of the country; the sizable monetary input required to finance its projects (including the construction of the new capital, Brasilia) left an unwanted legacy of inflationary tendencies, forcing the adoption of a monetary stabilization program in 1958.[3] One problem Brazil faced was US opposition to the Target Plan, which created external funding dilemmas.[4] The Eisenhower administration did not respond positively to Kubitschek's plan to boost industrial development (by promoting fifty years of progress in a five-year office term), and Ford and General Motors rejected the idea of installing factories in Brazil. Although Washington gave a loan to expand steel manufacturing at Volta Redonda, the Kubitschek administration's fledgling nuclear program caused major tension between the two countries.[5]

The next plan up was the Triennial Plan for Economic and Social Development promoted by economist Celso Furtado with the support of the João Goulart government (1963–1964). Under Furtado's leadership, the Ministry of Planning, Budget and Management was established in 1962. He would be followed as minister by Roberto Campos during the first stage of the military dictatorship. The Triennial Plan was negatively impacted by the intense political and social turmoil of the era, as well as inflation that reached 91 percent in 1964, the year of the coup. Here, one of the main limitations to projects and plans becomes clear: without a stable social, political, and economic climate, the best of programs cannot be implemented. Hence the Strategic Affairs Center concluded that the economy was a victim of politics, in the sense that "inflation and political crises [...] thwarted developmental objectives."[6] With that perspective in mind, the NAE understood that as well as political stability, development plans must address not only economic but also "macro-sectorial" planning, i.e. take account of all variables, both national and international.

With this in mind, other analysts emphasized the role of the US and international capital as destabilizing factors in national development. Moniz Bandeira remembers how, in 1959, Kubitschek denounced "the IMF and the enemies of an independent Brazil trying to force a national capitulation, so that industry falls into the hands of outsiders."[7] Such complaints found receptive ears in both the Military Club as well as the powerful Federation of Industries of the State of São Paulo (FIESP). In Bandeira's opinion, beginning in the early 1960s, the "crisis of class rule," which led to a growing political instability, contributed to tensions that took shape as "the impasse between the growing needs of Brazilian development and dominant U.S. interests."[8] The meddling of Washington included a "silent invasion" of all types of advisers, both military and civilian, raising the number of US citizens in Brazil to as many as 5,000 in 1962, which in turn increased support for right-wing paramilitary groups formed at the time.[9]

The military regime introduced an Economic Action Plan to address the structural causes of inflation. They managed to reduce inflation from 91 percent in 1964 to 22 percent in 1968, lower than expected, and to relaunch growth rates close to 10 percent by the end of the decade, with a strong push from industry, which grew around 15 percent annually.[10] The truth is that during the military regime (1964–1985) planning took a qualitative leap. Despite the anticommunist discourse and being ideologically against state intervention in the economy, the whole military period was characterized by robust state intervention that included a significant tax increase. "The model was never a prototype of free enterprise," an NAE report pointed out, and the interventionist tradition of the Getúlio Vargas period was continued with large infrastructural investments.[11]

In its assessment of planning during the military regime, the NAE valorizes the economic achievements as well as effective state reform in the areas of planning and taxation, which prepared the foundations for growth. The alliance between military leaders, technocrats, and diplomats, according to the NAE assessment, "left marks in the subsequent functioning of the Brazilian state, especially at the level of the tax burden and responsibilities in regulating and promoting development."[12] Among these reforms of a strategic nature, was the creation of the influential Institute of Applied Economic Research (IPEA) in 1964, which remains in place and as important today.[13] The IPEA mission is to provide technical and institutional support for the formulation of public policies and development programs. It is an important and robust institution that has been integrated since 2007 into the Secretariat of Strategic Affairs of the Presidency.

A series of administrative reforms—a key piece of which was 1967's Decree 200—helped consolidate a new mode of governance that ceded "a large part of the responsibility in conducting, with relative autonomy, the objective of intensifying the industrialization process" to planning institutions.[14] By order of Minister of Planning Roberto Campos, the IPEA developed the Ten-Year Economic and Social Development Plan for 1967–1976. Campos had a remarkable and curious career: under the Vargas government he was one of the creators of the BNDE (without the S of "social" at the time) and was its president from 1958 to 1959; he played an important part in the Target Plan with Kubitschek, and later was a minister under the military regime, becoming one of the architects of its planning strategy. A liberal first and a neoliberal later, he was also a strong developmentalist. Leaving office in March 1967, he outlined the ideas that inspired his approach to planning:

> We sought to develop a strategy for long-term development, to escape the constant habit of spontaneous improvisation, which sacrifices the future to the present, for not understanding the past [...] The plan is not an episode, it's a process; not commandments, but an outline; it is not a muzzle but an inspiration; it is not a mathematical exercise, but a calculated adventure. To plan is to prioritize, and prioritizing means delaying one thing for another.[15]

The IPEA has a Guidance Council of twenty people representing different strands of the recent history of the country and, through its ideological diversity, embodies the national project. Alongside the Worker's Party economist Marcio Pochman, president of IPEA, are prestigious economist Maria da Conceição Tavares, also PT; Antonio Delfim Netto, the most prestigious economist to arise from the military regime; engineer Eliezer Batista da Silva, a former president of the state mining company Vale do Rio Doce; Rubens Ricupero, finance minister in 1994 when they introduced the Real Plan; essayist Candido Mendes de Almeida; and Carlos Lessa, former director of the BNDES in the first Lula government; among others. I would like to point out that the ideological diversity and political integration of the advisory group embodies the continuities of the planning process in Brazil for over half a century. I am certain the words of Roberto Campos, quoted above, would be endorsed by every high-ranking official currently directing the country's destiny.

In 1972, the First National Development Plan was launched, prioritizing large scale integration projects in transportation and telecommunications, as well as export corridors. In 1974, the Second Plan expanded basic industries such as steel and petrochemicals in an attempt to achieve national autonomy in key basics. Both plans are hailed today as "the high point of government planning in Brazil," being more extensive and intensive than any others throughout the country's history.[16] The leaders of the military regime considered state enterprises as part of their arsenal of government policy, a concept that was floated again, decades later, by the Lula government. Among the achievements of this period are the construction of the Itaipu Dam, the Trans-Amazonian Highway, the Rio-Niterói Bridge, the first nuclear power plant, and key infrastructure, shipbuilding, mining, and communications works.

The Second National Development Plan, from 1974 to 1979, "paved the way for Brazil's profile as an emerging great power" and its becoming the eighth largest economy in the world.[17] This was made possible because its industrialization strategy no longer focused on producing consumer goods, but instead invested heavily in capital goods, basic materials like nonferrous metals, minerals, agro-chemicals and pulp, as well as energy infrastructure. However, the second oil shock of 1979 and the debt crisis in 1982 led to economic and political turmoil in the final stage of the dictatorship, and the growth of a huge movement for democracy. As economic and political crisis gripped Brazil once more, putting a brake on the "economic miracle," state planning was shelved, and a long period of stagnation and inflation began, marked by ad hoc and defensive stabilization plans that lasted until the introduction of the Real Plan in 1994.

To end this brief history of development plans, it is interesting to note the perspective of the NAE under the Lula government regarding the Real Plan launched by Fernando Henrique Cardoso, the PT's greatest political enemy. The NAE was willing to recognize that "for the first time in many years, the causes of inflation have been preemptively attacked, primarily the budget deficit, rather than attempting to simply minimize its effects through known mechanisms (wage and price controls)."[18] According to the NAE, Cardoso's actions led to not only economic stability but to "a return to government planning." In 1998, the Secretariat of Strategic Affairs prepared the tentative *Brazil 2020* project, which outlined exploratory scenarios for the future of the country, seeking to reflect the "dominant desires" of Brazilian society regarding its future.[19]

Brazil in 3 Phases: The country's centennial

Introducing the first NAE presentation in July 2004, Minister Luiz Gushiken established that the team's goal was to "articulate national intelligence dealing with strategic themes, developing information and analysis" with the objective of developing a national project.[20] The first goal set by the center was to design the *Brazil in 3 Phases* project with an eighteen-year plan: to 2022, with intermediate stops in 2007 and 2015. It explicitly proposed to overcome short-term pitfalls and to plan the future of the country for at least two decades.

The creation of the NAE was one of the first decisions taken by the Lula administration shortly after taking office. Its first executive secretary was Oswaldo Oliva Neto, brother of Senator Aloízio Mercadante, who played an important role in the crucial initial formulations of the center's role. We shall see that after leaving the NAE, Neto came to occupy other significant, but more discreet, posts. The NAE's first publication, *Brazil in 3 Phases*, "embodies the concept of national long-term planning," said Oliva Neto.[21] In 2005, the NAE think-tank was directly integrated into the office of the Presidency of the Republic and re-named the Secretariat of Strategic Affairs (SAE) in 2008.[22] The other government institution for strategic planning—the Institute of Applied Economic Research (IPEA)—is also linked to the SAE.

The National Space Program and the Sustainable Amazon Plan—products of major research and consultation carried out by these institutes—were approved in 2008. The Amazon Plan is a strategy of sustainable development for a region of critical importance to the country's future. The National Defense Strategy report was also published the same year, outlining a complete reorganization of the armed forces and priorities for investment in strategic sectors (nuclear, aerospace, information, and communication technology), as well as drawing up strategic planning cycles with the IPEA.

To develop *Brazil in 3 Phases* and long-term strategic management, a space was opened within the government, giving rise to a "Council of Ministers" in charge of coordinating the project, led by the NAE. Comprised of PT militants and confidantes of President Lula, this genuine think-tank was overseen by Oliva Neto and included the ministers of the Casa Civil (José Dirceu), General Secretariat of the Presidency (Luiz Soares Dulci), Economic and Social Development (Tarso Genro), and Government Communication and Strategic Management (Luiz Gushiken), all presidential appointments, as well as the Minister of Planning, Budget and Management (Guido Mantega). As we will see, participation was only opened up to people outside the inner circle of top PT leadership after the projects were already well defined.

The NAE formed working groups, convened round table discussions and meetings, and produced books and other publications outlining objectives in various sectors. With great pragmatism, the NAE concluded that previous national plans failed due to the static way they were conceived. Thus, the NAE analysts prioritized the concept of process and replaced the concept of "planning" with that of "management," allowing them to intervene and correct problems during a project's implementation.[23] In 2005 and 2006, the NAE undertook a broad nationwide analysis and allocated specialists to study specific sectors, which the center then modeled based on extensive consultation with the population, thereby combining both specialist knowledge and the "popular will."[24] In all, some 500 researchers and 50,000 people participated in the studies, producing a million and a half data entries "related to social perceptions of the future of key national strategic issues."[25]

Arising from this extensive research, fifty major, long-term strategic issues were recognized, which if realized, would place Brazil among the top developed nations. They include: quality of teaching, basic education, violence and crime, social inequality, and employment levels.[26] Between 2004 and 2007, in addition to the above-mentioned study, the NAE produced twelve reports on diverse topics from nanotechnology to climate change, and between 2008 and 2010 teamed up with the IPEA for further strategic planning.[27]

In December 2010, the *Brazil 2022* project was launched by Pinheiro Guimarães. Presenting the document, the Minister for Strategic Affairs explained the importance of long-term planning:

> The job of planning is extremely important for underdeveloped countries like Brazil, unlike the situation in highly developed countries. In highly developed capitalist countries, the maturity of the physical and social infrastructure, and the belief that market forces would guide, in the best manner possible, productive investment and the country's external relations, make planning seem less important. This statement should be qualified, because such developed countries do make very careful and persistent plans regarding the state's role in two key areas: defense and high technology, which are never left to the market and its pricing system.[28]

Pinheiro Guimarães supports the idea that China's growth is due to state planning and the regulation of private companies both in terms of geographical location as well as their commitments to technology transfer and the nationalization of investments and exports. He explains how thirty-seven working groups were formed in the elaboration of *Brazil 2022*, one for each ministry, made up of technical staff from the SAE, the IPEA, the Casa Civil, and each ministry. The document has four parts: "The World in 2022," "South America in 2022," "Brazil in 2022," and "Centennial Goals." The first two outline the perspective of Brazilian strategists on current global and regional realities.

Among the many challenges facing Brazil for 2022, one of the most pressing is the growing concentration of power in the core countries. The paper argues that the gap in military power between the US and the rest of the world will continue to be "a fundamental strategic fact," and will be widened by the evolution of military technology.[29] The global trend, according to the SAE, is towards an acceleration of scientific and technological development that will change the relations of power through intense competition between mega-corporations and states. Because of the huge impact of information technology, nanotechnology will transform the physical processes of production, leading to increasing market oligopolization. Biotechnology and genetic engineering will have an enormous effect on the competitiveness of agriculture, in addition to their effects on human health.

In the military field, armaments will become increasingly lethal, automated, miniaturized, and remotely controlled, increasing the power differential between the United States and the countries of the periphery. All indications are that the concentration of power will be the key tendency in the world, and therefore, "should be the main concern for Brazilian strategy in the international and domestic spheres."[30] To give just one example: the US invests $400 billion in research and registers 45,000 patents a year, while Brazil spends only $15 billion and registers 480 patents. For this reason, *Brazil 2022* proposes that the country must act on key international trends "to prevent the crystallization of the great powers' privileges, which hinder our development."[31]

The proposed strategy is based on what China has been doing: allowing access to its market and natural resources on the condition that industry is developed on its soil and that there is a transfer of technology. In parallel, as the global economic system becomes increasingly dominated by a few companies in the core countries, Brazil should stimulate its national companies to prevent the country from becoming "a mere production and export platform for the mega-multinationals, whose headquarters are located in highly developed countries."[32]

In short, the task is to compete on the same terrain, employing the same means. The main objective is to prevent Brazil's subordinate incorporation into any of the global power blocs, which is why they must lead the South American bloc. According to the *Brazil 2022* analysis, in order to achieve global influence, the South American region must form a bloc with other developing nations, based on its enormous natural resources: minerals, energy sources, arable land, water, and biodiversity. However, due to the heterogeneous nature of the region, with high levels of wealth concentration, poorly developed industry (except in Argentina and Brazil), and the export of raw materials, the task of regional trade integration is an enormous one. To this list of challenges, we can add the recent overwhelming threat from Chinese competition.

Moreover, the US free trade agreements signed with Chile, Peru, and Colombia after the failure of the Free Trade Agreement of the Americas (FTAA) seek to "impede the possibility of the formation of a customs union in South America."[33] To continue and deepen regional integration, Brazil should help overcome the enormous disparities among the twelve South American countries by assisting the development of the most backward. No doubt there are too many declarations and not enough concrete acts at this point, but at the very least, we are witnessing a shift from the previous discourse. But as *Brazil 2022* points out, the asymmetries among the countries of the region have structural features that are not easy to modify.

During the 1960s, all the region's countries had an export pattern overly concentrated in a few products, to the point that just three commodities accounted for some 70 percent of all exports. By 2010, this has changed, albeit only partially. Brazil's three main export products account for 20 percent of total exports. But for the region's next most important exporter, three products account for 40 percent of the total. Brazil's trade balance with its regional partners is quite uneven and its companies are much larger; heavyweight Brazilian companies are assuming increasing importance in other South American nations' economies. Consequently, there is a concern about eventual Brazilian hegemony.

The strategic planners in Brasilia believe their country has a special responsibility to begin reversing this situation. They argue that South America is similar to Europe after World War II, where the United States' Marshall Plan promoted development to prevent the region from falling into the hands of Soviet communism. Thus Brazil should "open its markets without demanding reciprocity, and finance the construction of its continental partners' infrastructure" by expanding the Mercosur Fund for Structural Convergence.[34] The Brazilian government's strategic plan ends on a cautionary note: If South America's most important country leaves the region open to the investment strategies of the market and the multinationals, regional tensions and resentments could increase, which could also affect Brazilian development.

Finally, they propose expansion into West Africa, where Brazil would face strong commercial, financial, and strategic competition from China. However, it has the advantage of not having a colonial past and can propose sharing the South Atlantic peacefully with its African neighbors, an ocean of strategic importance for Brazil's security.

Centennial goals

Brazilian strategic planners envision the Union of South American Nations (UNASUR) as the center of a South American axis by 2022. Mercosur would expand from a customs union into an economic union between the countries. Brazil would be a "fully sovereign country, with the necessary means to ensure the security of its borders, its waters, its airspace, and critical infrastructure against transnational threats, and capable of deterring any State seeking to limit its self-determination, economic security, or development."[35]

In terms of foreign policy, *Brazil 2022* emphasizes that Brazil would take its place on the international stage with giant steps in a short time. In 2003, Brazil helped create the G-20 and held the India-Brazil-South Africa (IBSA) summit. In 2004, it played an active role in the creation of MINUSTAH (UN Stabilization Mission in Haiti) and took over command of the military operation. Brazil formed the G-4 with India, Germany, and Japan in order to reform the UN Security Council. In 2005, the first Summit of South American-Arab Countries was held. In 2006, the Mercosur Structural Convergence Fund was created, operating as a cash transfer fund by Brazil and Argentina to support development in smaller countries like Paraguay and Uruguay. That same year saw the first South American-African Summit. In 2007, the Banco del Sur (Bank of the South) was established, and Brazil and the European Union signed a strategic alliance. In 2008, the Constitutive Treaty of UNASUR was approved. In 2009, Brazil signed trade agreements with India, the BRIC alliance (Brazil, Russia, India, and China) was institutionalized, and the OAS was compelled to revoke its 1962 exclusion of Cuba. Brazil also completed a strategic alliance with France, involving extensive military cooperation. In 2010, the first Latin American and Caribbean Summit was held without the presence of the United States, allowing for the creation of the Community of Latin American and Caribbean States (CELAC). The general boost to South-South policy meant that between 2003 and 2008 Brazil's trade grew 222 percent with Mercosur, 316 percent with Africa, 329 percent with Asia, and 370 percent with Arab countries.[36] One thing Brazilian diplomacy has not yet achieved is the coveted permanent seat on the United Nations Security Council.

The creation of UNASUR and the South American Defense Council (CDS) has played an important role in the region and shows how the strategy being constructed by Brazil is taking advantage of new opportunities opened by the increasing weakness of the United States.

The rejection of the Free Trade Area of the Americas (FTAA) treaty—the backbone of US regional policy—would have been impossible without the series of changes, from 1999 on, that led to the delegitimation of the Washington Consensus, the rise of strong social movements, and progressive and leftist governments coming to power. The Summit of the Americas in Mar del Plata, November 2005, buried Washington's integrationist proposal and simultaneously opened the door to Mercosur's expansion throughout the entire South American region, particularly to Venezuela. The firmness of Brazil's position, along with Argentina, was key to the change in relations. There was a clear *before* and *after* the presidential summit.

The creation of the Union of South American Nations (UNASUR) would not have been possible without this step. In December 2004, the presidents of the region signed the Cusco Declaration, forming the Community of South American Nations. After successive meetings, it adopted the name UNASUR in April, 2007. Following Colombia's air strike on the guerrilla camp of Raúl Reyes (member of the Secretariat of the FARC) in Ecuadorian territory on March 1, 2008—an attack that threatened to explode into a wider conflict in the Andean region—UNASUR decided to create the South American Council of Defense (CDS) to coordinate the region's armed forces, thus consolidating UNASUR's influence in the region.

Although the Treaty was signed in May 2008 in Brasilia, the new law was instituted on March 11, 2011 after meeting the requirement of getting at least nine signatures from the twelve member countries. As a regional project, UNASUR aims to build a participatory and consensual space of integration and union in the cultural, social, economic, and political development of its members, through political dialogue, social policies, education, energy, infrastructure, finance, and the environment, etc., to eliminate socio-economic inequality, for social inclusion, citizen participation, and to fortify democracy.[37]

UNASUR has displaced the OAS. During both the Bolivian right-wing offensive against the government of Evo Morales, in August and September 2008, and the police rebellion in Ecuador on September 30, 2010—which could have become a coup—the new regional alliance was decisive, occupying the center of the political stage and aligning all governments in defense of democracy. The OAS, a once-powerful diplomatic instrument subordinated to the White House, ceased to occupy the central place it had for so many decades.

Clearly the role of Brazil, and particularly the Foreign Ministry at Itamaraty,[38] was instrumental in promoting this shift. Political integration is being consolidated, but progress is needed in the economic field. The process is in place. The mega-infrastructure projects begun ten years ago and overseen by the IIRSA are closely linked to economic and political integration. The next step may be the implementation of a single regional currency, which could lead to a decoupling from the dollar economy.

The creation of the South American Defense Council (CDS) is another strategic move driven by Brazil. The organization was proposed by President Lula and officially launched in December 2008, though its the first planning meeting took place on March 10, 2008. Its origins were tied to the regional crisis between Colombia, Venezuela, and Ecuador around the aforementioned Colombian attack on the clandestine FARC camp in Ecuador. The Declaration of Santiago de Chile, March 2009, established cooperation on defense, tackled asymmetries in military spending, promoted conflict resolution through dialogue, and coordinated the nations' external security. It is not a military alliance but a first concrete step in addressing the complex and sensitive issue of defense.

The meeting of defense ministers, or the Defense Council of the UNASUR, held in Lima on November 11, 2011 agreed to undertake twenty-six actions (codified in the 2012 Action Plan) aimed at regional defense integration, the establishment of a peace zone in South America, and the creation of an aerospace agency. Projects were to be implemented in two to three years' time. Argentina will be responsible for producing the aircraft for training pilots, a process also involving Ecuador, Venezuela, Peru, and Brazil. Each will manufacture parts to be assembled in a place yet to be determined. Brazil, meanwhile, is in charge of a border-monitoring drone project.[39]

In many ways, the trajectory followed by South American countries toward defense integration mirrors the one taken by Brazil and Argentina. On September 5, 2011, the defense ministers of both countries, Arturo Puricelli and Celso Amorim, met to follow up on the agreement between presidents Cristina Fernandez and Dilma Rousseff, on July 29, 2011, reaffirming "the importance of the strategic relationship on defense between Argentina and Brazil." The Joint Declaration signed by the ministers establishes a Mechanism for Strategic Political Dialogue on a vice-ministerial level to intensify military cooperation. The second section defines areas of "cooperation in technology and production for defense" with several objectives: the production of the "Gaucho" jeep, the development of armored personnel carriers, cooperation in naval and aerospace industries as well as in informatics and cyber defense.[40]

Bilateral cooperation has already reached an advanced level in the manufacture of the KC-390 military cargo plane, designed by the Brazilian aeronautical company Embraer; it will feature parts made in Cordoba, Argentina, with a total investment of $1 billion. Such cooperation opens the way for bilateral approaches to production of the Brazilian "Guarani" armored vehicle and the "Gaucho" jeep.[41]

Changes in the region could have been more ambitious if proposals for the integration of energy infrastructure, such as the Southern Gas Pipeline project (which was never fully discussed), had been taken more seriously, and if the agreements that created the Bank of the South, which was to construct a new financial architecture, were implemented. In this respect, the aspirations of the axis formed around the Bolivarian Alliance for the Peoples of Our America (ALBA) are still far from being accepted by all the UNASUR countries.

Brazil's global advancement—one of its long-term strategic priorities—crested on May 16, 2010, when it reached an agreement with Turkey and Iran to resolve the crisis caused by US opposition to Iran's production of enriched uranium. The agreement is to exchange uranium with Turkey, not Iran, thereby avoiding new international sanctions.[42] Such actions put Brazil in direct and public opposition to Washington, but earn it a place on global forums. Furthermore, Brasilia has intensified South-South cooperation, increasing tenfold the resources for technical cooperation with developing countries, placing Itamaraty diplomacy in a good position to take the initiative with fellow southern countries.

The main objectives of the Centennial Goals, at least until 2022, are as follows:

Economy
- 7 percent growth annually.
- Increase the rate of investment to 25 percent of GDP.
- Reduce public debt to 25 percent of GDP (it was 43 percent in 2010).
- Get 100 percent of the adult population online.
- Double production and exports of agricultural produce.
- Increase agricultural productivity by 50 percent.
- Triple investment in agricultural research.
- Double food production.
- Increase in sustainable agriculture fivefold.
- Double the per capita consumption of fish and increase fishing catch by 50 percent.
- Increase the volume of exports fivefold and increase investment in media and high technology sixfold.
- Increase private investment in research and development to 1 percent of GDP.
- Increase total spending on research and development to 2.5 percent of GDP.
- Have 450,000 researchers and achieve 5 percent of global scientific production.
- Triple the number of engineers.

- Dominate microelectronic technologies and pharmaceutical production.
- Increase the number of patents tenfold.
- Ensure independence in the production of nuclear fuel.
- Dominate satellite manufacturing technologies and launch vehicles.

Society

- Eradicate extreme poverty and child labor.
- Reach the figure of 10 million college students.
- Get Brazil into the top ten of Olympic powers.
- Achieve autonomy in the production of strategic materials.
- Double spending on health.
- Universalize welfare.
- Pay equity between blacks and whites.

Infrastructure

- Increase the amount of renewable energy used in the energy matrix to 50 percent.
- Increase hydraulic power use to 60 percent (from 29 percent in 2007).
- Double per capita energy use.
- Install four new nuclear plants.
- Increase geological knowledge of the Amazon territory from 30 to 100 percent.
- Reduce fossil fuels by 40 percent.
- Increase port capacity to 1.7 billion tons.
- Ensure access to high bandwidth of 100 Mbps to all Brazilians.
- Launch two geostationary satellites into orbit.

State

- Increase resources to the Mercosur Structural Convergence Fund tenfold.
- Increase financial and technical cooperation with Africa tenfold.

- Consolidate UNASUR.
- Consolidate political ties with developing countries.
- Launch nuclear submarine.
- Launch the first satellite built in Brazil.

In the process of becoming a global powerhouse, Brazil is taking concrete steps to demonstrate its progress along the proposed trajectory. On the economic level, it achieved the world's sixth largest GDP in 2011, and remains ahead of powers like France. During President Lula's eight years in office, about 30 million Brazilians climbed out of poverty and swelled the middle classes. Social progress was made in education and health, although still an insufficient amount. A series of strategic plans were designed, like the National Defense Strategy. Brazil is now home to some of the largest multinationals in the world, and has achieved energy independence. Being chosen to host the 2014 World Cup and the 2016 Olympic Games (in Rio de Janeiro) is perhaps the best indication of Brazil's elevated global status.

Who's who in strategic planning

Some distinctive personalities have played a prominent role in Brazil's current strategic planning. Not all of them are from the PT, but have received public recognition from other political groups or as career-minded civil servants. In any case, the Lula government had the power to attract them and work with them during this fertile period, laying the foundations of a new national strategy.

Samuel Pinheiro Guimarães is a career diplomat, who served as the Secretary General of the Ministry of Foreign Affairs, Minister of Strategic Affairs, and when Lula left government, High Representative General of Mercosur. He taught at the University of Brasilia, in 2006 was voted "Intellectual of the Year" by the Brazilian Union of Writers, and published eighteen books, among them: *Quinhentos anos de periferia* (500 Years in the Periphery) in 1999 and *Desafios brasileiros na era dos gigantes* (Brazilian Challenges in the Era of Giants) in 2006. The latter book develops a vision for Brazil's strategic role, a process put in motion when he directed the SAE.

Indeed, Samuel Pinheiro is one of the most important Brazilian and Latin America intellectuals. He graduated with a degree in economics from Boston University, and received a law degree from the Federal University of Rio de Janeiro. He is a member of the Center for Strategic Studies at the Superior War School. He played an important role in the *Brazil 2022* project and the formulation of the National Defense Strategy. During the military dictatorship, he was fired from the leadership of the Northeast Development Superintendency (Sudene) for opposing USAID interference in the government of Marshal Humberto Castelo Branco (1964–1967). During the government of General João Figueiredo (1979–1985), he had to leave Embrafilme over a scandal caused by the film *Brasil pra frente* (Forward Brazil), which criticized the dictatorship. During the Collor de Melo government, he left the country, spending five years in France, and under President Fernando Henrique Cardoso (1995–2002), he openly criticized the Free Trade Area of the Americas (FTAA), for which he was removed from office as director of the Itamaraty Research Institute for International Relations.[43] Assessing his trajectory and political positions, he can be considered a left-wing nationalist, but is not a member of any political party.

During the first phase of the Lula administration, he served under Celso Amorim in Foreign Affairs. During that period, Brazil began its international ascent, playing a decisive role in the 2003 World Trade Organization (WTO) summit in Cancun with the creation of the "Group 20-plus," led by Brazil, China, India, and South Africa. His opponents describe him as anti-US, but it would be more accurate to describe him as a staunch supporter of Brazil.

In *Desafios brasileiros na era dos gigantes,* he establishes the three main challenges facing his country. The first is the gradual but steady elimination of internal disparities—which he identifies as the concentration of income and wealth, deprivation and cultural alienation, access to technology, gender and racial discrimination, and the influence of economic power over political decisions.[44]

The second challenge is related to Brazil's chronic external vulnerabilities, which are economic, political, technological, military, and ideological. Pinheiro argues that while economic weaknesses have long been the subject of debate, the question of technology and the country's reliance on imported technology often remain in the background. Military weakness is exacerbated because of reduced military spending in the 1990s under the neoliberal model, dependence on weapons imports, and because the country signed the nuclear nonproliferation treaty.

Pinheiro sees the third challenge as the most significant: for Brazil to fully realize "its economic, political and military power." Brazil is no small country; it is among the largest in the world, alongside China and United States in terms of population, area, and GDP. To develop this potential Brazil must commit to domestic market growth and productivity to drive "capital accumulation per capita" and technological development.[45] In geopolitical terms, Brazil borders ten countries, which should allow it "to develop a political and economic strategy that enables the articulation of a South American regional bloc with the capacity to project great power, *provided that* it is articulated in a nonhegemonic manner, with compensatory mechanisms and the effective reduction of disparities."[46]

Pinheiro argues that these three challenges may only be overcome if the Washington Consensus is challenged, which implies the need for a strong Brazilian state, a regulated economy that is not left to market forces, and strategic planning. He is aware that Brazil's rise to the level of global power will adjust the continental and global balance, and place it in competition with the United States, for whom "Latin America, contrary to what is claimed, is still their most important zone."[47]

Nevertheless, the main reason why these three challenges should be overcome is internal. Pinheiro anchors his analysis in a nationalism that subordinates social conflict to achieve the objectives of great Brazilian power:

> This Brazilian ascent to a position of global power should not be considered utopian, but a necessary national goal, because the failure to achieve these challenges would [...] usher the Brazilian state into a period of great instability

gg4e theratensio

(and possible internal conflicts), of democratic fragility, of growing foreign interference in Brazilian society that could, in the worst possible scenario, lead to territorial tensions and political fragmentation.[48]

The country's relationship with Argentina and the United States is key. He argues that Brazil has no reason to submit to US hegemony, a country that is, in his opinion, distrustful of multilateral solutions to global problems. Pinheiro denounces US policy as a form of "arrogant interventionist unilateralism" that puts their own interests above even international law, and that does not hesitate to resort to armed force.[49]

He asserts that the United States abandoned cooperation with periphery states, opting instead for a policy of control, promoting modernization, disarmament, and the adoption of "liberal democracy."[50] Brazil is surrounded by a collar of US military installations that carry out joint operations with countries in the region, and he believes that US strategy in general is the regionalization of Plan Colombia. To reverse this, "a strong and serene rejection of policies that subject the region to US strategic interests should be the focus of our strategy."[51]

He argues that Brazil must pursue the formation of a South American political union, and cooperation between Argentina and Brazil is essential to achieving this. Hence, the attempts, by Washington and its continental right-wing allies, to destabilize Argentinian governments that share Brazil's focus—which is to say, that prioritize regional unity.

That regional bloc, maintains Pinheiro, must confront three main short-term challenges: to resist US economic absorption through the FTAA, NAFTA, and gradual dollarization; to avoid and oppose possible US military intervention in Colombia that could extend to the Amazon region; and to regain control of their economic policies from under the influence of the IMF and the WTO.[52] His analysis was written in 2006. By 2011, when this book was started, many of these challenges had been overcome or were in the process of being overcome, demonstrating the ongoing success of Brazilian foreign policy.

Other challenges for developing Brazil's foreign policy, according to Pinheiro Guimarães, are in the military and security field: the need to re-equip the armed forces as a military deterrent, to improve military defense of the borders (especially the Amazon), to attain access to technology, and to preserve Brazil's political, economic, and military autonomy. Once having established a united regional bloc, with a consolidated Mercosur, national growth, and a capacity to defend itself, the next step for Brazil would be to prioritize South-South relations with countries like India, China, Russia, South Africa, Turkey, and Iran. These relationships could help address Brazil's military vulnerability through arms purchases from Russia and China.

Pinheiro outlines a strategy of concentric circles that expand simultaneously, where progress in one part reinforces the others, and vice versa. The danger, as experienced by other countries that have tried to realize their potential (or ascend to the level of a global power), is the risk of being attacked by the US. To understand the invasion of Iraq, according to Pinheiro, one must keep in mind the discovery of new oil reserves that had the potential of allowing Iraq to replace Saudi Arabia as the main producer, and to make good on Saddam Hussein's threat of abandoning the dollar standard in favor of the euro.[53] Brazil shares a similar trajectory: to develop their full national potential, which for a country of its size inevitably implies a confrontation with the global hegemonic powers.

Taking into account that the main trends are toward greater concentration of power (military and technological power) in the center of the system and increasing instability and fragility of the peripheries, Pinheiro maintains that there is "no individual solution for any South American country."[54] What's interesting about Samuel Pinheiro's analysis is that it is not anchored in ideology or prejudice, but is the logical conclusion of a perspective concerned with the interests of a strong periphery country. One of the goals set at that time was realized just two years later with the development of a defense strategy for Brazil and, thus, for the entire region.

Samuel Pinheiro is part of a long Brazilian nationalist tradition alongside presidents Getúlio Vargas and Juscelino Kubitschek, the economist Celso Furtado, and in his own way, General Ernesto Geisel, who was president from 1974 to 1979. Pinheiro is part of a genealogy with a long and eventful history in Brazil that cuts across democracy and dictatorship, embraced by civilians, military officers, and professionals alike.

Pinheiro has also articulated his views on nuclear energy and regional integration more recently. In an article entitled "Climate Change and Nuclear Energy," he indicates that 81 percent of the known reserves of uranium are concentrated in six countries, including Brazil, which has the sixth largest reserves despite having only explored 20 percent of its territory, giving it the potential to become the third largest.[55] Only five companies produce 71 percent of the world's uranium and only eight countries hold the technological knowledge for the complete cycle of uranium enrichment and the industrial capacity to cover all stages. Brazil is one of them.

Therefore he believes that Brazil should not sign the Additional Protocol to the Safeguards Agreements with the International Atomic Energy Agency (IAEA) under the Non-Proliferation Treaty (NPT), because it would mean that Brazilian uranium enrichment facilities would be controlled and inspected, as would their program for nuclear submarine development. He maintains that these agreements are instruments disguised to revise the NPT and limit the right of Brazil to develop its own nuclear technology. In conclusion, he writes: "Brazil has mastered the technological domain around the uranium enrichment cycle and has significant reserves of uranium. Only three countries—Brazil, the United States, and Russia—have such a privileged position."[56] This was written while Samuel Pinheiro was serving as Minister of Strategic Affairs.

In regards to regional unity, his article "South America in 2022" (later published in full as part of the *Brazil 2022* project) supports a mega-plan to assist other South American countries.[57] He views Brazil's proposal to launch a Marshall Plan to support regional countries as a sign of intellectual and political courage, and strategic determination. He encourages Brazil to oversee long-term economic development programs to "encourage and finance the economic transformation of the smaller countries."[58] He supports a dual strategy that would open up the Brazilian market to exports from its neighbors, overcoming trade obstacles as it has done with Argentina, and financing the construction of infrastructural projects such as the IIRSA—which also benefits large Brazilian construction companies and accelerates trade towards the Pacific, a route that the São Paulo bourgeoisie is keen on exploiting.

In conclusion, the quintessential intellectual and political influence of Samuel Pinheiro in Brazil's strategic projection cannot be overestimated.

Roberto Mangabeira Unger was the First Minister of Strategic Affairs in 2007, appointed by Lula to launch the new ministry, despite his declaration, just two years earlier, that Lula's government was "the most corrupt in our history," an indication of how the government prioritizes strategic planning goals over political infighting.[59] At twenty-five years of age, he became Professor of Law at Harvard University, the youngest professor in the history of the institution, where he went on to become both a tenured professor and a member of the American Academy of Arts and Sciences. His influence on the development of American legal thinking is such that Richard Rorty says that he contributed to "modifying the curricula of law schools and the self-image of our lawyers."[60] His body of work is considered one of the most extensive and ambitious contributions to intellectual thought on the reorganization of society.[61]

Toward the end of the military dictatorship, he was part of the Brazilian Democratic Movement and, with Ulysses Guimarães, he created the Brazilian Democratic Movement Party (PMDB), helping to draft its founding manifesto. He worked with Leonel Brizola in the PDT. In the 1998 and 2002 elections, he assisted with the candidacy of Ciro Gomes (PPS). He is the grandson of Otávio Mangabeira, who was one of the most important politicians of the Northeast right-wing, founder of the National Democratic Union, governor of Bahia, and chancellor under President Washington Luís (1926–1930). More recently, he was a founding member and vice president of the Republican Party, with the country's former Vice President, José Alencar.

Although little is known of Mangabeira Unger outside Brazil and the United States, his intellectual stature is remarkable. His most important books published in Brazil, although originally in English, are *False Necessity: Anti-Necessitarian Social Theory in the Service of Radical Democracy* (2005), *Politics* (2001), *A Second Way* (2001), *Passion: An Essay on Personality* (1998), and *Democracy Realized: The Progressive Alternative* (1996).[62] With Ciro Gomes, he wrote *O Proximo Passo: uma alternativa Prática para o Brasil* (The Next Step: A Practical Alternative for Brazil), a political/ electoral intervention on the Brazilian political scene. Mangabeira Unger designed a social theory that has been defined as "the most ambitious socio-theoretical project at the end of the twentieth century,"[63] and which, as a project "aimed at social reconstruction, has no contemporary parallel."[64]

This esteemed intellectual personality was appointed Prime Minister of Strategic Affairs by Lula. He was only in office for two years, from June 2007 to June 2009, but was key to the development of some of the most notable initiatives of Lula's eight years. The National Defense Strategy, bearing his signature, marks a turning point in the recent history of Brazil, and its importance deserves to be studied in detail. He also designed the first steps of regional initiatives for the Amazon, the Northeast and Midwest, sectoral initiatives in labor-capital relations in education and agriculture, as well as for a national agenda for public governance, and initiatives towards overcoming apartheid in health/social policy.[65]

In his *Programmatic Letter to Lula*, he argues that the social base of the project for a new model of development is the desire of the majority of the Brazilian people to follow the path of the "second middle class: mestizo, hailing from below, and composed of millions of Brazilians struggling to open small businesses, studying at night, and responsible for inaugurating a national culture of self-help and initiative."[66] Unlike the revolution of Getúlio Vargas, who oversaw a state alliance with organized sectors of society and the economy (employers and unions), the current revolution in Brazil is that the state is using its resources to follow the example of "this vanguard of emerging workers," who command the popular imagination.

Mangabeira Unger outlines some long-term ideas and proposals:

> We will not achieve this goal without doing something rare in our national history: innovate institutions. It is not enough solely to regulate the market economy. It is not enough to counterbalance inequalities generated by the market solely through social policies. It is necessary to reorganize the market to make it institutionally and socially inclusive and to expand opportunities. This is just one of many applications for institutional reconstruction that we lack. Without it, material public works, however justified, remain far from solving Brazil's problems, or even achieving their own goals.[67]

In one of the most interesting passages, he proposes redesigning labor-capital relations, which had remain unchanged since the period of Getúlio Vargas. Brazil faces the threat of "being squeezed in a vise between countries with high productivity and countries with cheap labor," so for reasons of national interest, he argues that it must escape the vise-grip by valorizing work and productivity and not by debasing labor. "Ours is not a future of China with less people."[68] He then proposes measures to address the problem of informal labor and profit-sharing within companies, something that is in the Constitution but has yet to become law.

In terms of strategic thinking, Mangabeira Unger has some things in common with Samuel Pinheiro: "Our country is destined to become great without becoming imperial."[69] During the Seventh Meeting on Strategic Studies, he proposed four great axes: defense, the Amazon, digital expansion, and the expansion of economic opportunities. There can be no development without a defense strategy, he said, proposing a reorganization of the armed forces towards a new form of territorial deployment, alongside consolidation of the defense industry and personnel training. He applauded Brazil's openness in terms of its defense policy debate.

Regarding the question of the Amazon, he asserts that it cannot be preserved as an area without economic activity, but nor should it be deforested to make way for cattle and soybeans. He argues for "a national project of economic and ecological zoning, with differential economic strategies for different regions," which implies "confronting completely new problems in the world."[70] One of the biggest challenges he identifies is how to preserve a decent quality of life and education for the dispersed Amazonian population.

Digital inclusion can be achieved, he argues, through developing a national Infovía network, stimulating domestic content production, and "a system of Internet governance in Brazil and in the world, to ensure the community management of the Internet by global civil society and not control by nation states or corporate interests."[71] To move in this direction, he advocates using state resources to support the majority of unorganized workers, 62 percent of whom work in the informal economy. While aware that a system based on inequalities will not be changed by social policies but only by finding a new model, he advocates a social policy premised on the training and education of the population. Regarding what he calls "the democratization of the market economy," he was more explicit than in the letter to Lula: it is about reorganizing the market, he says, about rebuilding institutions, which will not happen as "a gift from an enlightened technocracy and a passive population," but as a result of "popular pressure."[72]

Finally, he notes that one major obstacle to succeeding as a global power is that Brazilians still do not feel a sense of grandeur about their own country, in the sense that they cannot yet imagine a great destiny and are prisoners of a fatalistic view. Mangabeira Unger repeats over and over again the notion of "stature without empire." He believes that the world is being held prisoner due to a lack of alternatives to the systematic impoverishment of existing democracies. Brazil needs to discuss alternatives and embark on changing the world, as other countries had in other times and places. "Those nations that became powerful in the world, and whom we have become accustomed to imitate, were formed in the midst of economic crises and wars."[73] Brazil must learn to change without war and destruction, something that requires a new vocabulary and above all, the collective realization that this is one of the central problems of the country.

Retired Colonel Oswaldo Oliva Neto was the first General Secretary of the Strategic Affairs Center (NAE) in 2003; with the departure of Luis Gushiken in 2007, he became head of the agency. He is the brother of the historic PT leader Aloízio Mercadante and the son of influential General Oswaldo Muniz Oliva, who was commander of the Superior War School in the 1980s. He retired from the army in 1990 to become a consultant in strategic planning, his specialized area in the army.[74] Oliva Neto held a postdoctoral position in Policy, Strategy, and Senior Management at the School of Army Staff, studied several specialization courses at the Getulio Vargas Foundation, is author of the NAE methodology for long-term strategic planning, as well as the essay "PENTA: Strategic Foresight and Interaction Compared (A Strategic Management Methodology."[75]

During Lula's first government from 2003 to 2006, Oliva Neto was responsible for laying the foundations for strategic plans in several areas. In 2004, he went from being assistant to the commander of the army to NAE Executive Secretary. In 2006, he became Minister of the NAE, the agency that coordinated *Brazil in 3 Phases*, and oversaw strategic analyses in biofuels, climate change, nanotechnology, political reform, demographics, the fuel matrix, the macro-economic model, and digital inclusion. Under Lula's second administration, 2007–2010, he became first counselor to the president for the digital inclusion project in public schools, and then strategic planning consultant and director of the Penta Strategic Foresight Company.

In 2006, while still a member of the NAE, he proposed the creation of a "South American NATO," with the conviction that in the future there will be regional wars around access to water.[76] According to Oliva Neto, the regional military coordination targets would be: to defend natural resources, to deter extracontinental intervention in the Southern Cone, and to ease relations between South American countries. He saw this as part of the *Brazil in 3 Phases* project and noted that "when the problems of energy depletion, water, and raw materials become more acute, [other countries] beyond South America could turn their eyes to our region."[77]

In 2006, Oliva Neto gave a long interview on one of the NAE's priorities: energy. He stressed that a new ethanol energy network, cleaner than the current one, will be established in just twenty years. This indicates that, in his opinion, the country has very little time to add new energy sources to the matrix because, once the new network to replace petroleum is in place, the window of opportunity for other plans will have passed. The goal is to exploit Brazil's strong comparative advantage in ethanol production; a survey conducted by the NAE indicated that there are some 90 million hectares available for growing sugarcane, offering an opportunity to begin transforming the energy matrix.[78] He also talked about nanotechnology, an issue addressed by another extensive NAE study that involved the participation of specialized entrepreneurs and scientists from all over the world. If Brazil does not take the issue seriously, explained Oliva Neto, it could be out of the industrial market in ten years time, a disaster for a country with claims to be a global power.

In the same interview, one of the few given by the retired colonel, he emphasizes the danger faced by countries specializing in microelectronics—like South Korea—with the emergence of nanoelectronics, which has the potential to bypass the microelectronics market in just five to ten years. Brazil should learn from such examples as they develop their own industries, says Oliva Neto. "We are creating a critical mass of researchers, professors, and specialists that Brazil never had before," he said in reference to the fact that Brazil produces as many specialist graduates as France and Germany.[79] In Dilma's administration, the Ministry of Science and Technology is headed by Oliva Neto's brother, Aloízio Mercadante Oliva.

An agreement between Brazil and France, signed in September, 2009, for the purchase of fifty-one EC-725 military transport helicopters, four conventional submarines, and a nuclear submarine, presented a major new opportunity to the PT strategic planners. Brazil also announced the purchase of thirty-six Rafale fighters, although this part of the deal was later canceled by the Dilma administration. All the deals involve the transfer of technology and most of the assembly work will be done in Brazil—as proposed by the National Defense Strategy—thereby contributing to a revival of a powerful state-linked military industry.

With the creation of a burgeoning Brazilian military-industrial complex, Colonel Oliva Neto becomes a key figure. A highly trusted person within the Lula and Dilma administrations, he embodies the dual capability to both plan and execute strategies, and many of the steps the country has taken were designed with great care by Oliva Neto and his small team.

The deal for the manufacture of helicopters with the EADS Company, the largest European manufacturer of armaments, meant a corresponding Brazilian counterpart was needed, as none of the medium-sized businesses dominating the Brazilian military industry were appropriate.[80] The government decided to revive the old Engesa (Specialized Engineers SA) company, created in 1963 and prominent in the 1970s and 1980s in manufacturing armored vehicles and trucks, including the Urutu and Cascabel tanks. The company had gone bankrupt in 1993.

Creating Engesaer (or a new Engesa) is the result not only of the arms deals with France, but also Oliva Neto's quiet and patient work since 2008. The new company receives and processes technology transferred by EADS. The EC-725 helicopters are produced in the Helibras factory in Brazil, the only helicopter manufacturer in Latin America—although it is 70 percent owned by Eurocopter, a subsidiary of EADS and the leading manufacturer of civil helicopters in the world, linked to EADS. Nonetheless, Europeans will have only 20 percent of the Engesaer shares, with the remainder reserved for private domestic investors, pension funds, and the federal government.[81] According to the *Revista Istoé*, the entire process was undertaken in absolute secrecy by Oliva Neto.

A further decisive step was taken in May 2010 with the signing of a partnership deal between Odebrecht and EADS Defense & Security. Which is to say, a deal was cut between a global leader in aerospace and weapons and a Brazilian construction company, among the twenty largest in the world. The company's statement is very clear: "The alliance aims to become a competent and trusted partner of the armed forces, governmental organizations, and local companies."[82] EADS had revenues of $60 billion in 2009, producing civil and military aircraft, missiles, sensors, and a wide range of military equipment. Odebrecht claimed $25 billion in heavy construction, infrastructure, energy, oil, and petrochemicals; it is a family-based Brazilian multinational employing about 90,000 people. Oliva Neto became Director of Business Development in the new company, Odebrecht-EADS Defesa SA, based in São Paulo.

Three months later, in September 2010, Odebrecht took another important step with the creation of the Copa Gestão em Defesa (Copa Defense Management Company) with which it entered the growing and lucrative market for modernizing the armed forces. The new company has two minority partners, Atech, a technology company involved in the Surveillance System of the Amazon (SIVAM), and Neto Olive's company Penta.[83] In early 2011, it took control of Mectron, the largest Brazilian manufacturer of missiles and one of the largest defense companies.[84] The BNDES controlled 27 percent of the total capital in Mectron, and Odebrecht now controls a more than 50-percent stake, well placed to take advantage when a strategic restructuring of the sector occurs.

Odebrecht has a long relationship with the Worker's Party and Lula, reaching back to at least 1992, and has made significant economic contributions to their campaigns, to the point of creating a relationship of mutual trust. In 2008, Odebrecht had already been commissioned by the government, without bidding, to produce four conventional submarines and a nuclear submarine in partnership with the French company DCSN. The contract was estimated to be worth $10 billion, and included the construction of a shipyard at a naval base.[85] Oliva Neto embodies the alliance between the state led by the Worker's Party and the great Brazilian industrialists, involving military officers and civilian strategists in planning the course of Brazil towards its destiny as a great power.

One could also mention other important strategic planners and managers. Like Aloízio Mercadante, founder of PT, key man in the Senate during the two Lula governments, Minister of Science, Technology, and Innovation, and then later in the Education Ministry under the Dilma administration. Celso Amorim is another key figure in the PT governments. As Lula's Foreign Minister, he played an important role in global forums and in various regional crises, and was named the "world's best foreign minister" by the magazine *Foreign Policy*.[86] In Dilma's administration, he was the Minister of Defense at a strategic moment in the rearmament of the armed forces.

4

From a Resistance Strategy to a National Defense Strategy

"If we would like to be a great country, if we would like to be able to defend ourselves and not be intimidated, we need to arm ourselves, and to arm ourselves, we need a defense industry based on our capabilities."
—*Roberto Mangabeira Unger*

In late 2004, the Army general staff sent four senior officers to Vietnam to study the guerrilla techniques that defeated the United States forces three decades ago. The story of the mission was posted for several days on the Army website (www.exercito.gov.br), noting that "the visit was to make contact with the armed forces of that country in order to investigate the viability, in the near future, of conducting exchanges regarding the Resistance Strategy at strategic, tactical and operational levels."[1]

The mission included Lt. Col. Moraes José Carvalho Lopes and Captain Paul de Tarso Becerra Almeida, both from the Jungle Warfare Training Center, Major Cláudio Ricardo Hehl of the Officers Improvement School, and Colonel Luiz Alberto Alves of the Ground Operations Command. On the same website, General Claudio Barbosa Figueiredo, head of the Amazon Military

Command, explained that the mission visited the cities of Hanoi and Ho Chi Minh (formerly Saigon), as well as the Cu Chi province, which has preserved 250 kilometers of tunnels built during the war. He said that Brazil's Resistance Strategy "does not differ much from guerrilla warfare and is a resource that the army would not hesitate to adopt during a possible confrontation with a country or group of countries with greater economic and military potential than Brazil," adding that "one must have the rainforest itself as an ally to combat the invader."[2]

General Figueiredo is not exactly a man of the left. During the military regime, he was aide to President Marshal Arthur da Costa e Silva (between 1968 and 1969). He assumed command of the Amazon with the arrival of Lula in government in February 2003. Shortly after taking this position, he appeared before a parliamentary committee: "We need to employ a strategy that entails a high cost for any force that attempts to venture into the Amazon."[3] At the same meeting, he noted that "we are developing a resistance strategy in Brazil that transforms the forest into an ally, an enemy of our enemy." He was very clear that the strategy would be used against larger forces from "core countries," whose armies Brazil could not match in a conventional war.

The general was referring to a strategy designed a long time ago by the military—around 1998, he said—addressing concerns regarding the fall of Soviet socialism and the unilateral hegemony of the United States, which was eyeing the riches in the Amazon, and furthermore, was constructing a ring of military bases around the country.[4] The Resistance Strategy would have begun to be formulated in the early 1990s, by officers who had participated in the struggle against guerrillas in Araguaia River during the latter part of the 1970s, and who had been trained at the Jungle Warfare Training Center based in Manaus. In 1991, the commander of the Amazon, General Antenor de Santa Cruz Abreu, told the National Defense Commission of the House of Representatives that they would turn the jungle into a Vietnam if there was an invasion; that year the topic was discussed at the School of Army Command and the General Staff Headquarters, with the objective of designing a strategy to transform the regular forces into guerrilla forces in case of invasion.[5]

Even General Luis Gonzaga Lessa, former commander of the Amazon, said in 1990 that, with the end of the Cold War, the United States was left as the sole hegemonic power, and its assumed role as "world policeman" became "a concern for us all."[6] Around this time, the military began to develop the notion that a technologically superior power could invade part of the Amazon to seize their proven reserves of strategic metals (such as niobium, used in the aircraft industry) and water. This led to Military Command conducting guerrilla warfare training in the Amazon and to discussions, as early as 2001, around the need for the general population to participate in a Resistance Strategy.[7]

João Roberto Martins Filho, president of the Brazilian Association for Defense Studies, argues that by the mid-1990s the Resistance Strategy was already established and was revitalized by the end of the decade when the US approved Plan Colombia, which the Brazilian military saw as a threat to the Amazon.[8] The theme is interesting because it shows how the military has been able to set its own priorities even at a time when neoliberal governments had weakened the state apparatus and reduced the defense budget. The nationalist spirit of the military persevered under both military rule and the Washington Consensus, and the armed forces maintained their independence of thought with or without the support of those in political power.

According to historian of Brazilian external relations, Luiz Alberto Moniz Bandeira, the military never trusted the intentions of the United States, a position aggravated when the US intensified its military presence in Colombia, Ecuador, and Peru under the pretext of fighting drug trafficking and guerrillas. The US military presence in the region has both increased and diversified since deactivating Howard Base in Panama in 1999. In the early 2000s, the Southern Command had responsibility for the bases at Guantánamo (Cuba), Fort Buchanan and the Roosevelt Roads Naval Reservation (Puerto Rico), Soto Cano (Honduras), Comalapa (El Salvador), and the newly created air bases Manta

(Ecuador), Queen Beatrix (Aruba), and Hato Rey (Curacao). It also operated a network of seventeen ground-based radar garrisons: three in Peru, four in Colombia, and the rest—mobile and clandestine—in other Andean and Caribbean countries.[9] In the mid-2000s, Colombia became the fourth largest recipient of US military aid in the world, behind Israel, Egypt, and Iraq, and the US embassy in Bogotá is the second largest in the world after Iraq.

In the 1990s, there were huge differences of opinion between the military and the neoliberal governments in Brazil over the weakening of the defense industry; during the 1970s and 1980s the defense industry was producing about 70 percent of the equipment used by the armed forces, then came a reversal—tanks (previously exported) were now imported, as were armor, bazookas, and ammunition. These policies appeared to originate in Washington and increased nationalist sentiment among Brazilian officers "where the vast majority blamed the US for neoliberal policies imposed by the IMF and World Bank."[10]

Brazil was firmly opposed to Plan Colombia. During the Fourth Conference of Defense Ministers of the Americas, held in Manaus in October 2000, then-President Cardoso rejected the possibility of involving the Brazilian army in the fight against drugs, as the Clinton administration proposed. In response to Plan Colombia, Brazil launched Plan Cobra (an acronym for Colombia and Brazil) to prevent the conflict from spreading to the Brazilian Amazon, and Plan Calha North to prevent guerrillas and drug traffickers from crossing the border.[11]

The Brazilian military felt surrounded by US bases in that period and reaffirmed a commitment to strengthening its autonomy. A comprehensive report appeared in the conservative newspaper *Zero Hora*, in March 2001, detailing the positioning of US armed forces. The image in the report mapped a ring of United States military bases around Brazil: "The United States has established a presence in South America and nearby islands over the past two years, creating a '*cordon sanitaire*' of 20 military garrisons, divided between aerial and radar bases."[12] According to the report, the relationship between the armed forces of Brazil and the United States is one of "noncooperation," the Brazilians refusing to allow US bases on its territory, or participate in joint maneuvers with the US, and receiving almost no funding to combat drug trafficking.

Fernando Sampaio, rector of the School of Geopolitics and Strategy (dedicated to the study of military matters), sums up Brazil's perception of Plan Colombia and the Pentagon's military deployment in the region: "It is a dispute over regional hegemony. Brazil does not want to be another satellite in this US-sponsored war constellation."[13]

The growing rapprochement between Argentina and Brazil, which began taking shape in the 1980s and materialized with the creation of Mercosur in 1990, helped to modify the traditional hypothesis, held since independence, that Brazil's main military threat came from Argentina. During the colonial period, this hypothesis was prioritized, and it was reiterated by the military dictatorship after 1964, but global geopolitical changes, especially the collapse of the USSR and the formation of a unipolar world, as well as Argentina becoming a strategic ally through Mercosur integration, helped undo perceived notions about Brazil's greatest enemy. Although it is possible that the discovery of vast petroleum reserves in the "pre-salt layer" on the coastline—the so-called "Blue Amazon"—has played an important role in redefining defense priorities.

The hypothesis guiding this book is that with Lula's arrival at Planalto Palace, the military again figure prominently in the plan to turn Brazil into a global power. Or, in other words, I am arguing that there is a confluence between the regional and the global project put forward by the PT government and the old nationalist aspirations of the armed forces, which allows them to build a powerful alliance that goes far beyond the immediate political context to project toward long-term objectives. The formulation of the National Defense Strategy, in 2008, was a turning point that revealed an interpenetration of influences existing between the new administration and the military nationalists.

The National Defense Strategy

On 6 September 2007, President Lula issued a decree creating an interministerial committee for the formulation of a National Defense Strategy (END). It was chaired by the Minister of Defense, Nelson Jobim, and coordinated by the Minister of Strategic Affairs, Roberto Mangabeira Unger. Other committee members included the Minister of Planning, Budget and Management, the Minister of Finance, and the Minister of Science and Technology, with support from the commanders of the three armed services. The committee heard expert views (both civil and military) on defense over the course of a year and, on December 17, 2008, ministers Jobim and Mangabeira Unger presented a fifty-eight-page document to the president. It would be the first time that Brazil had ever formulated a long-term defense strategy.

Three priorities defined the National Defense Strategy document: First, the reorganization of the armed forces and the redefinition of the role of the Ministry of Defense; second, the restructuring of the defense industry to equip the armed forces based on technologies under national control; and third, a new relationship between society and the armed forces, one that returned to a republican ideal, and that reflected in its composition the integration of the country.

Some key themes of Brazilian strategists are reiterated in the initial pages of the END report: "Brazil will rise to the forefront of the world without exerting hegemony or domination" and "expand without being imperialist."[14] Defense strategy is inseparable from national development strategy, so one supports the other: development needs to be defended, and the armed force needs to provide a shield to development. Defense is, according to the END report, the capacity of saying *no*, when necessary.

The country's independence is based on three pillars: mobilization of physical, financial, and human resources; autonomous technological training; and democratization of educational and economic opportunities, because "Brazil will not be independent if a part of its population lacks conditions for learning, working, and producing."[15] The END report provides twenty-three guidelines that summarize the philosophy of and objectives for an effective national defense strategy. Logically, the starting point is deterrence and combat capability, establishing that even the most sophisticated technology is not an alternative but simply an instrument of combat. Being a country of vast land and sea frontiers, "strategic mobility" is crucial for Brazil, necessitating the capacity to monitor and control those borders.

This task requires the operational unity of the three branches of the armed forces because, separately, they cannot guarantee the protection of so vast a country. Three strategic sectors are emphasized: aerospace, cyberspace, and nuclear. Regarding the third sector, the END document asserts the need to master the entire nuclear cycle with technological independence and the capacity to produce nuclear submarines.[16]

One of the most important guidelines—one that is already being implemented—is the repositioning of troops:

> The main army units are stationed in the Southeast and the South. The navy squadron is concentrated in Rio de Janeiro. The technological installations of the air force are almost all located in São José dos Campos, in the state of São Paulo. [The National Defense Strategy] however identifies the greatest defense concerns geographically in the North, the West and the South Atlantic.[17]

The traditional deployment of the armed forces was a legacy of the historic rivalry between the Portuguese and Spanish since colonial times, leading to a deep mistrust between the elites and the populations of Brazil and Argentina. This historical mistrust was further stirred up by the United States, realizing that cooperation between the two countries would create a center of power in South America that would affect its political, economic, and military influence.[18] Hence the significance of the shift that began in the 1990s with Mercosur, a change in regional relations that is further consolidated in the END report, with the awareness that Brazil needs to defend the Amazon and its new oil deposits in the South Atlantic from outside powers other than Argentina.

As part of the new plan, the Navy would deploy in the basins of the Amazon and the Paraguay-Paraná estuary, the Army would place its strategic reserves in the center of the country as a launching base from which it could deploy anywhere, and the presence and density of all three branches would be increased at the borders. A section of the report is devoted to what it defines as the priority region, the Amazon. Aware that powers in the Global North seek to exercise international authority over its wealth, the Ministry of Defense remains defiant: "Brazil guards the Brazilian Amazon in the service of humanity, and for Brazil itself."[19]

South American integration features prominently in the National Defense Strategy. It proposes to create a South American Defense Council and defines how, confronted with a possible deterioration of the international scenario, Brazil must protect both its territory and its maritime trade lines and oil rigs. Two new strategic concerns are introduced here. The first is the discovery of large oil reserves off the Atlantic coast, ensuring energy independence for Brazil and needing to be defended by a fleet of submarines the country has yet to procure. Secondly, foreign trade lines extend beyond the southern borders to Pacific ports, meaning that the IIRSA corridors also need to be guarded. Therefore, regional integration is of a strategic nature. Regional energy sources including large hydroelectric dams in neighboring countries must also be considered strategic points to be defended by the military.

The END report urges national autonomy in essential defense technologies. Brazil's military industry merits its own special chapter, but suffice it to mention that the END report recommends the state ensure that the military industry attains the highest level of technology possible without allowing it to be subject to the logic of the market, as has happened in the past. On one hand, it seeks to phase out the purchase of imported military hardware, and on the other, to develop a military-university-industrial complex capable of supplying the whole region.

For each arm of the military, the National Defense Strategy proposes specific objectives. The navy should be able to deny the use of the sea to any hostile power, defend oil platforms, and to this end, build a major submarine naval force with both conventional and nuclear submarines. In addition to the South Atlantic submarine base, it should establish a second naval base at the mouth of the Amazon River, similar to the one at Rio de Janeiro. The territorial army must master guerrilla warfare as well as tactics of concentration and dispersal, and its basic ground combat units should be completely restructured. Strategic Action Rapid Forces should be formed, with each combat brigade a separate module comprised of about 3,000 men. The whole force must assume a new strategic outlook: "The transformation of the entire army into a vanguard, based on the brigade module, takes precedence over the strategy of maintaining a presence."[20] The army should be capable of launching a formidable air defense, which requires mastering satellite technology and clandestine cyber warfare. Defense strategy however, is not considered a goal in itself: The defense of the Amazon region is not simply understood in terms of the armed forces but in relation to its sustainable development. Defending the Amazon, asserts the END report, means solving the land problem, whether that is the land conflict between the landless and the landowners, or the state of legal uncertainty regarding ownership. The Army must assume the imperatives of asymmetric war[21] because it may have to confront more powerful enemies, thus it must combine conventional with unconventional action, turning an asymmetric war into a "war of national resistance."[22]

The Air Force, meanwhile, faces a short-term challenge to replace the current outdated fleet of fighter jets. The force needs aircraft to transport strategic reserve brigades from the center of the country to any territorial point in just a few hours. Aviation units are to be placed in the center of the country near the strategic reserve of ground forces. Technological independence is necessary in this field, therefore the END proposes strengthening the São José dos Campos scientific and technological complex in São Paulo state. However concentration of the aircraft industry in this city becomes a strategic vulnerability, requiring "the gradual dispersal of some of the most sensitive parts of the complex."[23]

The Air Force's current vulnerability requires quick decisions and then long-term consideration. Two potential paths have been proposed: the first would be to form a strategic partnership with an international company to design and manufacture, in Brazil, a fifth-generation jet fighter like those that already exist on the global market. The second possibility would be to purchase fifth-generation fighters in a deal that includes a comprehensive and complete transfer of technology, including all source code. The purchase would be the first step towards national production of the jet fighters by a Brazilian company with state involvement, which would eventually be capable of the entire manufacturing process. This second solution was the part of the aforementioned deal between Brazil and France for the purchase and manufacture of submarines and military transport helicopters, which would culminate in the purchase of thirty-six Rafale fighters that, beginning with the sixth plane, would be built in Brazil. However, the latter part of this agreement was postponed in order to explore other possibilities.

As a indication of how highly Brazilian authorities value strategic change, many of the proposals in the END report have already been implemented with some urgency. To illustrate the point, here are three examples. The first concerns the restructuring of the Army to relocate itself in the Amazon. In April 2010, *Zero Hora* reported an ebullient spirit in military barracks because "the biggest change for the troops in the country since the military took power in 1964 is underway."[24] However, the newspaper notes, now it is not about ideology but geopolitics: infantry brigades are being transferred from the coast to the center plateau and the Amazon.

Twenty-eight new military posts were created in the Amazon frontier on top of the existing twenty-one, and in addition to the movement of Rio Grande do Sul and Parana armored divisions to the region. To this end, the army plans to invest nearly $90 billion in restructuring by 2030. When the process of relocation and restructuring is finished in the next few years, the army will have added 59,000 new troops to the existing 210,000, and the war machine will be more agile with the addition of up-to-date equipment. This process forms part of the Defense Ministry's "Strong Arm Strategy," which includes the "Protected Amazon" and "Homeland Sentinel" programs. To get a sense of the preference for Amazon defense, 40 percent of all new soldiers will be placed in that region, almost doubling the number to 49,000 soldiers.

The Brazilian Navy established the Submarine Development Program (PROSUB) in the wake of purchasing submarines from France in 2009, to oversee the construction of a huge shipyard in Itaguai, Rio de Janeiro, where the four conventional submarines and Brazil's first nuclear submarine are to be made. The submarines will be instrumental in the Navy's monitoring and defending of the South Atlantic oil fields. The shipyard was originally owned by the Navy, but has been ceded to a partnership of Odebrecht (49 percent ownership) and France's DCNS (50 percent). The remaining 1 percent belongs to the Navy, which has veto power over strategic decisions made by the two companies.

Itaguaí shipyard, still under construction at the time of writing, will be responsible for manufacturing the first of four conventional submarines by 2015, though the initial production stages will be in France. From that point, the shipyard will produce one sub every two years and, by 2023, the nuclear submarine will be ready, pending transfer of the necessary technology from France, as provided in the deal. The Nuclep company, industrial arm of the Brazilian nuclear complex, is responsible for making the hulls of the ships. A submarine base will be added to the shipyard, built by Odebrecht, in a complex on the Bay of Sepetiba. In the long term, by 2047, the shipyard will build at least twenty submarines, and several nuclear subs, and will modernize Brazil's current five conventional submarines, thus making it the largest South Atlantic fleet.[25]

Regarding the manufacture of helicopters, the deal with France included the purchase of fifty-one military transport EC-725 helicopters that are being manufactured by Helibras. Helibras set up in Itajubá (Minas Gerais) in 1978 with a majority participation from Eurocopter and a minority participation from the Brazilian State. In thirty-three years it has produced some 500 helicopters, mostly civil transport, but the agreement for the construction of the EC-725 represents a quantum leap for the company that ranks among the four largest manufacturers of military helicopters in the world, alongside Sikorsky and Bell in the US, and Agusta in Italy.[26]

The first three EC-725s were delivered in December 2010 to equip the three branches of the armed forces.[27] By mid-2013, Helibras will be able to oversee all production in Brazil.[28] Of the two major projects signed with France, this one is moving faster. The projection is that 50 percent of the manufacturing of the EC-725s will be done by Brazil by 2020, when Helibras will have the ability to design, develop, and produce on its own. Helibras's president, Lutz Bertling, describes this as "a process of nationalization of helicopters," and hopes to expand it beyond the EC-725.[29]

Although significant, these three examples are just the beginning of the changes being introduced by the National Defense Strategy. In August 2010, the Senate approved the restructuring of the armed forces, unifying the three branches through a Joint Chief of Staff working closely with the Defense Minister.[30] This move strengthens the unified leadership of senior command and advances the centralization and coordination of forces.

Brazil has a 7,491-kilometer coastline, sometimes referred to as the "Blue Amazon" in plans, emphasizing its strategic importance on a par with the "green" Amazon jungle. At this point in time, Brazil's maritime area stretches 200 miles from the coastline, and includes 3.5 million square kilometers in what is called the Exclusive Economic Zone. But Brazil is litigating in the United Nations' Commission on the Limits of the Continental Shelf to extend these limits to 350 miles, due to the particular characteristics of its continental shelf. If this lawsuit succeeds, maritime areas of Brazil will extend to 4.5 million square kilometers, an area larger than the "green" Amazon.[31]

To defend this huge, resource-rich area, and its oil, requires strong military deployment. In July 2010, the Atlantic II maneuvers were carried out, with the participation of all three military branches and some 10,000 soldiers. The Navy employed thirty ships. The exercises were held on July 19–30, encompassing the states of Rio de Janeiro, Espirito Santo, and São Paulo, as well as the islands of the Fernando de Noronha archipelago and the São Pedro and São Paulo archipelago (a thousand miles from the coast), and the exercises involved a simulated defense of oil infra-structure and ports, landing exercises, protection of nuclear power plants as well as a simulated recovery of the P-43 platform for Petrobras, in the Campos Basin, by a Marines Special Group.[32]

It was the first exercise in military maneuvers to defend the newly discovered oil fields. Admiral Paulo Ricardo Medici, deputy chief of Naval Operations Command, told Reuters that when Brazil possessed a nuclear submarine "no country will have the courage and conditions to approach our coast."[33] The specialized military website Defesabr.com made a hypothetical calculation of the needs of the Navy to defend the extensive Blue Amazon coast and the oil rigs: 140 patrol craft, 42 escorts, 28 conventional submarines and 14 nuclear.[34] These numbers seem exaggerated but they are not far from those outlined in the country's actual defense plans.

During the NATO Lisbon Summit on November 19–20, 2010, the heads of state noted that the military alliance—created in 1949 to defend the Euro-Atlantic area—had realized its voca-tion to become a global intervention force. "The citizens of our countries rely on NATO to defend the allied nations, to mobilize our robust military forces when and where required for our secu-rity, and to promote the common security of our allies around the globe," reads the document they signed.[35]

The expansion of NATO military powers was interpreted by critics as an ambition to maintain its nuclear arsenal in perpetu-ity and become the world's policeman, an instrument for Pentagon military strategy (as embodied by Operation Infinite War and Full Spectrum Dominance).[36] With the reactivation of the Fourth Fleet, the deployment of new military bases in Colombia and Panama, the military occupation of Haiti under the guise of earthquake relief (January 12, 2010), and the coup in Honduras (June 28, 2009), Brazil responded quickly to this latest reassertion of US military power, which they feared could negatively affect the region.

The Brazilian Defense Minister Nelson Jobim registered his concern about the risk of armed NATO incursions into the South Atlantic, which he defined as a "geostrategic area of vital interest to Brazil."[37] The minister noted the need to separate the issues of the North and the South Atlantic, and that they deserve "differentiated responses." He said that the reasons NATO had been created "had ceased to exist" since the threat posed by the Soviet Union had disappeared. He charged that NATO had become "an instrument for the advancement of the interests of its leading member, the United States," and criticized "extreme European dependence on US military capabilities within NATO," which prevented it "from becoming a geopolitical actor at the height of its economic clout."[38]

On November 3, at the opening of the Seventh International Fort Copacabana Security Conference, Jobim returned to the same subject. He stressed that Brazil and South America cannot accept the US and NATO's "self proclaimed" right to intervene anywhere in the world and, in particular, to "cross the line" separating the North and South Atlantic.[39] He rejected the Pentagon's idea of "shared sovereignty" over this region: "What sovereignty does the United States want to share, theirs or ours?... We will not be allies of the US to maintain their role in the world." He went on to maintain that "international politics cannot be defined from whatever perspective suits the United States."[40] He said he refused to discuss the South Atlantic with a country that does not even respect Brazil's claim to its 350 miles of maritime sovereignty, as recognized by the UN. Jobim defended Brazil and other South American countries' right to "build a deterrent device to address threats from outside the region." Here he is articulating one of the cornerstones of the National Defense Strategy—the capacity to confront every challenge to the region, diplomatic or military, conventional or nonconventional.

On November 21, shortly after the Defense Minister's speech, *O Estado de São Paulo* reported that the Brazilian Navy had a plan to acquire a fleet of six nuclear submarines and twenty conventional ones for 2047, a date corresponding to NATO's "strategic concept" plan.[41]

Map 1: Blue Amazon

A new military-industrial complex

The END document clearly defines Brazil's need to build a "military-university-business complex at the cutting edge of technology with a dual military and civilian role."[42] It further states that in relation to the military-industrial complex, the state will have "special powers over private companies, beyond the limits of the overall regulatory authority," in the form of "golden shares" able to block decisions deemed strategic to state interests.[43] The report also notes that Brazil will no longer be an arms buyer but a partner or ally to international companies selling weapons, increasing its capability of producing weapons with the transfer of technology. To this end, the END proposed creating a Secretary of Defense Products in the Defense Ministry, responsible for the area of Science and Technology, appointed directly by the president.

Under the Lula government military spending grew 45 percent, as much as it had during the military period.[44] Following the END reports recommendations, Lula strengthen the three military branches. Total investments planned for armaments comes to at least $260 billion over twenty years, almost 10 percent of annual GDP.

It is interesting to note how the authorities understand that military spending can place Brazil in a prominent global position. The defense minister believes that the modernization of the armed forces is closely linked to the powerful regional and global role the country will play in the next two decades. "We have the potential not only in the South American context but also in West Africa and in parts of the world where Brazil's vital interests are at stake," Jobim said during the passing of a law guaranteeing military investment "in perpetuity." Brazilian legislators are looking at the Chilean model where a portion of the profits from their national copper goes automatically to the military forces; Brazil could legislate similarly in relation to future oil income.[45]

The recent historical experience of military dictatorship casts a shadow over the relationship between the armed forces and other sectors linked to the military-industrial complex. Between 1974 and 1983, military industry exports reached $16 billion, but in the 1994–2003 period, sales fell to only $287 million.[46] The so-called golden years of military industry exports were concentrated on Iraq and Libya, and limited to a narrow range of weapons: Tucano aircraft manufactured by Embraer, Cascabel and Urutu tanks manufactured by Engesa, and air defense systems from Avibras.[47] With the end of the Iraq-Iran war, exports to Iraq collapsed and the industry entered into a deep crisis from which it never recuperated.[48] During the 1990s and 2000s, there were years in which weapon exports were zero. The contradiction is very strong: A country that is among the ten largest industrial powers in the world (sixth in 2011), is number thirty-seven in the list of arms exporters and twenty-sixth among the importers.[49]

This gap explains the need for such a great power—again, it's soon to have one of the five largest GDPs in the world—to create an equivalent defense industry. To break that inertia does not take much political will and the Lula government started down that road shortly after taking office. In 2003, the government announced a series of discussions around the area of Defense and Security—thus fulfilling a campaign promise—with civil and military participation lasting until July 2004. The discussions were published in four volumes by the Ministry of Defense and identified budget cycle problems: 82 percent of the budget goes to salaries and only 5.3 percent to investments.[50] In contrast, the US spends only 35 percent of the military budget on salaries and more than 20 percent on investments.

Four years after these discussions ended, the National Defense Strategy was adopted. The deal with France in December 2009 marked a huge step forward for the Brazilian defense industry, both in the amount involved ($8 billion) as well as the prospects opened. For many years, economic and political problems prevented the country from maintaining a long-term strategic course. What happened with the Air Force is symptomatic of these problems.

A *Veja* magazine report from 2009 states that the Air Force has a hundred fighter jets, 90 percent of them made in the 1970s and 1980s and about to become obsolete.[51] Other countries in the region have much more modern military fleets: Venezuela purchased twenty-four Sukhoi 30 Russian fighters, considered among the most advanced in the world, and Chile has twenty-eight F-16s, Israel's preferred aircraft. The program to purchase a new generation of fighters, called FX-2, has moved slowly since 1998. The situation is pressing because the old fighters can only detect targets at 20 kilometers while the current models have a target range of 170 kilometers. And the Brazilian Air Force has to protect a vast territory of continental size. The deal with France was scuttled due to budget problems: Each Rafale costs $80 million and a cheaper offer came in from the Swedish Gripen company. There were also probably political differences with France over Brazil's geopolitical rapprochement with Iran (2010) as well as the Brazilian position on the Arab uprisings (2011).

The truth of the matter is that when a country achieves the purchase of jet fighters along with a transfer of the technology involved, it has taken a phenomenal step in terms of expanding its military-industrial complex. Brazil is poised to be the eleventh country to manufacture fifth generation jet fighters. As we have seen, it will be one of the major manufacturers of helicopters and it will enter the select club of those who produce nuclear submarines. This all represents a new and revitalized military industry.

The military-industrial complex is undergoing enormous changes in a very short time: New foreign companies are setting up in Brazil, the largest Brazilian companies are starting up defense wings and hoping to benefit from the state budget to upgrade weapons, and national groups are buying small and medium sized companies based in the technology hub of São José dos Campos. In sum, the defense sector is really moving since the committee for the formulation of a National Defense Strategy gave the go ahead in December 2008 and especially since the signing of the French deal a year later. But such deals, although very important, are only the beginning. What has happened since the French deal was signed?

On a business level, a lot of activity has been registered at Odebrecht and Embraer, as both companies have substantial ventures in the defense sector. In the previous chapter, I mentioned that Odebrecht had reached a strategic agreement with the European EADS in May 2010 for the manufacture of submarines, and that one of the principle players in the Brazilian multinational is the retired Col. Oswaldo Oliva Neto. In 2011, the creation of Odebrecht Defense and Technology, to consolidate Odebrecht's presence in the defense area, was announced. Previously, in 2010, it had started the Defesa em Gestão SA Group in partnership with the Penta and Atech companies.[52] The partnership is crucial: Odebrecht is one of the three largest business groups in Brazil, and EADS is the second largest corporation in the world's defense sector.

A decisive step was taken by Odebrecht, in March 2011, to acquire Mectron, manufacturer of missiles and high technology products for the aerospace market. Mectron has produced radars since 1991, and will now be used in the modernization of fighter aircraft, air-to-air missiles, anti-tank missiles, and fourth-generation missiles. The deal was closely followed by the Lula government, which was now supporting the restructuring of the sector and encouraging the creation of business blocs within the defense industry that are capable of making risky investments to develop products of interest to the military. As Roberto Simões, a director at Odebrecht, said, "our goal is to strengthen and transform the company based on product exportation and services promoting the national industry, aligned with one of the principles of the National Defense Strategy."[53] It is possible that Odebrecht could win the contract to produce some sixty patrol vessels for the protection of oil rigs, which would be a deal as important as their submarine contract.[54]

Meanwhile, Embraer, the third largest manufacturer of aircraft in the world, created the subsidiary Embraer Defesa e Segurança in late 2010 to reinforce their commitment "to the Brazilian state to ensure the training and technological autonomy that the country needs," in line with National Strategy Defense plans.[55] The company aims not only to supply the Brazilian armed forces—having already supplied over thirty aircraft—but also to help them become players on the world stage.

In March 2011, Embraer bought the Orbisat company, a strategic step to increase its participation in the defense industry.[56] Orbisat was created in 1998, has BNDES equity interest, and went on to develop cutting-edge technology for remote and radar surveillance of air, sea, and land. Announcing the purchase, Embraer pointed out Orbisat's work in developing, in conjunction with the army, the SABER M60 radar, which will be the basis of the Border Surveillance System (SisFron), which can remotely monitor terrain beneath a canopy of trees "with the best accuracy in the world," for cartographic mapping of the Amazon region.

Shortly afterwards, Embraer bought 50 percent of Atech, the company responsible for the Amazon surveillance system (Sivam) and which produces air traffic control systems.[57] Embraer is in competition with Odebrecht for a portion of Brazil's nuclear defense needs. The aircraft manufacturer is investing in product research and development and is the only candidate in line to make Brazilian fighter aircraft—the French Rafale model, the Swedish Gripen, or any other model the authorities choose. Meanwhile, the project to build a military transport cargo plane—dubbed KC-390—is well on its way to compete with the legendary C-130 Hercules from Lockheed Martin, which has cornered the market since the 1950s.

The Embraer cargo plane has several advantages over the Hercules: higher speed, lower price, larger load capacity, and the ability to supply aircraft in flight.[58] The deal signed between the Air Force and Embraer in April 2009 envisages the production of 180 aircraft starting in 2015. Brazil's air force ordered twenty-eight units, although it is estimated that it will need between sixty and eighty units in total, and they already have orders from eight other countries to purchase another sixty. With two other companies involved in its construction, the Czech Aero Vodochody and Argentina's Aircraft Factory, it is estimated that KC-390 could capture 30 percent of the world market for this sector.[59]

The IVECO company (part of the Italian FIAT Group, which manufactures trucks in Brazil) has begun production of 2,044 amphibious armored vehicles for the army. The Guarani model will be manufactured in the company's factory in Sete Lagoas, Minas Gerais, between 2012 and 2030, designed jointly by the company and the Science and Technology Department of the army. It will replace the old Urutu made by Engesa, weighs eighteen tons, carries eleven soldiers, and Brazil controls 60 percent of its production.[60]

Aerospace Avibras is another expanding Brazilian company. It fabricates telecommunications antennas, sounding rockets, fiber-optic guided missiles, and air defense rockets. The company went through difficult times in 2011, entering into talks with the government to discuss its future. "We are looking at several options, including selling our majority share in the company, but in conjunction with the government to ensure the national identity of the company," said company president Sami Hassuani.[61] The expectation is that the government will participate in the restructuring of debt so they control 15 to 20 percent of the shares. The 2020 Astros Program expects Avibras to develop artillery rocket launchers for the army, an option enthusiastically supported by the Metal Union of São José dos Campos, in the interest of saving workers' jobs.[62]

Besides the expansion of both Brazilian and international companies, new businesses are setting up in the country, such as the German KMW (Krauss-Maffei Wegman), manufacturer of armored vehicles, to be located in Santa Maria, Rio Grande do Sul. In its first phase, KMW will oversee the maintenance of the 250 Leopard tanks bought in Germany, but they are also in talks with the army to develop a new armored vehicle that could also be exported around the region. The commander of the Third Army Division, Sergio Westphalen Etchegoyen, said that since it was approved by the END, they no longer buy guns but acquire technology packages, as happened with the Leopard: "What was bought was a combat tank along with necessary technology to allow us to continue to develop it, with the KMW company setting up here. The same goes for the purchase of the French helicopters."[63] According to Nelson Düring, editor of the *Defesanet* portal, KMW's presence in Brazil will have a huge technological impact, and a new generation of tank, the "Embraer Terrestrial," will be developed within a decade.[64]

In the coming years more changes are in the pipeline. The navy is negotiating with Germany, South Korea, Spain, France, Italy, and England for the manufacture of eleven ships in Brazil. The British BAE Systems closed a contract in April 2011 to upgrade some of the army's 574 M-113 armored vehicles.[65] The Federation of Industries of the State of São Paulo (FIESP) has stated that in 2014 programs formulated by the END will be given the go ahead for Brazilian industry. "From that point, companies will be discussing and improving technology transfer processes and working to remove the legal barriers that have always hindered the growth of domestic production."[66]

To all of the above, we must add the Space Program outlined in the END proposals, which includes the development and launch of a geostationary satellite to provide secure communications and meteorology, as well as environmental monitoring satellites. It also proposes to develop launch vehicles and satellite systems to assure access to space while encouraging national industry to meet these objectives.[67]

Behind the nuclear weapon

The END analysis says that Brazil must acquire the knowledge for the entire nuclear cycle, and to complete the mapping, exploration, and development of Brazil's uranium reserves. It should also *not* adhere to the Additional Protocol to the Treaty on the Nonproliferation of Nuclear Weapons that require countries to open their facilities to inspection by the IAEA (International Atomic Energy Agency). In 2004, the IAEA asked to inspect the Resende nuclear base, on the suspicion that it was enriching more uranium than necessary. The authorities refused to allow inspectors access to Resende or any nuclear submarine production facilities. In September 2009, a report circulated that Brazil had gained the knowledge and technology needed to make an atomic weapon.[68] No official source denied the claim.

It was not the first time that a rumor had spread regarding the possibility of Brazil working to get nuclear weapons. Brazil has a long nuclear history, dating back to the 1930s when the University of São Paulo conducted nuclear research and located the country's first uranium reserves.[69] In 1945, an agreement was signed with the United States for exclusive radioactive mineral exports, and in 1946, the Plan Baruch attempted to internationalize radioactive mineral reserves to "correct the injustices of nature."[70] In the 1950s, successive confrontations occurred between the US and Brazil as the Getúlio Vargas administration proposed an autonomous nuclear program without external interference. In 1951, US diplomats reported that the government of Vargas had "large quantities" of strategic minerals like uranium.[71]

Vargas opted to sell these minerals in exchange for Washington buying products manufactured in Brazil. In 1952, monazite and thorium oxide were exported, but in return Brazil demanded technical assistance and the necessary materials for reactors to produce nuclear energy. The government soon concluded that the United States would never facilitate that step, so they went to Germany instead. In January 1953, Brazil began to install three ultra-centrifuges for a uranium enrichment plant. Juscelino Kubitschek, governor of Minas Gerais and later president of the country, was one of those responsible for initiating the clandestine project with a small group of admirals.[72]

The US government knew that Brazil was enriching uranium and the pressure on the Vargas government became untenable, to the point that it forced him to stop exporting strategic minerals. Even more serious was the manipulation of coffee prices, Brazil's main export. The US was the main buyer of Brazilian coffee and, aware of the South American country's dependency on it, they reduced imports, leaving the country with an impending trade deficit. Between 1953 and 1954, Brazilian coffee exports to the US fell sixfold.[73] The US was tightening the noose around Vargas and his incipient nuclear program. In Germany, Brazilian negotiators in July 1954 were closely monitored by British and American secret services. Vargas committed suicide in August, leading some analysts to see the nuclear issue as putting the most pressure on his administration.

In 1956, President Kubitschek canceled the radioactive mineral export deal with the US, and created the National Commission for Nuclear Energy, and the centrifuges arrived in Brazil despite Washington's attempt to embargo them. The Army Command declared themselves against the export deals claiming they had not been consulted by the government of João Café Filho who succeeded Vargas. Nevertheless, the export of the strategic minerals continued, albeit clandestinely.

Disagreements with Washington continued and even intensified in the wake of the military coup in 1964. In 1967, General Costa e Silva announced an independent line in nuclear policy,

and when the nuclear powers established the Nuclear Nonproliferation Treaty (NPT) in 1968—determining that uranium and
all other nuclear materials should be controlled—Brazil decided
not to accept the treaty. In 1975, the military regime signed a
cooperation agreement with West Germany that included the
construction of eight nuclear power plants. According to the Brazilian nuclear physicist José Goldemberg, the agreement covered
all stages of nuclear technology and, based on the records of the
National Security Council in 1975, assured that the project was
for peaceful ends, "but it kept the military option open."[74] The
United States opposed the deal. The debt crisis of the 1980s made
it impossible for Brazil to devote adequate funds to the development of the nuclear program, and only one of the eight proposed
nuclear power stations could be built.

However, the agreement with Germany allowed the Brazilian
technicians who trained at the Nuclear Research Center in Karl-
sruhe and Siemens plants to transfer centrifuge technology to Brazil, although not under the auspices of the International Atomic
Energy Agency.[75] In 1979, Brazil began its Autonomous Program
for Nuclear Technology Development, undertaken by the armed
forces, creating the technology for the construction of centrifuges
developed by the navy. The first nuclear power plant, Angra I, was
built in 1985.[76] In 1987, President José Sarney announced that
Brazil had officially gained complete mastery of uranium enrichment technology by means of the centrifuges.[77]

In retaliation, Brazil was placed on an international "blacklist"
that prevented it from importing materials used in the nuclear
field. In June 1991, Brazil circumvented the NPT by signing an
agreement with Argentina for the peaceful use of nuclear energy,
creating the Argentina-Brazil Agency for Accounting and Control
of Nuclear Materials (ABACC). The deal was successful and had
the support of the IAEA, which signed a four-part agreement with
Argentina, Brazil, and the ABACC.[78]

Despite this, President Fernando Henrique Cardoso signed the
Nuclear Nonproliferation Treaty in 1997. Cardoso argued that
the failure to sign the NPT was becoming an obstacle to Brazil's

technological development, and by accepting US hegemony, the country would "win, in terms of international prestige and participation in decision-making mechanisms," in reference to the possibility of joining the United Nations Security Council.[79]

In 2003, shortly after Lula assumed the presidency, the Ministry of Science and Technology made nuclear issues "a strategic priority" according to Odair Dias Gonçalves, president of the National Nuclear Energy Commission (CNEN).[80] In 2004, after a visit to China, Lula asked the commission to develop a nuclear proposal. In 2007, the Ministry of Mines and Energy recommended building four to eight nuclear power plants by 2030. The CNEN authorized the construction of Angra III (Angra II had commenced operations in 2002) and initiated studies to build a fourth plant.[81]

Brazil did not sign the Additional Protocol to the NPT, which would give IAEA inspectors access, without notice, to any facility they consider relevant. Since the nuclear weapon states (the US, Russia, China, France, and Britain) had not proceeded with the disarmament and elimination of nuclear arsenals as provided in Article VI of the NPT, Brazil saw no need to make concessions. The CNEN president goes even further. He believes Brazil has the second or even the largest world's reserves of uranium and is one of three countries with the capability of mastering the entire fuel cycle and enriching uranium to 20 percent, enough to make a nuclear submarine reactor. It is, therefore, "one of the three countries that has both the technology and the uranium."[82]

Brazil aims to raise the amount of nuclear power in its national energy grid to 5.7 percent, which is almost double the current amount. It also seeks total nuclear self-sufficiency by 2014, as part of the process of enriching is still done outside. Uranium is extracted in the Catieté mine in Bahia state, then it undergoes a process of purification and separation in order to be concentrated into a salt known as yellowcake. After this first stage, it is sent to Canada where it is converted into uranium hexafluoride gas. The third stage takes place in Europe where the enriched uranium is converted into small pellets to be used as solid fuel in the Angra plants.[83]

The Catieté mine, which can extract up to 1,200 tons of uranium per year (although until 2009 it produced only 400), will be complemented by the Santa Quitéria mine, in Ceará, which became operational in 2012 and will produce about 1,100 tons per year. Thus production will have increased five- or sixfold by the time Angra III goes online in 2015. Brazil plans to commission a new nuclear plant every four years.[84]

In order to build a nuclear submarine, Brazil needs to undertake the whole process of enriching uranium within the country. Of course, everything related to uranium enrichment is a matter of state secrecy under the Ministry of Science and Technology, which is led by Aloízio Mercadante, brother of Colonel Oliva Neto, during the Rousseff presidency.

At the Aramar military complex, in São Paulo, the first 100 percent Brazilian nuclear reactor was built (Angra I and II were made in the United States and Germany). The same facilities will be used to equip the country's first nuclear submarine, to be operational by 2020.[85] Brazil has established a strategic alliance with China and France and intends to export enriched uranium to supply thirty nuclear plants under construction in China, as well as the French multinational Areva, the largest producer of enriched uranium in the world and a partner in the construction of Angra III. The alliance with these two countries was promoted by the IPEA and realized towards the end of Lula's term, combining Brazilian uranium with Chinese and French enrichment technology.[86]

The question remains: Is Brazil building an atomic bomb? Vice President José Alencar was very clear during an informal conversation with journalists in Brasilia in September 2009: "The nuclear weapon used as an instrument of deterrence is of great importance for a country that has 15,000 kilometers of border in the west and a territorial sea—if you include the pre-salt—of more than four million square kilometers." He cited the case of Pakistan, which despite being a poor country, is respected and participates on various international bodies: "They sit at the table because they have nuclear weapons." He concluded by suggesting a military budget increase of 3 or 5 percent of GDP.[87]

It is not known conclusively if Brazil is building atomic weapons. But what is certain it that it has the capability to do so. Hans Rühle, former director of the German defense ministry between 1982 and 1988, published an article in *Der Spiegel* stating that the construction of the nuclear submarine "could be a cover for a nuclear weapons program" and that "in 1990, the Brazilian military were ready to build a bomb."[88] With the end of the military regime, democratic governments abandoned the secret nuclear programs, but it seemed certain, "a few months after Lula's inauguration in 2003, the country officially resumed the development of a nuclear submarine."[89]

Although not asserting that Brazil already has nuclear weapons, Rühle does suggest that it can make them any time it wishes to, and claims that the Brazilian program is more advanced than the Iranian one. Interviewed by *Deutsche Welle*, he said that the US nuclear laboratories at Los Alamos and Livermore claim that "Brazil can build nuclear weapons in three years time, if desired."[90]

That appears to be the point: Brazil can at any time obtain nuclear weapons. Whether it has them or not is a purely political decision, linked to the costs and benefits of making the knowledge public.

5
The Reorganization of Brazilian Capitalism

"The state acts like the central intelligence of the whole process, to the extent that it guides the expansion of the bourgeois order, the concentration and verticalization of capital, and the rationalization of the production system, and strives to maximize the possibilities of internal and external expansion."
—*Luiz Werneck Vianna*

The Brazilian Development Bank (BNDES) and the pension funds are like great levers being used to redirect Brazilian capitalism in the strategic interests of the new ruling elite. In the first decade of the century, disbursements from the BNDES grew by a fabulous 470 percent; they also soared during the global crisis, and this largely explains how Brazil strengthened its economic course during that period. In 2010, the development bank's disbursements totaled $100 billion, about 7 percent of GDP, the main recipients being industry and infrastructure.[1]

During the current systemic crisis, which is causing a long-term rearrangement of the balance of power around the globe, the BNDES has become the largest development bank in the world. To give an idea of its size: In the fiscal year 2009–2010, the Inter-American Development Bank (IDB) approved loans in forty-eight countries for a total of $15.5 billion and the World Bank disbursed a figure of $40.3 billion during the same biennium, less than half of what the BNDES disbursed.[2] Brazilian bank assets can only be compared with their Chinese counterparts, and sit well above the German development bank, one of the most powerful in the world. The BNDES is responsible for 70 percent of long-term financing in Brazil alone, and its influence is felt in all sectors of the country.

The decisions taken by the bank are crucial for businesses and have the ability to change the entire productive sector, promote mergers, and create giant monopolistic or oligopolistic firms. During the second presidency of Getúlio Vargas (1951–1954), the development bank was instrumental in the process of industrialization and in the construction of infrastructure, while during the 1970s, in the hands of the military dictatorship, it largely supported the process of import substitution. Under Cardoso's neoliberal government in the 1990s, the bank financed privatization and deregulation, helping 30 percent of GDP to change hands and promote the birth of a new bourgeoisie.[3] Under Lula, the BNDES changed its orientation once more.

Under the Workers' Party administration, the bank's enormous sums of money are employed as part of a state plan for the reorganization of Brazilian capitalism, and to avoid bankruptcies and prevent the purchase of large companies by foreign multinationals. The economist Marcio Pochmann, PT member, and former director of the Institute of Applied Economic Research (IPEA), maintains that since the debt crisis in the 1980s, Brazil is now undergoing its third capitalist restructuring attempt, this one creating large economic groups that have a presence in private capital, the state, and the pension funds of state enterprises. He describes the choices made by Lula's Brazil with a frankness that deserves attention:

> What we are seeing during the last decades of dominant globalization—particularly financial—is the deregulation of the state, and the formation of large transnational corporations. Before the 2008 crisis there was talk of the emergence of at least 500 large transnational

corporations that would dominate all sectors of economic activity. In this circuit of hyper-monopolization of capital, the countries that do not have large economic groups that might become one of those 500 would, in some way, be left outside, out of the running. This would leave them with a passive role, subordinate to the decisions of the 500 groups within the circuit. Therefore Brazil has chosen to involve itself in concentration of these giants, in order to be part of that circuit through a few, but huge, companies [...] We are moving into a phase in which it is not the countries that have the companies, but the companies that have countries, given the size of corporations with profits many times greater than any national GDP. So there is no alternative, in my view, than to go about constructing those groups.[4]

Brazilian strategists do not hide the fact that they are inspired by the Chinese model. Pochmann reaffirms this, noting that the Chinese own 150 of the 500 largest global groups. He argues that Brazil should have a similar plan and "the role of government is to reorganize these economic groups in order to compete within the new international economic order."[5]

The two Lula administrations, in particular his second term (2007–2010), have deployed the state in a dual role: as financier of large businesses to strengthen economic groups, and as an investor in major infrastructure projects, under the Growth Acceleration Program (PAC). Some leftist intellectuals are critical of the path Lula has chosen because it promotes a concentration and centralization of capital, favoring large corporations and weakening labor. In this chapter, we will see how the state deals with large companies, using some notable examples, and then investigate the role of the state in building infrastructure.

The reorganization begins

One characteristic of Brazilian capitalism in recent years is for the state to designate "national champions" among the business sector, in order to promote a company's global competitiveness.

This is not simply a matter of the state supporting business, but of a state becoming an actor in mergers and mega-deals—becoming, in effect, a partner of the largest companies in the country. Here are some examples:

• *The merger of Sadia and Perdigão in May 2009 led to the creation of Brasil Foods, the largest exporter of beef in the world.* Both companies had already become large businesses in various countries. Sadia was a conglomerate of nineteen companies, Brazil's largest processor of poultry, industrialized meat, pork, and cattle, with 55,000 employees. But the 2008 crisis, as well as speculation in financial derivatives, resulted in its first loss in sixty-four years of business, bringing the company to the brink of bankruptcy.

Perdigão had forty-two industrial units, was slightly smaller than Sadia, and did not play in the financial market. Their merger created the tenth-largest food company in the Americas, the second-largest food company in Brazil (behind JBS Friboi), and the third-largest exporter behind Petrobras and Vale. It controls almost 25 percent of the world's poultry market, with factories in Europe, and has a controlling stake of 57 percent of the Brazilian market for processed meat.[6] The merged company is one of the largest employers in the country, with 120,000 employees and sales totaling $15 billion annually. Brasil Foods' largest individual shareholder is the pension fund Previ (of Banco do Brasil) with a 13.6 percent stake, consolidating its previous investments that it already had in Perdigão and Sadia.[7] The BNDES disbursed $235 million to buy 3 percent of shares.[8]

Luiz Fernando Furlan played a key role in the merger—as former president of Sadia, current co-president of Brasil Foods, and former Minister of Industry and Trade in the first Lula government. The government not only supported the merger but signed an agreement with China in order to open up this huge market to Brazilian exports for the first time.

• *The merger of Friboi JBS and Bertin food processors in September 2009.* The BNDES invested about $4.7 billion in both food processing companies. JBS is the largest meat processing company in the world and has undergone a huge expansion in recent years, doubling its slaughter capacity since 2006. In 2007,with the capitalization support of BNDES—which acquired 14 percent of JBS—it bought US Swift Foods to gain access to the US market. In 2008, the BNDES also supported Bertin (an exporter of meat, milk, and leather with 35,000 employees and thirty-eight production units), acquiring 27 percent of the company. With this investment in the merged company, the BNDES has a 22.4 percent stake.[9]

Today the JBS Group has twenty-one subsidiaries and operates in 110 countries. It has the capacity to slaughter 51,000 cattle daily and employs 125,000 workers. With the purchase of Bertin, it acquired 64 percent of Pilgrim's Pride, the second-largest meat processor in the United States.[10] "We are locating groups that can be strengthened to compete internationally," said Development Minister Miguel Jorge, when the government bought Swift through JBS with the support of BNDES.[11]

• *The merger of Aracruz and Votorantim Pulp and Paper (VCP) in September 2009, which created Fibria, the world's largest short fiber company and the fourth-largest pulp company.* The two companies suffered losses on investments in derivatives, similar to Sadia, and entered into difficulties in 2008. The BNDES was already a minority shareholder in both. During the crisis, the Swedish-Finnish Stora Enso company intervened to invest in both companies, while the BNDES put a total of $1.4 billion into the new company, allowing them to take a 26 percent share.[12]

The agreement stipulates that the bank has the right to veto important decisions until 2014. "The merger fulfilled the long-held dream that Brazil would have a strong global player, financed with national capital, in this arena, where our competitiveness is unbeatable," said one of the merger's negotiators.[13]

• *The purchase of Brasil Telecom by Oi, creating a giant "national network."* In April 2008, the BNDES released substantial funds for Oi to buy Brasil Telecom. The telephone sector privatizations under Cardoso's neoliberal government had led to the division in 1998 of the state-wide and monopolistic Telebras into twelve companies, the largest of them being Telemar, which operated in sixteen states under different names. In 2001, the companies were unified, and in 2007, the entire company was named Oi, with the BNDES controlling 25 percent of the capital.

Brasil Telecom, another of the major companies arising from the privatization of Telebras, was purchased by the Brazilian investment bank Opportunity and Telecom Italia. Oi, the new telecommunications company arising from the purchase of Brasil Telecom, is the leader in fixed-line telephones in Latin America with 22 million connections, and ended 2011 with 45 million mobile phone customers, making it the fourth largest in Brazil with 19 percent of a market that grows almost 20 percent annually.[14] Furthermore, and this has been decisive for the involvement of the BNDES and pension funds, a 100 percent Brazilian company has been created, with a presence throughout the country and that is capable of expanding within and beyond national borders. In some sense, this process reverses the process of foreign take-over of Brazilian industry, which was a product of privatization. It also gives the state influence in a strategic sector. The BNDES invested a total of $2.5 billion for the purchase of Brasil Telecom, which has a market value of $7.65 billion.[15]

Oi shares were distributed as follows: Andrade Gutierrez and La Fonte received 20 percent each, while Oi's pension fund retained 10 percent. The public sector controlled the remaining 50 percent: BNDES with 16.8 percent, Previ with 12.9 percent, and Petros and Funcef funds with 10 percent each.[16] In any case, the agreements stipulate that for certain key decisions the new company must have larger voting majorities, ranging from 66 to 84 percent, ensuring a role for the state in the future of the company.

• *State support for Braskem to make it one of the ten largest petrochemical companies in the world.* In this case, the State acted through Petrobras, facilitating the growth of Braskem, a company within the Odebrecht Group. The company was formed in 2001 by the consolidation of six companies, including Copene (Northeast Petrochemical Company) bought by the construction company Odebrecht and the Mariano group. In November 2007, Braskem joined Petrobras in the biggest merger in Brazilian history, and purchased several oil-related companies such as Companhia Petroquímica do Sul, Ipiranga Química, Ipiranga Petrochemical, Petrochemical Paulínia, and Petrochemical Triunfo. Petrobras now holds a 25 percent stake in Braskem.[17]

At that point Braskem was the third-largest American petrochemical company, behind only Exxon and Dow Chemical, and was among the eleven largest in the world. In 2010, Braskem purchased Quattor, controlled by Petrobras and Unipar, in order to open up the international market, in particular the United States. This formed a "petrochemical giant" that became the largest in the Americas and eighth worldwide. The sector was now dominated by two companies: Petrobras and Braskem, both with strong state ties. Shortly after, Braskem continued to grow with the acquisition of the US Sunoco company and a technology center in Pittsburgh, Pennsylvania.

In 2011, Braskem shares were still controlled by Odebrecht with 38 percent equity, but Petrobras had 31 percent as well as a minority presence in Previ and Petros pension funds.[18] The president of Sindipolo (Metalworkers Union of Triunfo Petrochemical) stressed that the government was "clearing the ground" so that Braskem would take an 80 percent share of the industry. "The official government position is that they are restructuring the sector to ensure increased competitiveness. In our opinion, there is some shadowy relationship with the Odebrecht group," and "decisions are not made by Petrobras but by the federal government."[19] Once more, the influence or partnership between the state and private multinational companies is an undeniable fact. At the same time, a high level of concentration was carried out: together, Odebrecht and Petrobras get 100 percent control of the petrochemical industry in Brazil.

Petrobras, the crown jewel

The capitalization of the oil industry in September 2010 was one of the most successful projects of the Lula government. In this chapter, I intend to reflect on how the government worked to recover substantial control over Petrobras, which had been abandoned during the neoliberal governments of the 1990s. The company was created in 1953 by Getúlio Vargas as a state monopoly for the exploitation of oil. Later, under the military dictatorship, it began to trade internationally in crude oil.[20]

By the end of the 1970s, Brazilian production was only 200,000 barrels of oil a day, but consumption reached over a million barrels. Petrobras drilled for offshore oil in deep ocean waters, searching for large deposits, and with the inauguration of the P-50 platform in 2006—the country's biggest—Brazil achieved full self-sufficiency. 70 percent of oil production is based in deep and ultra-deep waters, a process of exploration and extraction in which Petrobras is becoming a specialized global leader through technological innovations.[21] In 2007, the company could refine 1.9 million barrels of oil daily, thereby eliminating the need to import refined oil and other derivatives. By late 2010 it was extracting an average of 2.6 million barrels a day.[22]

In 2006 and 2007, Petrobras announced the discovery of huge oil reserves off the coasts of the states of Santa Catarina and Espirito Santo. The medium- and high-quality oil and natural gas lies below a 2,000-meter layer of salt, itself below an approximately 2,000-meter layer of rock under 2,000–3,000 meters of the Atlantic (therefore called "pre-salt"). The Tupi, Iara, and Whale Park fields increase Brazil's reserves from fourteen to thirty-three billion barrels, but other sources estimate that its reserves could rise to seventy billion barrels.[23] The Tupi and Iracema fields alone, baptized *Lula* and *Cernambi*, contain eight billion barrels of reserves, being the largest oil discovery in the world since 2000.[24] The pre-salt reserves are found along a long sea stretch of almost a thousand kilometers from the city of Florianópolis (Santa Catarina) to Vitória (Espírito Santo).

IPEA analysts estimate that Brazil's "pre-salt province" is one of the ten largest in the world, which will "strengthen Brazil's international autonomy" and represents a very real strategic leap forward for the country.[25] The country will produce about five million barrels a day by 2020 and, even factoring in an increase in domestic demand, Brazil will have a surplus of 2 million barrels

Map 2: Petroleum basins of Santos and Campos

LOCALIZAÇÃO
NOVAS RESERVAS DE PETRÓLEO

MG

ES

BACIA DO
ESPÍRITO
SANTO

SP

RIO DE
JANEIRO

RJ

BACIA DE
CAMPOS

SÃO PAULO ●

PR

CURITIBA

SC

BACIA DE
SANTOS

Campo de Tupi
Quantidade estimada:
5 a 8 bilhões de barris

FLORIANÓPOLIS

RS

OCEANO ATLÂNTICO

Map 3: Campo de Tupi

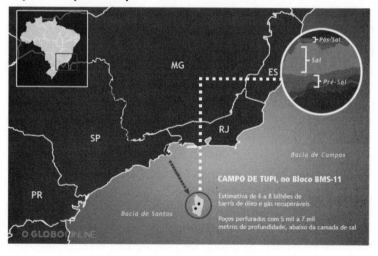

MG

ES

Pós-Sal
Sal
Pré-Sal

SP

RJ

Bacia de Campos

PR

Bacia de Santos

CAMPO DE TUPI, no Bloco BMS-11

Estimativa de 6 a 8 bilhões de
barris de óleo e gás recuperáveis

Poços perfurados com 5 mil a 7 mil
metros de profundidade, abaixo da camada de sal

O GLOBO ONLINE

a day. In a few short years, Brazil will have gone from being a net importer to a net exporter of oil, which changes its global standing. It is the only emerging power that has both a powerful industrial base and surplus energy.

The discoveries in the pre-salt layer, specifically the Tupi field/ *Lula*, delineate a before and after in the history of the Petrobras company, in that the value of the company tripled.[26] With the exploitation of these fabulous reserves, Brazil will become one of the major oil producers in the world. As you can imagine, there has been intense debate around the most appropriate ways to exploit these riches, and it is interesting to note how the government has responded. Its starting point was that the partial privatization of Petrobras weakens the government's role in oil exploration. In 2000, the state share in the company was only 61 percent, which fell to 39.9 percent by 2005. The remainder was in private hands: 20 percent domestic and 40 percent foreign.[27] To reverse this situation and raise funds for the expansion of Petrobras—which requires substantial investment for pre-salt extraction—the Lula administration decided to promote its capitalization with the biggest share sale in history.

The investment plan for 2010–2014 is $224 billion (half the GDP of Argentina), something no oil company in the world is capable of doing, hence the need for fresh funds and state intervention.[28] Between 60 and 80 percent of the investment is expected to be provided by Brazilian industry. With that amount of investment and the pre-salt reserves, Brazil can join the top five oil producers in the world by 2020. Even before the capitalization in late 2009, Petrobras was the fourth largest oil company, behind only Petro China, Exxon, and BHP.[29] This continuing rise of the oil company explains the remarkable success of the capitalization.

The transfer of oil from the Tupi field to Petrobras was part of the capitalization that did not materialize in money but increased the shares held by the state. Which is to say, the government increased its stake in Petrobras by yielding six billion barrels from the Tupi field to the company. In September 2010, Petrobras conducted the largest share sale in history, when US$72.8 billion worth of shares in the company were sold on the BM&F Bovespa stock exchange. The second largest capitalization in history was conducted by Nippon Telegraph and Telephone in 1987, and was $36.8 billion.[30]

With this capitalization the market value of Petrobras rose to $283 billion ranking it second in the world behind the US Exxon.[31] But the most important thing for the Brazilian state is that it increased its stake in the company, to over 50 percent. Before the share sale, the state had 40 percent of the shares, and with the capitalization its stake rose to 48 percent (with BNDESPar), to which can be added the 3.2 percent stake of Previ, which allows it to directly or indirectly control more than 50 percent of the total capital.[32]

The whole exercise shows the advantage for the state in employing strategic plans with long-term objectives. In effect, the Brazilian state is reversing the loss of control of the state oil company through privatization in the 1990s, because Petrobras is a key strategic element to the ambitious plans.

The Petrobras investment plan seems at times like a piece of science fiction. On one hand, there is the technological challenge posed in extracting oil at deep sea, below the bedrock and salt layers. One platform has been constructed in the area that should have the capability to store large amounts of oil offshore, but an estimated ten more are to be built by 2016, as well as a 400-mile pipeline to the coast of Rio de Janeiro. The exploitation of the maritime oil field is supported by four air bases in the states of São Paulo and Rio de Janeiro. But the most interesting thing under consideration is the construction of "hub platforms," which Petrobras engineers define as "terminals at sea," from which another dozen platforms can be controlled.[33] In total, it is estimated that there will be fifty platforms on the pre-salt layer, with plans for drilling 2,000 wells.

To lower costs, Petrobras is studying the possibility of "underwater cities" on the seabed, at a depth of 2,000 meters, where the platform operating equipment can be installed, using a high level of automation and robotics. "Our goal over the next ten years is to eliminate the need for platforms," said Carlos Tadeo Fraga, executive manager of Petrobras Research Center.[34] The plan is to install processing plants and compression systems for the separation of oil, water, gas, and sand on the sea bed, alongside the necessary modules to generate power to run the complex. The underwater operations would be controlled and monitored from land-based facilities. Currently, all these operations are situated on floating platforms.

In the first quarter of 2011, an underwater oil and water separator began operating in the Marlim field in the Campos Basin, the first step towards installing a processing plant on the seabed. Exploitation of deep wells in a hostile environment requires reducing operating costs, and to do so, Petrobras needs to make a technological leap. The other objective is to extract more oil with fewer wells. Currently a single well can extract 40,000 barrels per day, which was once the total output of an entire platform.[35]

Alongside its giant step forward in the petroleum field, Petrobras is also playing an important role in the production of ethanol, an area of production where the government is also attempting to reverse the rapid de-nationalization of recent years.

Petrobras and the foreign takeover of ethanol

In response to the 1973 global oil crisis, ethanol was added as a fuel to the Brazilian energy matrix in 1975. The National Alcohol Program was created to replace petrol with ethanol in cars. The program aimed to reduce oil dependency because, at that time, the country was importing most of its oil. The crisis was further compounded in 1979 with the sharp increases in the price of hydrocarbons. Initially, between 1976 and 1986, ethanol production tripled, but the programs were abandoned in the neo-liberal decade, in part because international oil prices dropped. During the government of Fernando Collor, the ethanol program almost disappeared.[36]

During the 1990s, there were shortages of biofuels and users stopped buying cars that ran on ethanol. With rising oil prices around 2000, consumers, particularly in São Paulo, began to mix hydrated alcohol with gasoline in their car tanks to reduce costs.

"Given the spread of this practice, carmakers began to develop cars with flexi-fuel engines, that were launched publicly with the support of President Lula in March 2003. In practice, this was essential in restoring confidence in biofuels."[37]

Cane production grew from 120 million tons in 1975 to 320 million in 2003 when Lula took office, and rose to 590 million tons in 2009.[38] Ethanol production has doubled over the course of the 2000s.[39] In 2008, Brazil was the first country in the world to use more ethanol than gasoline to power its automobile fleet.[40] Global ethanol production quadrupled between 2000 and 2008 according to the United Nations' Food and Agriculture Organization, largely because it is a renewable energy and contributes towards reducing global warming. In the next ten years, global ethanol production is expected to double again.

In Brazil, there are almost 7 million hectares of sugarcane, half of it dedicated to sugar production and half to ethanol, representing a quarter of the country's agricultural output. Advances in the genetic enhancement of sugarcane improved the crop, and that, along with an improvement in the industrial chain, has led to an astonishing growth in productivity: between 1975 and 2000 production went from 2,024 liters of ethanol per hectare to 5,500.[41] Towards the end of the decade, productivity continued to grow, reaching about 7,000 liters per hectare compared to only 3,800 liters of US corn, its main competitor.[42] The price of sugarcane ethanol is 30 percent lower than that of maize, it has much higher energy efficiency, and furthermore, it reduces greenhouse gases emissions by more than double.[43]

Brazil is the world's largest global producer of ethanol, driven by its strong domestic market, and alongside the US, it controls two-thirds of world production.[44] By 2012, seventy-seven ethanol plants were built, involving an investment of $2.5 billion, with most of the capital coming from the United States. "Up to last year, 3.4 percent of the industry was controlled by foreign interests. In ten years, half will no longer be Brazilian," points out Maurilio Biagi, who sold one of the largest ethanol plants, Cevasa, to the agribusiness multinational Cargill in 2006.[45] Part of this investment will come from major multinationals, since all the companies producing GM crops—Syngenta, Monsanto, Dupont, Dow, Bayer, BASF—have investments in the production of biofuels like ethanol and biodiesel.[46] Some of these companies are positioning themselves in Brazil to increase productivity of ethanol crops with genetically modified seeds.

The importance Brazil attaches to biofuels is reflected in studies conducted by the Strategic Affairs Center (NAE). The biofuels report, which relied on twenty specialists, was the second to be published by the research center and the first devoted to a specific sector.[47] IPEA investigators, advising the Secretary of Strategic Affairs, expressed official alarm at the increasing internationalization of the sector, and warned that the rapid growth of direct foreign investment in the ethanol industry was producing "a significant process of concentration and de-nationalization [...] without a corresponding international expansion of domestic firms."[48] Although they recognize that the process contains aspects that can help turn ethanol into an international commodity, they believe that the penetration of foreign capital should be monitored because it can affect "national sovereignty in resource exploitation."[49]

In the 2000s, direct foreign investment in Brazil occurred mainly in agriculture and industry. Whether in agriculture or in industry, foreign investment sought to situate itself in the production of commodities, with particular interest in oil, natural gas, biofuels, and iron ore.[50] "Increased foreign presence has caused significant changes in the production structure," noted the IPEA in relation to the sugar-alcohol industry, "with implications for the domestic market and for broader political strategies in the ethanol industry."[51]

Investing in ethanol is tempting for international capital because the market is growing both domestically and internationally. In the domestic market, 25 percent of the Brazilian fleet is already flexi-fuel, but it is estimated that by 2015 that figure will climb to 65 percent, and Brazil is now the fourth-largest producer and seller of vehicles in the world. On the international market, enormous profits are to be made from ethanol due to its higher productivity. The official concern of the Brazilian government is that, while control by foreign interests means industrial concentration, it is at the expense of Brazilian business:

> The entry of international companies is not accompanied by an equal capacity of domestic firms to move outwards. On the contrary, this movement raises barriers to the Brazilian government's strategy of exporting technologies and equipment developed in the domestic market, so as to stimulate Brazilian companies' insertion into the international market.[52]

Ethanol production in Brazil is a widely dispersed industry in the hands of hundreds of families. The recent concentration of the industry has been very rapid: between 2000 and 2009 there were ninety-nine mergers and acquisitions in the industry, to the point that the market share of the five largest groups in the sector grew from 12 percent to 21.5 percent.[53] Within that process, groups such as Bunge, Cargill, and George Soros's Adecoagro began aggressively carving out space, as did the giant Cosan, which controlled nearly 10 percent of the sector. The sugar and the alcohol industry has about 400 plants operated by 200 groups. In 2008, for example, of the fourteen mergers and acquisitions in the sector, eight involved foreign capital. The same was more or less true in 2009, so that, of the five largest ethanol plants, two are linked to international capital, with plenty of complex partnerships, income investments, and strategic agreements that do little to give the industry a transparent profile.[54]

To contain the "foreign invasion," the Lula government gave Petrobras a dynamic role in the sector, with the aim of consolidating a large national ethanol company. The logic is similar to how it has operated in other sectors, like petroleum. Some analysts speculate that alarm bells started ringing when Shell and Cosan reached a $12 billion deal in early 2010, turning them into the world leaders in ethanol. At the same time, British Petroleum and the Brazilian groups Moema and Santelisa Vale joined to form

Tropical Bioenergy, which meant that two oil majors entered the ethanol game, "a traditionally green and yellow sector."[55]

Petrobras put in an offer to acquire 40 percent of ETH, the sector's second-largest company, for $2 billion as ETH was opening nine new plants in 2012. It also bought 46 percent of Acucar Guarani, the fourth-largest processor of cane sugar in the country.[56] Many analysts believe that Petrobras is arriving too late to compete in the sector and needs to invest heavily if it is to reverse the growing dominance of foreign capital.

Investment in infrastructure and energy

On January 28, 2007, four weeks after starting his second term, Lula launched the Growth Acceleration Program (PAC), a four-year investment program with a budget of $291 billion representing (at that time) 23 percent of GDP. Major investments were planned in the area of infrastructure with the expectation that for every *real* invested by the public sector there would be 1.5 reals invested by the private sector.[57]

Most of the investment went into electrical power and housing projects. The rest was spent on biofuels, sanitation, the Light for All project, and the construction of highways, railways, ports, airports, and waterways. To get an idea of the scale of investment over the four years, it included the construction or restoration of 45,000 kilometers of roads, 2,500 kilometers of railways, the expansion of twelve airports and twenty ports, the generation of 12,000 additional MW of electricity and 14,000 kilometers of transmission lines, four new petrochemical refineries, 4,500 kilometers of pipelines, forty-six biodiesel and seventy-seven ethanol plants, 4 million houses and sanitation for 22 million families.[58]

In 2010, PAC 2 was launched, with similar criteria, but with three times the resources: $933 billion, 43 percent of the GDP for four years. Urban infrastructure was extended with the goal of universal access to electricity and water and the construction of 2 million homes, mostly aimed at low-income families. Although most of the programs have a clear social purpose, two-thirds of the investments are focused on the energy sector.

TABLE 3: PAC 2 Investments (in billions of dollars)

	2011–2014	After 2014	TOTAL
BETTER CITY	33.5	-	**33.5**
CITIZEN COMMUNITY	13.5	-	**13.5**
MY HOUSE, MY LIFE	162.6	-	**163.6**
WATER/LIGHT FOR ALL	18	-	**18**
TRANSPORT	61.4	2.7	**64.1**
ENERGY	271.5	368.7	**640.2**
TOTAL	**561.6**	**371.3**	**932.9**

Source: PAC 2, 32.

Investments destined for the energy sector generally go towards petroleum and natural gas, which are basically investments in Petrobras. The second most important category is the generation of electricity. Brazil had a power-grid generation capacity of 106,000 MW in 2009, including hydroelectric, thermal, wind, and nuclear power. Hydro generation was 75,500 MW that year but the potential of Brazil's rivers to produce electricity is 260,000 MW, the highest in the world.[59]

The Brazilian energy matrix is one of the "cleanest" on the planet. While the global average for renewable energy supply is 12 percent, Brazil's is 47.3 percent. The biggest difference is the growing role of sugarcane, ethanol, and biofuels, which are close to 20 percent of total supply, with hydropower contributing around 15 percent to the power grid compared to only 2 percent globally.[60] We have seen the growing importance of cane alcohol as transport fuel. Energy produced from sugarcane derivatives is growing and has displaced hydropower as the second largest energy source in Brazil.[61]

The PAC 2 program includes the construction of fifty-four hydroelectric plants.[62] Since the Paraná and San Francisco river basins are close to their limit, the bulk of future dams will be built in the Amazon basin, the most sensitive region from an environmental and social perspective.

Table 4: Energy Matrix in the World and in Brazil

(percent of energy by source)

Source	World*	Brazil**
Petrol	34	37.9
Carbon	26.5	8.7
Natural Gas	20.9	4.7
Nuclear	5.9	1.4
Hydro	2.2	15.2
Cane/Wood/Renewables	9.8	28.2
Others	0.7	3.9
TOTAL	100 percent	100 percent

* 2007 ** 2009 | Source: Balanço Energético Nacional 2010

The Belo Monte Dam on the Xingu River, which forms part of the PAC, will be the world's third largest after China's Three Gorges and the Brazilian-Paraguayan Itaipu dam. The Belo Monte dam has become a symbol for the social and environmental consequences of Brazil's growth. The project was a flagship of the military dictatorship and has been in the making for more than thirty years, but was put on hold because of resistance from a formidable social movement comprised mainly of environmentalists and the indigenous. Nevertheless, the Lula government relaunched the dam project, citing Brazil's increased energy needs for growth, and hydropower's clean, renewable qualities, necessary in the fight against global warming.

Belo Monte is certainly one of the most controversial projects in recent decades. It is located in the Volta Grande on the Xingu River, a tributary of the Amazon, and the proposal is not only to divert the original course of the river but also to open it up to river traffic, to expedite the transit of agricultural products in Mato Grosso and Pará. The power generated by the plant will be 11,200 MW, and the project will affect a hundred-kilometer stretch of the river, forming a 516-square-kilometer lake. It is earmarked to supply twenty-six million people, and will cost $11 billion— although critics believe the ultimate cost may double.[63] As shown in the map below, a wall will split the river, and from there channels will divert its course towards the turbines. The river current will be seriously reduced for hundreds of kilometers.

Map 4: Belo Monte project

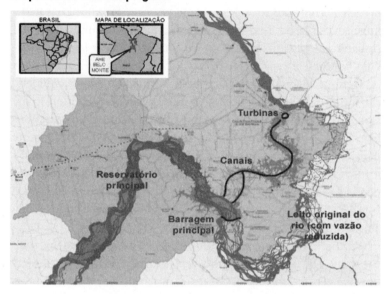

Resistance to the dam, spanning three decades, has been led by the Bishop of Xingu, Erwin Kräutler, who has lived in the state of Pará for forty years. In 1975, the state company Eletronorte hired the National Consortium of Consulting Engineers to conduct a feasibility study of the plant. The study was completed in 1979, and the proposed dam was to be named Kararaô, *nom de guerre* of the Kayapó people, although the local people were never consulted. In February 1989, the First Meeting of Xingúin Indigenous Nations was held in Altamira, bringing together 600 war-painted Indians to resist the dam.[64] A dramatic photo of the indigenous leader Tuíra pointing a machete at the face of the Eletronorte president José Antonio Munis Lopes went global, becoming a potent symbol of resistance to the dam. Shortly afterward, the project was suspended.[65]

In the late 1990s, the project resurfaced, renamed Belo Monte, probably a vain attempt to distance itself from the failed Kararaô attempt. During the 2002 election campaign, Lula came out clearly against Belo Monte, but later changed his position and began to advocate the project, making it one of the priorities of PAC 3.[66] The "monstrosity" that the bishop denounced has had a huge social impact in the region before it is even finished: 50,000 Indians and peasants have been expelled from their lands, permanent flooding affects the nearby city of Altamira as well as nineteen indigenous villages. The current has decreased by 80 percent along the hundred kilometers of river causing a major disruption to life along its banks. Dozens of social and ecclesiastic organizations have spoken out against Belo Monte, and a 600,000-signature petition protesting the dam was delivered to the government.[67] The Order of Lawyers of Brazil requested that construction be suspended, claiming that the project has only a partial license issued by IBAMA (Brazilian Institute for the Environment and Renewable Natural Resources) on February 1, 2010.[68]

Furthermore, there are technical and economic problems with the dam. The Xingu riverbed is very irregular, increasing to overflow in winter and decreasing to almost nothing in summer, so the power supply will average only 40 percent of installed capacity, which is "one of the worst power-to-energy ratios in the whole Brazilian electricity system."[69] This would affect investor profitability and has hampered the formation of a construction consortium to participate in the auction to win the contract to build the dam.

The auction finally happened on April 20, 2010, and was a contentious process. Of the three companies who oversaw the initial environmental impact studies (which is to say, those most familiar with the project) two withdrew from the project (Odebrecht and Camargo Corrêa). The third, Andrade Gutierrez, presented a proposal designed to fail. The business's returns would be very low and the risks very high. So the government had to pressure a group of companies to form the Norte Energia Consortium, which took over the project. The consortium was made up of nine companies with the State of San Francisco Hydroelectric

Company (which belongs to the Eletrobras group) as the main shareholder, with 49.98 percent.[70] The other eight investors had much less involvement.

In the months following the auction, it was learned that state pension funds (Previ, Petros, and Funcef) would be investing in the winning consortium, increasing state involvement with about a 10 percent stake each.[71] The three largest Brazilian construction companies, Odebrecht, Camargo Corrêa, and Andrade Gutierrez, are involved in the construction, but none of them are prepared to assume the risks of a venture they consider "economically unviable."[72] Although the Belo Monte dam is in the final stages of construction and due to begin operating in 2015 as planned, the controversy will continue. Other controversial dams include a mega-project on the Madeira River, near the Bolivian border, the Inambari project in Peru, and the Tapajós Complex (five dams in Pará slated to produce about 10,600 MW, almost as much as Belo Monte). These projects are the tip of an iceberg that will change the Amazon forever. The impact will not only be felt by indigenous and small farmers in Brazil, but populations from neighboring countries as well, particularly Bolivia and Peru.

Eletrobras president José da Costa Carvalho Neto announced a joint investment with the private sector of $123 billion in hydropower this decade in an attempt to internationalize Eletrobras and make it "the energy sector's equivalent to Petrobras, with investment in Argentina, Colombia, Peru, and Venezuela."[73] That figure exceeds the combined GDP of Uruguay, Bolivia, and Paraguay. In Peru alone, they estimate constructing twenty hydropower dams to produce 20,000 MW, twice the capacity of Belo Monte.

State and capital

On August 5, 2010, during the campaign to elect a successor to Lula, the five leading newspapers published a manifesto defending the BNDES against the barrage of criticism it faced. Titled "In Defense of Investments," it was signed by twelve industry associations that collectively accounted for 21 percent of GDP, and employed some 2.5 million workers.[74]

Criticism had come from many fronts: from the financial sector to social movements, from the right and left. The banking sector was unhappy that the state has capitalized BNDES, which then loans that money at a lower rate than the commercial banks. The National Treasury's rate is 10.75 percent while BNDES lends to companies at 6 percent.[75]

For other critics, the BNDES loans concentrate wealth and facilitate the creation of monopolies. They point out that 57 percent of the bank's loans went to just twelve companies, including two state companies (Petrobras and Eletrobras) and the three private construction companies "friendly" to the government: Odebrecht, Camargo Corrêa, and Andrade Gutierrez. The list of twelve also includes Brazilian multinationals Vale, Votorantim, and JBS.[76] In the same vein, critics charge that, as a state bank, BNDES should fund innovation and small and medium enterprises, but instead it funds large company groups, which, in effect, is "transferring worker's funds to a few shareholders, further concentrating income in an already very unequal country."[77]

It is striking to note that what were previously large family-run businesses in each sector have since become diversified conglomerates with substantial state support, following the same process of global capital in the early-twentieth century. The reporter Vinicius Torres Freire synthesizes it thus: "Fernando Henrique Cardoso privatizes, Lula conglomerates."[78] The data speaks for itself. In 1996, there was BNDES participation in thirty major Brazilian companies. In 2003, Lula's first year, BNDES was a shareholder in fifty-three companies, and by 2009, that figure reached ninety. If we add to this the presence of Petros, Previ, and Funcef pension funds, the state has a presence in 119 companies.[79] The sector that gained most between 1996 and 2009 were the pension funds of large state enterprises: Previ controls seventy-eight companies, including giants like Vale; Petros controls thirty-one; Funcef has a decisive role in eighteen; and Funcesp in fourteen.[80]

The entanglement of private companies and state actors did not begin with the Lula government, although the process did intensify during his eight-year rule. According to Sérgio Lazzarini, the private and state sectors really started working together during the privatizations under Cardoso. Between 1990 and 2002, 165 state agencies were privatized but a "reverse" process took hold in 2004, as the state took back control of many of them. Through its close association with the BNDES and state pension funds, the state carefully positioned itself as a key partner in many private companies.[81]

During the privatization auctions of the 1990s, the Cardoso administration helped create mixed consortia with state involvement, as a way to mitigate antineoliberal criticism and "to make the political process of privatizations viable."[82] Here, we can revisit the case of Vale, formerly Vale do Rio Doce, a state enterprise whose privatization was resisted by the left and social movements. It was Brazil's largest privatization ever and made possible by the backing of the BNDES and the formation of Valepar S. A., which controls the Board of Directors with a 53 percent majority. Valepar is dominated in turn by four pension funds led by Previ (with a 58 percent stake) and the Bradesco Group (17 percent), followed by the Japanese multinational Mitsui (15 percent) and the BNDES (9.5 percent). Thus, through pension funds and the BNDES, the "privatized" Vale was controlled by the state or, more precisely, by the new breed of pension fund managers intertwined with major Brazilian companies and the BNDES. This marks a first decisive difference with other privatization processes.

The second is the manner in which the auctions were carried out. While in northern countries the trend is towards dividing up the shares among many small investors, in Brazil the dominant tendency is purchase by large corporate blocks. "The winning consortium, supported by a shareholders' agreement defining the rights and responsibilities of the parties, takes over the new privatized company."[83]

In this manner a "coalition of support" was formed, consisting of local economic groups, new investors like state pension funds, and public resources, acting in partnership to compensate for the lack of support for the privatization process on the part of the elites and the political class.[84] But a third aspect appears under the

Lula government: the exponential growth of the joint role of the BNDES and pension funds. While domestic and foreign private companies held the same roles they had before, the BNDES/pension funds duo becomes the key node of the Brazilian economy, alongside a handful of private companies, particularly Odebrecht, Camargo Corrêa, and Andrade Gutierrez construction companies; the financial groups Unibanco and Itaú; and the Votorantim group:

> Being spread throughout various companies and, at the same time, active in their control structures, pension funds became pivotal in diverse local corporate agglomerations. Partnering with the funds in a given societal context made it possible to coerce other shareholders, co-opt allies, or increase the funds' level of influence in company decisions. Even without being majority shareholders in each firm, the centrality of the pension funds simply created multiple opportunities for coalition and negotiation between various operatives in the companies where they were present.[85]

The investments made by pension funds and the BNDES naturally drive the process of concentration of capital. They focus on large economic groups, leaders in their sectors, in order to get partial or sometimes almost entire control over the global supply chain of certain products. Based on the studies of sociologist Gary Gereffi, Brazilian economist Mansueto Almeida explains how companies and countries benefit in international trade depending on their degree of integration into the global production chain. In his view, the creation of giant companies benefits those companies, but not necessarily the country or those who place their savings in pension funds.[86]

In that sense, the market choices made by the pension funds are questionable. In 2010, Petros decided to enter the block that controls Itaú-Unibanco, the largest bank in Brazil and one of the ten largest in the world. By investing $1.5 billion in the construction company Camargo Corrêa, Petros obtained 11 percent of the voting capital and Camargo Correa's seat on the Board of

Directors of the huge bank.[87] Such power has brought waves of criticism from diverse sectors.

In July 2007, the "BNDES Platform" was created, a coalition of NGOs and citizens advocating for greater transparency in the development bank.[88] The platform's principle goal is to democratize the bank as a public instrument for the good of the country's development, to re-politicize the economy and subject BNDES investments to independent public control. On July 9, 2007, the group delivered a proposal to the bank president Luciano Coutinho, arguing for transparency, for investments to reduce social inequalities, and a commitment to protecting the environment. In dialogue with bank officials, the platform outlined five priority areas to work on: ethanol, hydropower, pulp and paper, social infrastructure (sanitation), and regional integration.[89]

In November 2009, the South American Meeting of People Impacted by Projects Financed by the BNDES was held in Rio de Janeiro, with delegates from Brazil, Bolivia, and Ecuador. The "Charter of People Affected by the BNDES" criticized BNDES's support for sugarcane and eucalyptus monoculture, unsustainable meat production, exploitation of minerals, pulp mills, agro-energy and hydropower production plants, as well as large infrastructure projects like ports, gas and slurry pipelines, railways, and roads.[90] The BNDES Platform reiterated that the institution's funds come from public monies in the National Treasury and the Worker Support Fund, but serve only to increase the profits of a small group of large companies. The regional integration plan promoted by the bank, argued the Platform, relies on a high concentration of capital and the control and use of indigenous territories to produce goods for export.

Members of the Brazilian Network on Multilateral Financial Institutions—an NGO lobbying for citizen participation in decision-making on economic policy and projects financed by international financial institutions—are also voicing their criticism of the BNDES, emphasizing the role it played in previous periods, before the consolidation of the import substitution model, and later, in the process of privatization. They further criticize the

BNDES for financing foreign capital along with Brazilian companies. Many of the companies BNDES consider Brazilian are, according to the lobby, actually companies incubated by foreign or international capital for the purpose of "leveraging the country's advantageous institutional structure to expand and monopolize certain segments of transnational production chains."[91]

The huge construction projects necessary to host the World Cup and the Olympics will extend and intensify the involvement of the state in restructuring Brazil, or specifically, the involvement of a small core of pension fund managers and BNDES operatives. In addition to questions about the PT government's restructuring of capitalism, opponents to this path need to think more deeply about what specific sort of capitalism is promoting Brazil's rise into the exclusive club of the five major world powers, behind China, the US, India, and Japan. In order to understand if Brazil's rise is a typical case of "imperialism" or whether we are witnessing the ascent of a new kind of power, we need to delve deeper into state strategies in areas like defense, the character of Brazilian multinationals, and the kind of regional integration being fostered.

6
Brazilian Multinationals in Latin America

"Brazil is undergoing a profound change with its integration into the global economy and global politics. Never before in its history has this country produced, exported, and invested so much, especially across borders, developing transnational corporations based in Brazil. Never before has Brazil's foreign policy been so independent, based on the exploitation of economic resources in Latin America and the competition for markets and investment opportunities in Africa. Never before has Brazil been so participatory, to the point that large capitalists support the compensatory policies of the 'left.' Never before has Brazil been so imperialist."

—João Bernardo

"Things happen, there is no program for life, there is no script," said a man in his seventies while touring the famous Anuga food fair in Germany. This is a man who only studied up to fourth grade and started working when he was fifteen. After completing his military service, he sold cattle to butchers in the small town of Annapolis, with population of about 50,000, in the state of Goiânia. When President Juscelino Kubitschek called on

Brazilians to come construct their new capital, Brasilia, this man saw opportunities because "the government were offering four tax-free years for those who wanted to work there." So he decided to set up a slaughterhouse, big enough to slaughter twenty-five cattle a day—which he sold to feed construction workers. As the city grew, so did his business. Half a century later, in 2007, this same man bought US Swift Foods for $1.4 billion. The family business, turned meat giant, is called JBS, the initials of its owner: Jose Batista Sobrinho.[1]

During his trip to Germany, Batista Sobrinho granted the first interview in his life. The founder of the Friboi meat processing company, now part of JBS, looked back on his long career: How he opened a butcher shop in Annapolis in 1953, set up in Brasilia in 1957, rented a slaughterhouse in Luziânia in 1962, and in 1969, bought the Formosa Industrial Slaughterhouse, naming the company Friboi. A family business that employed his six children (three boys and three girls), who all left school to devote their time to the family business. "Our knowledge is not academic, we learned from life," said his son Wesley in an interview with *Forbes* magazine that probed the secrets of the world's largest beef, and second-largest poultry company.[2]

The family business expanded in Brazil during the 1990s and then around South America. Its major acquisition was Anglo in 1995, then Sadia in the meat sector. In subsequent years, they bought up Mouran, Araputanga, and Frigovira meat companies, and formed an alliance with Bertin, another Brazilian meat giant, that eventually culminated in a merger. In 2005, they bought Swift Armour S.A., the largest producer and exporter of beef in Argentina, and in 2007, they turned their attention towards the US giant Swift Foods. Like most of the companies JBS acquired, Swift was in economic trouble and, in order to make an acquisition of such size and importance, JBS allied itself with the BNDES. In 2007, the development bank made its first investment in the meat giant. It currently controls 20.6 percent of the company.[3]

In 2011, JBS owned eighteen slaughterhouses in Brazil, six in Argentina, eight in the US, and four in Australia. In the US, the largest market for beef in the world, JBS supplies 22 percent of the total. In 2010, it had revenues of $35 billion.

JBS Friboi's trajectory is not unusual among Brazilian multinationals. You could say there are two genealogies. The first is large state enterprises that were partly or wholly privatized during the government of Fernando Henrique Cardoso—such as Petrobras, Vale do Rio Doce and Embraer—in which the state maintains a strong presence through the BNDES and pension funds. The second genealogy is the type of family business founded by Jose Batista Sobrinho: Norberto Odebrecht, Camargo Corrêa, Gerdau, Andrade Gutierrez, Votorantim, and many others. These family-based companies also have state involvement. After growing rapidly with the support of the BNDES, JBS Friboi was no longer in the hands of the Batista family as main shareholder. By 2011, the BNDES occupied that position with 35 percent of total capital, compared to the founding family's 24.2 percent.[4]

Both business genealogies have common traits. They are businesses with either familial or local/regional beginnings, and they expanded exponentially during the Kubitschek government (1956–1961), either by capitalizing on large state investments in infrastructure or due to the expansion of the domestic market. In the ensuing decades, they became important national companies, and during the period of globalization, they began their international expansion, first in South America and then the rest of the world, especially Africa.

The internationalization of Brazilian companies

The large companies followed a similar trajectory, with a few slight differences. Those linked to the exploitation of natural resources, Petrobras and Vale, went abroad in search of new deposits. The big construction companies used the experience gained at home to expand their business networks around the region and all over the world. Manufacturing industries, for their part, only began pushing beyond Brazil's boundaries in the 1990s. The history of these varied multinationals goes back to the period after the 1930 revolution led by Getúlio Vargas.

In that era, Brazil was an agricultural country exporting coffee. The first industries were created early in the twentieth century by European immigrants and a few landowners. As the influence of agricultural oligarchies weakened, large companies linked to the exploitation of natural resources arose: Companhia Siderurgica Nacional (founded in 1941), Vale do Rio Doce (1942), and Petrobras (1953). All three are progeny of the *Estado Novo*, the period from 1937 to 1945, which began when Vargas imposed a new, authoritarian constitution in a coup d'état, shut down Congress, and assumed dictatorial powers.

After the 1929 world economic crisis, Brazil instituted a policy of import substitution, resulting in the growth of national industry. Exports of Brazilian textiles and footwear were established by the 1970s. At the same time, foreign investment from the United States and Europe grew, focusing on consumer durables (cars and appliances), most prominently from companies like Ford, GM, Volkswagen, Whirlpool, Scania, Volvo, and Mercedes Benz. With the imposition of the military regime, national construction companies (Odebrecht, Camargo Corrêa, and Andrade Gutierrez) expanded, and in 1969, the aeronautical company Embraer was established, as was a petrochemical industry based on an alliance between the state, private, and foreign capital.[5]

The three construction companies provide the most notable examples of internationalization. All of them were created in the 1940s as local or regional companies linked to a family base. Camargo Corrêa was founded in 1939 by Sebastian Camargo in a small town in the interior of São Paulo. A son of ranchers, he traveled a similar path as Jose Batista Sobrinho. His studies ended in third grade, and at seventeen, he began working in construction. His small business expanded during the country's period of growth and the construction of Brasilia, leading to work on the Itaipu dam, as well as several other hydroelectric projects and the Rio-Niteroi Bridge.

Today the Camargo family is one of the wealthiest in the country and the company has diversified into construction, cement, footwear, textiles, steel, and energy, forming an economic group that operates in more than twenty countries.[6]

Table 5: Internationalization of Brazilian multinationals
(Top 20 companies of 2011)

COMPANY	SECTOR	% OF STAFF ABROAD	% OF INCOME ABROAD
JBS-FRIBOI	Food	61.7	77.4
GERDAU	Metal	45.3	52
ODEBRECHT	Construction	45	59.8
METALFRIO	Electronics	47.4	40
IBOPE	Services	55.2	29.7
ANDRADE GUTIERREZ	Construction	44.7	33.3
COTEMINAS	Minerals	21.9	88.5
VALE	Minerals	20.8	56.6
MARFRIG	Food	37.2	39
AMBEV	Food	28.5	32
STEFANINI	Information	37	35.7
SABÓ	Vehicles	35.7	43.2
MARCOPOLO	Vehicles	26	29.8
WEG	Mechanics	16.0	39.2
EMBRAER	Vehicles	5	34.9
MAGNESITA	Food	17	29.2
ARTECOLA	Chemicals	20.6	17.7
CAMARGO CORRÊA	Business Group	17	17.3
VOTORANTIM	Business Group	11.6	21.1
REMI	Mechanics	13.1	6.5

Source: Valor, *"Multinacionais brasileiras,"* September 2011, 308.

Norberto Odebrecht was created in Salvador, Bahia, in 1944, by a family of German descent who came to Santa Catarina in the mid-nineteenth century. It grew to become the largest construction company in the country, and controls Braskem, the largest petrochemical company in Latin America, exporting to twenty countries. Andrade Gutierrez was created in 1948 by two families. It became one of the largest infrastructure conglomerates in the country operating in various sectors from construction to telecommunications, and has a presence in thirty countries.[7] The other major construction companies were established in the same period in the Northeast: Queiroz Galvão, founded by three brothers in 1953 in Pernambuco, and the OAS, founded in 1976 in Salvador.[8]

Under Kubitschek, 20,000 km of roads and 1,000 km of railway lines were constructed, but the most profitable work was in hydroelectric dams and projects commissioned by Petrobras, including refineries and platforms.[9] The creation of the National Housing Bank (BNH) during the military regime was important for the growth of the construction industry, which also benefited with public works like the Trans-Amazonian highway, large dams like Itaipu, Tucuri I and II, and thousands of miles of roads. Construction was one of the three fastest growing sectors in the country in that era, alongside production and the financial sector. A side effect of the dictatorship's "economic miracle" was the rapid expansion of a handful of family businesses responsible for the huge public works.

In the late 1970s, the major construction companies began their monopolistic concentration and expansion beyond national borders. Between 1969 and 1973, Mendes Júnior built a hydroelectric plant in Bolivia, and between 1975 and 1979, a highway in Mauritania—the first Brazilian multinational to work there.[10] In 1979, Odebrecht oversaw public works in Chile and Peru, and Camargo Corrêa built the Guri hydroelectric plant in Venezuela. In 1983, Andrade Gutierrez began its first contracts abroad with the construction of a highway in Congo, and Queiroz Galvão made its international debut building a dam in Uruguay.

Large Brazilian construction companies began their international expansion in South America because of the geographical proximity and obvious cultural affinities, and then moved further afield to Africa and Portugal. Many others companies followed suit, to the point where there are currently 885 Brazilian companies working abroad with investments in fifty-two countries, indicating that it is not only the large companies who travel but medium-sized ones as well.[11] Research reveals a preference for South America and Africa, although this could also be linked to the fact that in these regions "there are no other companies powerful enough to compete with the large Brazilian companies."[12]

In the final stages of the military dictatorship—with which the construction companies had excellent relations—there was a significant reduction in the amount of large-scale public works, coinciding with a period of acute economic crisis. The construction companies adapted to the new situation by focusing outside the country and diversifying. They shed their original profile as construction companies and instead became "monopolistic conglomerates with diverse investment portfolios, with infrastructure construction assuming a smaller component."[13] Odebrecht, for example, bought the much larger Braskem petrochemical. By 2006, almost 70 percent of Odebrecht's revenues were coming from the petrochemical sector against only 30 percent from construction and engineering.

The other construction companies followed suit. Andrade Gutierrez invested in Oi telecommunications and Brasil Telecom, a sector that accounts for 60 percent of the companies' sales. Camargo Corrêa, the most diversified of all, bought Topper and Havaianas footwear brands in addition to Levi's, Lee, and Santista Textiles; they also entered the agricultural field, real estate, shipbuilding, cement, as well as purchasing Loma Negra and Alpargatas in Argentina. They invested in Usiminas steel works and Itaú bank, and by 2003, construction represented just over 20 percent of Camargo Corrêa enterprises.[14]

The trend of initially investing in neighboring countries appears to be the natural way of all internationalization processes. During the economic crisis, this trend was enhanced even more: between 2008 and 2009 Brazilian companies withdrew their investments from developed countries—by 47 percent in North America and

18 percent in Europe—but increased them by 36 percent in Asia, 126 percent in Africa, and 15 percent in Latin America.[15]

Economic deregulation promoted by the Washington Consensus, resulting in a massive inflow of foreign capital into Brazil and the region, was one of the driving forces of internationalization for large Brazilian companies looking to improve their competitiveness. The profile of the top 500 companies in Latin America changed between 1991 and 2001: Foreign multinationals went from 27 percent to 39 percent.[16] According to a United Nations Economic Commission for Latin America and the Caribbean (CEPAL) study, "increased competition put pressure on national groups, which traditionally provided products and services to their local markets," and this impelled them to seek new markets abroad.[17]

The creation of Mercosur was, in that sense, a way to open regional markets for local companies to compete, and in turn, to protect them from the increasing pressure of the big multinationals. However, being competitive internationally was also the key to maintaining a strong presence in the domestic market, as the growing interdependence of world markets ends up affecting each and every actor.[18]

Between 1995 and 2004, Brazilian companies carried out ninety mergers and acquisitions abroad, with the following geographical distribution: twenty-nine in developed countries and sixty-one in developing countries, of which thirty-two were in Argentina, four in Colombia, Peru and Venezuela and three in Bolivia.[19] Of the twenty most important projects for Brazilian companies setting up abroad between 2002 and 2004, fourteen were located in South America, one in Central America, three in Portugal, one in Iran, and one in Norway.[20]

The expansion in the South American region has been marked by conflicts between companies and governments. However, some multinationals attempt to present themselves as representatives of Brazil and its government policy, leading to a confusion of business interests with national interests. For example, Odebrecht's advertising during the Latin American summit held in

Table 6: Localization of Brazilian company subsidiaries *(Top 20 in 2009)*

Company	Total countries	Latin America	N.America	Europe	Africa	Asia	Oceania
Vale	33	15%	6%	15%	21%	36%	6%
Petrobras	26	38%	8%	12%	19%	19%	4%
Banco do Brasil	23	43%	4%	30%	4%	17%	0%
Votorantim	21	19%	10%	29%	24%	14%	5%
WEG	20	25%	5%	40%	0%	25%	5%
Brasil Foods	20	25%	0%	45%	0%	30%	0%
Odebrecht	17	47%	6%	12%	24%	12%	0%
Stefanini	16	50%	13%	25%	6%	6%	0%
Camargo Corrêa	14	71%	7%	7%	14%	0%	0%
Gerdau	14	71%	14%	7%	0%	7%	0%
IBOPE	14	93%	7%	0%	0%	0%	0%
Marfrig	12	33%	8%	42%	8%	8%	0%
Randon	10	30%	10%	10%	30%	20%	0%
TOTVS	10	80%	0%	10%	10%	0%	0%
Eletrobras	10	100%	0%	0%	0%	0%	0%
TIGRE	9	89%	11%	0%	0%	0%	0%
Localiza	9	100%	0%	0%	0%	0%	0%
Natura	9	78%	11%	11%	0%	0%	0%
JBS	7	43%	14%	14%	0%	14%	14%
Regional Average*		52.95%%	9.18%	16.89%	5.43%	14.66%	0.89%

*Over 38 companies Source: Ranking das Transnacionais Brasileiras, FDC, 10.

Bahia in December 2008 presented it as "the construction company of regional integration."[21] This at a time when the company was involved in a bitter dispute with the Ecuadorian government over the construction of a dam.

Foreign investment in Brazil

There is general agreement that Brazilian investments abroad are actually still very small in relation to GDP, but they could grow significantly in the coming years. Brazil was and still is a major recipient of FDI (foreign direct investment), but in the 1990s, it became an exporter of capital (direct Brazilian investment, or DBI). In some years, Brazilian investment exceeded foreign investment in the country, as part of a deep global realignment of capital flows driven by crisis in the central economies and growing geopolitical fragmentation. A brief look back will let us see the underlying trends. To do so, we need to look at three sets of data in the evolution of foreign investment.

The first reflects the evolution of overall FDI. Until the triennium 1978–1980, 97 percent of foreign direct investments went to developed economies and only 3 percent from developing economies. But in the first decade of the century, the developing and emerging economies began to attract more and more capital. By 2005, these economies attracted 12 percent of the global flows of capital, and by 2009, some 21 percent. The major turning point came in 2010, when emerging and developing economies attracted more capital than developed countries: 53.1 percent versus 46.9 percent. "For the first time since the start of the United Nations Conference on Trade and Development (UNCTAD) reports in 1970, developed countries received less than half of global FDI flows."[22] The UNCTAD reports show the profound spatial reorganization of the capitalist system, which has become more pronounced since the financial crisis of 2008.

The second set of data refers to the evolution of FDI received by Brazil and the region. The available UNCTAD reports since 1950 indicate that Brazil attracted more investment in the decade from 1970 to 1980, about half of all Latin America.[23] Afterwards,

Table 7: Foreign direct investment in South America and Mexico

(2000–2010 in billions of dollars)

Country	1990–1994*	1995–2000*	2000–2005*	2006	2007	2008	2009	2010	2011**
S. America Total	8,941	47,195	37,969	43,410	71,227	91,329	54,550	85,143	121,318
Brazil	1,703	21,755	19,197	18,822	34,585	45,058	25,949	48,462	66,700
Argentina	2,971	10,742	4,296	5,537	6,473	9,726	4,017	6,193	7,240
Chile	1,219	5,058	5,012	7,298	12,534	15,150	12,874	15,095	17,300
Colombia	818	2,505	3,683	6,656	9,049	10,596	7,137	6,760	13,200
Perú	785	2,022	1,604	3,467	5,491	6,924	5,576	7,328	7,600
Venezuela	836	3,416	2,546	-508	1,008	349	-3,105	-1,404	5,300
México	5,430	11,265	22,722	19,779	29,714	25,864	15,206	17,726	17,900

*Yearly averages **Preliminary

Sources: Ziga Vodusek, "Inversión extranjera directa en América Latina," cit. 21; and CEPAL, "La inversión extranjera directa en América Latina y el Caribe," 2010, cit. 45 and 2011, 34; and UNCTAD, "Investment Trend Monitor," No. 8, United Nations, New York, 24 January, 2012.

investments in Brazil decreased, with Argentina and Mexico becoming the main destination of transnational investment capital. From 1990–1994, Brazil only attracted 19 percent of the investment in South America, while it doubled in Argentina—which was undergoing an intense period of privatization of state enterprises—and Mexico received three times more investment than Brazil.[24]

The trend changed in the mid-1990s, with Brazil capturing half of all foreign direct investment in South America, well above the other countries.[25]

Estimates for 2011 anticipated a new wave of foreign investment in Brazil with a 35 percent growth over the previous year.[26] Brazil became the fifth global investment destination close to China. But the table mapping the capital also shows the evolution of the other countries. As Brazil grows exponentially, Argentina slips behind Chile and Peru, while Colombia becomes something of a star, with double the flow of investments received by Argentina in 2012.[27] Mexico tends to recede, largely due to its dependence on the US market, the epicenter of the 2008 crisis. Capital tends to flee from Venezuela.

The third set of data focuses on Direct Brazilian Investment (DBI), an area that is experiencing a breakthrough, reflecting the maturity of large multinational companies and the sustained support from the state through the BNDES. Although companies have about $150 billion invested abroad, Brazil has one of the lowest rates of foreign direct investment in the world, below even developing countries and others in the South American region. Developed countries invest about 2 percent of GDP abroad. In Latin America in recent years, direct investment abroad by Chile has been 5 percent of GDP, Colombia and Mexico 1.3 percent to 0.9 percent, while in Brazil it has been less than 0.5 percent.[28]

It can be argued that this low investment level is due to the lack of a credit policy to finance operations abroad, the high cost of capital, reduced ability to invest due to a long history of protectionism, and entrepreneurs' lack of preparation.[29] The 1990s would not have been conducive to the expansion of Brazilian multinationals, largely due to internal difficulties. In 2003, there were only three Brazilian companies among the fifty biggest non-financial transnational corporations (TNCs) from developing countries (Petrobras, Vale, and Gerdau).[30] However, in recent years, this situation is changing.

Indeed, Brazilian investments abroad took a major leap forward in the first decade of the new century, to the point that, in 2006, they exceeded foreign investments in Brazil.[31] That year Brazil was the number twelve investor in the world, ahead of Russia and China, and several developed countries. Table 8 summarizes the events of the last decade in the region, in which the Andean countries stand out as powerful exporters of capital.

These figures indicate that Brazil and Chile account for two-thirds of South American investment abroad. Brazil has placed a huge amount of capital in foreign investments, close to 10 percent of GDP, and that figure continues to grow despite the global crisis. The Brazilian Capital Abroad (BCE) survey begun in 2001 gives a visualization of changes in the past decade: foreign investment increased almost fourfold in less than a decade, to a total of $165 billion.[32] Most significantly, it grew during the crisis when global capital retracted, seeking refuge in speculative markets.

Brazil is building a state policy to encourage foreign investment, although the process is still inconsistent, a shortcoming identified by a study on Brazilian foreign investment: "It is

Table 8: Direct investment abroad by Latin American countries
(2001–2010 in millions of dollars)

	2001	2002	2003	2004	2005	2006	2007	2008	2009	2010
Argentina	161	-627	774	676	1,311	2,439	1,504	1,391	710	946
Brazil	2,258	2,482	249	9,807	2,517	28,202	7,067	20,457	10,084	11,500
Chile	1,610	343	1,606	1,563	2,183	2,171	2,573	8,040	8,061	8,744
Colombia	16	857	938	142	4,662	1,098	913	2,254	3,088	6,504
México	4,404	891	1,253	4,432	6,474	5,758	8,256	1,157	7,019	12,694

Source: CEPAL, *"La inversión extranjera directa en América Latina y el Caribe,"* 2009, 85; and 2010, 75.

impossible to clearly identify a strategic vision for the Brazilian public sector in relation to these investments and the role they can play in the economic development of the country; nor is there a set of well-defined policies to support and promote investment."[33]

An analyst with a longer-term view argues that, since 2003, the BNDES, one of Brazil's major economic policy instruments, rescued the practice of "competitive insertion," through which Brazil seeks an advantageous repositioning in the international division of labor, which translates into a concentration and centralization of capital to compete abroad.[34] During the Lula government, the BNDES decided to promote large, Brazil-based companies—even if they were subsidiaries of foreign multinationals—and to support their key initiatives. For then-president of BNDES, Luciano Coutinho, the "objective criteria" for receiving support from the bank are "the company's bottom line in terms of the results and figures."[35]

BNDES studies confirm that its managers overseeing loans to Brazilian companies understood that "without internationally competitive firms, a country cannot improve its economic performance."[36] The development bank concluded that, in 1990, the 420 largest companies in the world were responsible for half of all international trade, and that multinationals were the main source of private research and development in technology. For this reason, they believe internationalization has several positive effects: it gives access to resources and markets, it facilitates corporate restructuring, and the exports generate the hard currency that funds imports and sustains growth.[37]

In 2002, even before Lula's victory, a BNDES working group was created to study credit lines for investments abroad. The evolution of investments in South America since 2000 shows that Brazil became an intermediary link between the region and the world market, because of the comparative advantages presented by its huge internal market and its great abundance of natural resources.

While the economies of its neighbors were restricted to agricultural and mineral production, or subjected to processes of deindustrialization, Brazil managed to upgrade its industrial base through intracompany transactions that kept it in a position to produce and export manufactured goods at a competitive cost. Then, having survived the global economic crisis, "the contradiction of markets in the developed countries, and the adoption of new protectionist barriers, absorbing residual markets in Latin American countries became crucial for [Brazilian] capital."[38]

In 2008, BNDES published its five strategic objectives for the development of production and business. The first was to make Brazil a *world leader*, for which it would be necessary to "position production systems or Brazilian companies among the top five global players in their activity," in sectors like mining, steel, aeronautics, and ethanol.[39] The second objective was the *conquest of markets*, which means positioning certain major companies as the principal global exporters in their field, "combining meaningful participation in international trade flows with the preservation of their position in the domestic market."[40] Consumer durables and capital goods are the backbone of this strategy.

Specialization was the third BNDES strategy—building competitiveness in technology-dense areas, giving support to sectors such as information technology, the health-industrial complex, and the capital goods industry. The fourth strategy was *differentiation*, upgrading Brazilian brands so that each is positioned among the top five in each sector for semidurable or nondurable consumer goods. Finally, the fifth strategy involved *expanding access to mass consumption* in fields such as broadband services, consumer goods, and housing.[41]

The BNDES document also defined four long-term "macro targets." The internationalization of Brazil is key, based on the growth of exports and direct foreign investment to install production plants and establish commercial representation abroad. What distinguishes Brazil from other South American countries is that the state is actively planning to support large companies to expand abroad. To this end, it has opened a credit line of industry support, freeing 210 billion reals between 2008 and 2010.[42] It has also opened lines for innovation via a vigorous expansion of public investment in science and technology.

Brazil proposes to use its economic, diplomatic, and political power to promote Mercosur for the economic integration of Latin America and the Caribbean. It aims to augment production chains and increase intraregional trade to expand the scale and productivity of domestic industry. In reference to the Initiative for the Integration of the Regional Infrastructure of South America (IIRSA), the BNDES says, "In this context, the integration of logistics and energy infrastructure in South America remains the great challenge and opportunity."[43] It proposes similar aims in respect to Africa, with increased trade and a greater presence of large Brazilian companies.

In 2003, the BNDES amended its statutes to support establishing Brazilian companies abroad. The first major intervention was financing Friboi's purchase of 85 percent of Swift Armour, Argentina's leading meat company.[44] Support for this kind of investment in the region goes hand in hand with the strategic role that Brazil wants to play in the world, based on its hegemony in South America. The increase in exports of goods and capital is a fundamental step towards this end.

The results are obvious. Brazil is third in a ranking of the hundred largest companies in emerging countries, behind China and India, with fourteen companies such as Petrobras, Vale, and the construction and steel companies, some of which have doubled their revenues due to increased business in the region. These companies have assumed the role of flagship for Brazil's new power. The expansion of these Brazilian multinationals has powerfully impacted their neighbors: 20 percent of foreign investment in Bolivia comes from Petrobras, 80 percent of soybeans produced in Paraguay are owned by Brazilian ranchers, and in Argentina, 25 percent of the companies purchased between 2003 and 2004 were bought by Brazilian capital.[45]

Green-yellow entrepreneurs

On May 11, 2011 President Dilma Rousseff launched the Chamber of Policies for Management, Performance, and Competitiveness. The body consists of four "civil society" representatives "with renowned expertise and leadership in the areas of management and competitiveness," announced the President's Office.[46] These four are the entrepreneurs Jorge Gerdau Johannpeter, who chairs the Board of Directors of the Gerdau Group; Abilio Diniz, owner of Grupo Pao de Acucar; Antonio Maciel Neto, president of Suzano Pulp and Paper; and Henri Philippe Reichstul, former president of Petrobras. Attending on behalf of the government were Antonio Palocci, Minister of Casa Civil, Finance Minister Guido Mantega, Minister of Planning Miriam Belchior, and the Minister for Development, Industry and Foreign Trade, Fernando Pimentel.[47]

Gerdau is close to Rousseff, and the president considers him "the minister of her dreams," according to close associates.[48] His position is unpaid because it is considered an important public service. Some of the objectives of the Chamber are to increase competitiveness, reduce state bureaucracy, and stimulate exports. In her weekly radio program *Coffee with the President*, Rousseff said the Chamber "will find ways to cut red tape impeding businesses in trading with other countries" and that "government and business will work together in creating good administrative practices."[49]

Gerdau was one of the first big-business leaders to publicly support Lula in the 2002 election campaign, to the point that he showed up in electoral propaganda. Rousseff had wanted to appoint him to the Secretariat of Strategic Affairs or the Ministry of Development, Industry, and Trade, proposals the businessman rejected. During the Lula administration, Gerdau joined the Federal Council of Economic and Social Development and before that he was on the Board of Directors of Petrobras and the Brazilian Steel Institute, as well as participating in other state and business institutions such as Rio Grande do Sul's Quality and Productivity Board.

The Gerdau Group is not only a leading multinational in the country but it also represents a kind of typically Brazilian family business. Jorge Gerdau is the great-grandson of João Gerdau, founder of the company, who emigrated from Germany in 1869, settling in Agudo, a small town in Rio Grande do Sul. He went into business and in 1901, bought a nail factory in Porto Alegre, which grew rapidly. In 1933, he built a second nail factory in Passo Fundo, administered by his son Hugo Gerdau.

In the late 1940s, the company was taken over by Curt Johannpeter, Hugo's son-in-law, and it purchased the Siderúrica Riograndense (iron and steel) company, entering into a promising new sector of industrial expansion. Jorge Gerdau Johannpeter was born in 1936, and is one of Curt's four sons. At fourteen, Jorge began working in the nail factory during school holidays. In 1957, he took a course as an aspiring reserve officer in the Cavalry division of the Armed Forces, and in 1961, studied law at the Federal University of Rio Grande do Sul.

In the 1960s, the company expanded with Jorge Gerdau playing a key role. They acquired São Judas Alambres factory in São Paulo and Açonorte Iron and Steel in Pernambuco, and then in 1972, they bought Guanabara Iron and Steel Company, as the family decided to expand beyond Rio Grande do Sul. In 1986, Jorge became chair of the Board of Directors, and by 2010, the group was operating in over a hundred countries. Gerdau now owned forty-eight steel mills, twenty-one processing units, eighty commercial units, four lines of iron ore extraction, two private port terminals, as well as dozens of other interests; a total of 337 industrial interests in fourteen countries with a market value of $22 billion.

The Gerdau Group is one of Brazil's most internationalized companies. Its international expansion began in 1980 with the purchase of a small business in Uruguay, followed by the acquisition of power plants in Canada, Chile, and Argentina. The biggest purchase was the acquisition of 75 percent of AmeriSteel, the second largest producer of steel in the US. That allowed the company to triple production outside of Brazil and forcefully enter the US market. In 2001, Gerdau made purchases in Colombia and Europe, where it has 40 percent stake of the Spanish company Sidenor. This streak of acquisitions continued in Peru, Mexico, the Dominican Republic, Venezuela, and the United States, where it gained control of Chaparral Steel, one of the largest producers of structural beams.

Despite having become a major multinational, the thirteenth largest steelmaker in the world with the capacity to produce twenty-six million tons of steel, Gerdau leadership remains firmly within the family. The Board consists of nine members, and four Gerdau Johannpeter brothers occupy the positions of president (Jorge) and three vice presidents. Along with two of their children, they make up the majority of the group's governing body. Among nonfamily members on the board, two are economists, Affonso Celso Pastore, president of the Central Bank from 1983 to 1985, and André Pinheiro de Lara Resende who was also a Central Bank director during the period of Fernando Henrique Cardoso's Real Plan. Cardoso presented him with the presidency of the BNDES in 1998, a position from which he subsequently resigned due to allegations of corruption during the privatization of Telebras.

Gerdau rose from being a small local company to the rank of a major multinational, always allied to political power in its various manifestations, and always retaining a family-based and nationalistic profile. Many other successful Brazilian businesses share a similar trajectory: The construction industry, as we have seen, began in regions where large, public infrastructural projects were being built, and subsequently expanded nationally and then internationally, with a measure of political help. These companies benefited by getting public works contracts, either through the PAC (Growth Acceleration Program) or municipal and state connections.

These state donations are, according to the recipients, part of a Brazilian "republican vision," favoring "democracy and the economic and social development of the country, within the limits and conditions imposed by legislation" as Odebrecht has asserted.[50] At this point all the companies express their respect for state legislation, even though their behavior sometimes indicates otherwise. Worse still, they talk about democracy, yet were nurtured under the military regime.

The close relationship between business groups and the state is clearly revealed in the trajectory of the family that controls the Votorantim Group, in particular José Ermírio de Moraes and his son Antonio—one of the richest men in Brazil. His grandfather, and founder of the family business, Antônio Pereira Inácio, emigrated from Portugal in 1886 and learned the shoemaking trade in São Paulo. In 1918, he bought a troubled cotton company in the Sorocaba neighborhood. It was the beginning of an impressive ascent. His grandson amassed a $10 billion fortune, becoming the seventy-seventh wealthiest person in the world in 2010.[51] In turn, the Votorantim Group is among the top five economic groups in the country, dealing in cement, chemicals, aluminum, pulp and paper, electricity, and steel. In 2005, it won the Swiss IMD Business School award as the best family business in the world.[52]

José Ermirio de Moraes married the daughter of Antonio Pereira after studying engineering in the US, and became administrator of the company, which he converted into the powerful Votorantim Group. The company grew as other family businesses did, taking advantage of opportunities like the 1929 crisis, which triggered import substitution and allowed a few businesses to take a great leap forward. José Ermirio began operating the Brazilian Aluminum Company (CBA) in 1955, which was the first company in that industry in Brazil.

Votorantim funded 90 percent of the project, and maintained the controlling interest in the company, which Antônio Ermirio headed. Before long competition from multinationals forced him to postpone the project. The US Alcoa and the Canadian Alcan monopolized sales of aluminum and would not allow the formation of a national company they didn't control. Both were part of the "six sisters" of aluminum, formed in 1901, which controlled quarries for bauxite, the production and trade of which is strategic to the industry.

The first difficulty faced by CBA was purchasing factory equipment, as their efforts were boycotted by northern-based multinationals.[53] The company eventually managed to get equipment in Italy, but the Canadian Light company had a monopoly on electrical power and prevented de Moraes from getting enough of it to produce aluminum. CBA overcame the difficulty by building its own power generators, which led to Votorantim becoming, in 1984, the largest private producer of electricity in Brazil. The business insisted on technology transfer as part of its strategy of independence within the international business world. Perhaps that is why the richest man in Brazil became politically active on the left. First, he participated in the Chamber of Commerce of São Paulo, then joined the laborist PDT (Workers Democratic Party), and in 1962, was elected senator in Pernambuco. In 1964, he was Minister of Agriculture in the João Goulart government. Despite strained relations with the military regime, his company grew steadily during this period.

Many large Brazilian companies had similar trajectories, though without José Ermirio de Moraes's exceptional forays into partisan politics. The family business of Abilio Diniz (the eighth richest man in the country and a member of the Chamber of Policy Management, Performance and Competitiveness with Jorge Gerdau), for example, began in 1948 with his father's candy store, and grew to become the largest supermarket chain in the country. Both Pão de Açúcar and Casas Bahia, whose merger has created the largest national retail chain, began in the same period (1948 and 1952 respectively) as small businessmen.

The multinational Odebrecht is another rags-to-riches family business. The first family members arrived in Brazil in 1856, part of a wave of German immigration. The engineer Norberto Odebrecht took over his father's company and in 1944 founded a construction company in Bahia, whose growth was facilitated by the scarcity of imported materials during World War II. Nearly four decades later, Emilio succeeded his father, and in 2008 the founder's grandson, Marcelo, just forty, was elected president of Odebrecht, which had become one of Brazil's leading multinationals.

Like all the great companies, Odebrecht grew during Brazil's three decisive epochs: the industrial boom of the 1950s, the military regime's economic miracle in the 1960s and 1970s, and the current period in which Brazil is emerging as a global power. In each of the three historical phases, the state oversaw huge infrastructural projects allowing Odebrecht to become a major national construction company, and ultimately the world leader in construction of hydroelectric projects. In 2010, it had 130,000 employees worldwide and revenues of $32 billion.[54]

The company expanded to become a business group, with 40,000 employees in Angola alone.[55] In 1979, Odebrecht bought Braskem, one of the largest petrochemical companies in the world with thirty-one plants in Brazil and the US and a research center in Pittsburgh. Although its main business remains infrastructure works, the company expanded into the area of biofuels with ETH Bioenergy in 2007, where Odebrecht invested $3 billion to process 45 million tons of sugarcane by 2015 and become the leader in the sector.[56] One of ETH's innovative developments is to produce plastic from ethanol instead of petroleum.

The current president of Odebrecht Group, the third member of the family dynasty to head the firm, acknowledged the debt of the business to the Superior War School (ESG). In the ESG Alumni Association newspaper he said: "The dissemination of the ESG Doctrine for State Planning in their courses has effectively contributed to the process of national development."[57]

CHAPTER 7
The New Conquest of the Amazon

"This country is going to become a major economic power in the coming years. And it is thanks to the pre-salt, it is thanks to the Amazon, it is thanks to our biodiversity."

— *Luiz Inácio Lula da Silva*

On the afternoon of March 15, 2011, a violent dispute between a construction worker and a bus driver led to an uprising among a portion of the 20,000 workers constructing the Jirau dam on the Madeira River. Hundreds of workers set fire to the buses that take them from their barracks to the worksite. At least forty-five buses and fifteen vehicles were quickly burned, as were the offices of the construction firm, Camargo Corrêa, half the workers' dormitories, and at least three bank ATMs. Some 8,000 workers went into the jungle to escape the violence. The police were overwhelmed, and only managed to protect the facilities where the explosives used to alter the course of the river were stored. Calm was only restored when the President Dilma Rousseff sent 600 military police troops to take control of the situation. But the workers went back to their places of origin rather than returning to work.[1]

At the nearby Santo Antonio construction site, a work stoppage began that involved 17,000 workers who were building yet another generating plant on the Madeira River—this one near Porto Velho, the capital of the state of Rondônia. In just one week, the wave of strikes spread through the huge worksites: 20,000 workers left their jobs at the Abreu e Lima refinery in Pernambuco, another 14,000 at the Saupe petrochemical plant in the same city, and another 5,000 in Pecém, in the state of Ceará.

What these strikes have in common is that they all have taken place on the gigantic projects of the Growth Acceleration Program (PAC), and they have challenged the biggest construction firms in the country, the Brazilian multinationals contracted by the national government.

The Madeira River is the Amazon's main tributary. Starting at the convergence of the Beni and Mamoré rivers, near the city of Vila Bela on the border of Brazil and Bolivia, it is 4,207 km long—one of the twenty longest rivers in the world, and among the top ten in volume. It is fed by runoff from the Andes mountains in Bolivia and southern Peru, and thus has great potential for hydroelectric generation.

The Madeira River complex includes the construction of four hydroelectric dams, two of which have already begun, the Jirau and Santo Antônio, in the Brazilian section between the border and Porto Velho. The Jirau plant will produce 3,350 MW and Santo Antônio 3,150 MW. They are two priority PAC projects that will connect the two isolated systems in the states of Acre (neighboring Rondônia) and Maranhão (in the northeast) to the national electrical grid.[2] The aim is to use Amazon hydroelectric potential for the benefit of central and southern regions, which have the largest industrial parks, and to boost industry that relies heavily on electricity consumption such as mining, metallurgy and cement production. It would also support the agribusiness sector, "the main advocate for Brazil's expansion to the Pacific."[3]

The Jirau plant went on the block in May 2008 and was acquired by the Sustainable Energy consortium of Suez Energy Brazil (50.1 percent), Camargo Corrêa (9.9 percent), Eletrosul (20 percent), and San Francisco Hydroelectric Company (Chesf, with 20 percent). Its initial cost of $5.5 billion was financed by the BNDES. From the start, the plant was subject to intense criticism. It would endanger the existence of indigenous peoples who live in intentional isolation. The Institute of Environment (IBAMA) granted authorization for the plant in July 2007 under political pressure and against the opinion of experts. The company changed the location of the site, moving nine miles downriver to reduce costs, without an environmental impact study on the new site. In February 2009, IBAMA interceded to stop the work and applied a heavy penalty, citing use of an unauthorized area.[4] In June 2009, however, the official environmental permits to proceed were issued amid protests and demonstrations by environmental groups.

Bolivia also criticized the project so near its borders, due to concerns that the large lakes behind the dams could increase the incidence of diseases like malaria and dengue fever. According to the Brazilian media, cases of malaria had increased 63 percent in the project area in the first seven months of 2009, compared to the previous year.[5]

To the environmental question, we must add the social. The two projects now under construction employ about 40,000 workers, 70 percent of whom are from other Brazilian states. At Jirau alone there are some 20,000 employees, the great majority poorly paid laborers (wages are around 1,000 reals per month, about $600). They come to the isolated jungle work sites from distant places in the northeast, far north, and even the south of Brazil, often tricked by labor recruiters (called *gatos*, cats) who make false promises regarding wages and working conditions, and who charge a fee for their "services." When they arrive on the site, workers are already in debt, and food and medicines purchased from company stores are expensive. Many are housed in wooden barracks where they sleep on mattresses on the floor. The bathrooms are few and distant, there is no electricity, and conditions are crowded. Maria Ozânia da Silva, of the Migrant Pastoral Service in Rondônia, says that the workers "feel frustrated by their wages, and for the unexplained deductions taken from them."[6]

The "revolt of the laborers" is not about wages but about dignity, says journalist Leonardo Sakamoto. The protesters' ten main demands included: ending the aggression of supervisors and security guards, who use private jails; respectful treatment of those who come back to the barracks inebriated; an end to the bullying of laborers by their foremen; payment for the transportation time of long commutes to the worksite; efficient service in the dining halls so the entire break isn't spent waiting in line; and basic rations with costs based on local prices.[7]

According to Sakamoto contemporary laborers are quite different from those who worked in construction in the 1990s. Today, they use cell phones and the Internet, they know what is happening in the world, they are proud of dressing well, they demand respectful treatment, and they often use the word "dignity." They are concerned about the precarious condition of the buildings and dormitories and by being isolated and far from their families. The least mistreatment sets them off. Silvio Areco, an engineer with experience on large projects, also notes the change: "Before, whoever gave the orders on the worksite was almost a colonel; he had authority. Nowadays, that doesn't work. A common laborer has more independence."[8]

In September 2009, the Ministry of Labor freed thirty-eight people who worked in slavery-like conditions, and in June 2010, it reported 330 violations of labor conditions at Jirau.[9] The main problem is insecurity. In Da Silva's opinion, the migrants become an easy target for labor recruiters and construction companies because they have no protection from abuses. But the problems are not limited to the workplace. Aluisio Vidal is the pastor of Jaci-Paraná, a town near Jirau, and the president of the Party of Socialism and Freedom (PSOL) for the state of Rondônia. He complains of the increase in crime and prostitution. Between 2008 and 2010, the population of Porto Velho grew 12 percent (it has half a million inhabitants), but in the same period homicides increased 44 percent and, according to the child protection court, the abuse of minors increased some 76 percent.[10]

According to the social activist organizations in the region, who have joined forces in the Amazon Rivers Alliance (Aliança dos Rios da Amazônia), "All possible problems are concentrated in Jirau: At an uncontrolled pace, the project has brought to the region the 'development' of prostitution, drug abuse among young fishermen and in riverbank settlements, real estate speculation, a rise in food prices, unattended disease, and all types of violence."[11] Elias Dobrovolski, a coordinator in the Movement of those Affected by Dams, who has followed the situation of the workers since the beginning of the project, states that the districts around Jirau are experiencing very serious problems. "Towns that had 2,000 inhabitants now house 20,000. There is no infrastructure for so many people—not enough schools, health clinics, nor police to support all the people that came in with the projects."[12]

In addition to all this, the huge projects of the Growth Acceleration Program have above-average rates of job-related deaths. The rate is double that of the United States or Spain, even though the large construction firms "have sufficient technology to protect the workers."[13] The Movement of those Affected by Dams also denounces work days longer than twelve hours, and epidemics in the worksites. To make matters worse, the companies hired ex-colonels whom people suspect of secretly committing sabotage, which is then blamed on the unions.[14]

The revolt of the laborers attacked the symbols of power. "Witnesses of the attacks said that the men who came to destroy the living quarters first set fire to those of the supervisors and engineers."[15] The revolt in Jirau also took everyone by surprise— government, business owners, and the unions. Víctor Paranhos, president of the construction consortium, said: "It is troubling because we don't know the motive. There are not even leaders."[16] The union leaders' position is curiously similar. "In these revolts in Jirau, we can't find any leader who might negotiate a truce," said Paulo Pereira da Silva, of the Força Sindical.[17] The Central Única dos Trabalhadores (CUT), not to be left out, defended the government against the workers: "They have to return to work. I am Brazilian and I want to see this plant in operation."[18]

Brazil's economic growth implies turning the Amazon and all its resources into commodities. It is a grand project that has few organized detractors, as unions and bosses alike, from both left and right, are on board with the plans. The Jirau revolt is the response of the poorest sector, the unskilled laborers of Brazil, to the ambitious project of modernization and the deepening of capitalism. Gilberto Cervinski, of MAB, summarizes the problem: "To build the generating plants of the Madeira River is to open the Amazon region to dozens of other hydroelectric projects, without even discussing questions that we believe are fundamental: Energy for what? And for whom?"[19]

Just three months after the revolt of Jirau, the population of Puno, a southern Peruvian department, staged a major uprising that forced the government of Alan Garcia to suspend the Inambari hydroelectric project.[20] The uprising is part of a growing resistance to mining in Peru and the region. But the events in Puno mark a new trend. It was a long and intense struggle: forty-five days of strikes in which six people were killed and thirty wounded. Twice, the protesters tried to take the airport of Juliaca, the department's principal city with 30,000 inhabitants. They succeeded, but the ensuing crackdown left five dead.

In response, the crowds besieged the city, burning the Azángaro police station and attacking the offices of several transnational companies in Juliaca.[21] Aymara and Quechua communities participated in the protests, alongside peasants, urban workers, shopkeepers, students, and professionals—creating a broad social front that had the support of local authorities. The Defense of the Natural Resources of Southern Puno Front was one of the main actors, and they formed a broad convergence among local and grassroots organizations and the Conacami (National Confederation of Peru's Communities Affected by Mining).

Resistance was centered in the Inambari hydroelectric project, a set of five dams intended to provide power to Brazil, and in the process thousands of peasants were displaced and ecosystems affected. It also opposed the Canadian Bear Creek Mining company in Santa Ana, as well the contamination of the Ramis River by formal and informal mining. The protests were a clear rejection of mining projects in this, one of the poorest areas of the country.

The Peruvian government was forced to take a step back and cancel the license of a project the Brazilian press called "instrumental in the internationalization of the Eletrobras group."[22] It would appear that outgoing president Alan Garcia decided to pass on his most pressing social problems to his successor, Ollanta Humala, who won the elections in part due to the fervent support of the Brazilian government, in the form of two electoral advisors who had worked on Lula's campaign.[23] In 2010, the two countries signed an agreement for a joint supply of hydroelectricity.[24]

One of the current axes of capital accumulation in Brazil revolves around exploiting the Amazon so that it becomes "an export platform for commodities."[25] The current process is an updated version of the expansion under the military regime in the 1970s: the state promotes major infrastructure works for "national" capital to develop their supply chains towards export and not towards endogenous regional development.

The production of meat, soybeans, wood, sugarcane, aluminum, and iron ore for export is encouraged, roads and waterways are constructed to ease goods transportation, and hydroelectric plants are built to supply plenty of cheap electricity. The environmental and social impacts are not included in the price of these commodities, which cross the oceans along trade corridors between the Pacific and Atlantic, connecting the Amazon with ports in Asia.

Thanks to this externalization of environmental and social costs, Brazil has become the world's leading exporter of beef and an important exporter of biofuels, soybeans, and iron ore. Large dams supply energy to commodity-exporting companies like Gerdau, Alcoa, Votorantim, Vale, and CSN. Vale alone consumes 4.5 percent of Brazil's energy.[26] Under this reinvigoration of the export model, multinational companies gain at the expense of the Amazonian people and the country.

This predatory process knows no boundaries. It has an imperialist slant, in that it is designed by and for the São Paulo-based business sector, Latin America's only genuine bourgeoisie. The most damaging projects are: large hydropower plants on the

Madeira, Xingu, Tapajós, and Teles Pires rivers in the Amazon, and the construction of the IIRSA project's dozen transport corridors that interconnect and bleed the region. It is striking to note that the methods and results of this accumulation process—turning nature into commodities—are identical within and beyond Brazil's borders. Cross-border expansion follows the same pattern as internal expansion. If there is any Brazilian imperialism in the South American region, then it is an extension of this domestic imperialism that is turning the Amazon into a vast pasture.

Dams in the Amazon

Emerging countries have a thirst for energy, and plenty of fresh money for investing in large infrastructure projects. China has eighty-one hydropower projects on the Mekong, Yangtze, and Salween rivers, and is building dams in many other countries, including some in Latin America.[27] Brazil will build twenty-four hydroelectric dams between 2016 and 2020, in addition to those currently under construction, and not counting those projected in other parts of South America such as Inambari in Peru, Cachuela Esperanza in Bolivia, and Garabí on the Argentine border. Almost all the dams will be on the Amazonian river network, including the first of five plants for the Tapajós complex, which will have a power capacity of 6,133 MW.[28]

Brazil is the country best prepared to take advantage of Amazon energy and "the only one putting forward a comprehensive proposal to appropriate this strategic wealth in the short and medium term."[29] There are plans for Brazil to build hydroelectric plants in seven Latin American countries: Peru, Bolivia, Argentina, Nicaragua, Guyana, Suriname, and French Guyana.[30] The most important projects are in Peru and Bolivia, and two binational plants with Argentina on the Uruguay River that will generate 2,000 MW. Even in the small country of Guyana, Eletrobrás has mapped all the hydropower potential, and is considering building a plant with a 1,500 MW capacity. Written into all these ventures is the export of energy to Brazil as part of a CEPAL proposal to double electricity generation in the region by 2030.[31]

The military regime had previously made an inventory of Brazilian rivers in order to harness their hydropower potential, but many of their plans were shelved, considered too controversial, or technically infeasible. The Lula government reinitiated many of the plans, like Belo Monte, and followed this with a similar pattern of studying the potential in the Amazon rivers. The reason in both historical periods is the same: to provide power to export industries that consume large amounts of water and electricity. In 2008, the industrial sector consumed 46 percent of national energy, while the residential sector consumed only 24 percent.[32] Furthermore, the costly construction of large dams represents enormous profits for construction companies.

To understand the new offensive on the Amazon River and the multiple impacts it is having, one must leave aside the idea that dams are limited, localized interventions in geographic space, because isolated initiatives no longer exist—large projects are complex sets of interrelated ventures. This implies multiple impacts upon a river, its tributaries, and their surroundings; building a chain of dams involves the construction of ports and locks to navigate waterways. We are dealing with a global-scale intervention to modify the rivers as part of a much more ambitious project to turn the entire region into a platform for freight movement and transfer nature into exchange values. The Tapajos complex includes five dams; the Madeira River complex will have four dams and various construction projects to make it navigable; and Belo Monte will be much more than just a large dam, and will affect more than a hundred kilometers of the river Xingu.

The second element to consider is the plan to build "platform plants" in the Amazon, a concept devised by the Ministry of Mines and Energy to mitigate social and environmental impacts. The "platform plants" are a political and technical response to criticism from environmental groups for the enormous damage accompanying the dam's construction phase. But, it is simultaneously an attempt to neutralize the labor struggles that have consistently transformed huge public work projects into spaces of resistance.

Corriente Continua, the magazine of state company Eletronorte, was the first publication to report on the new platform plants concept, a kind of jungle rig inspired by oil platforms. Instead of constructing housing units, workers would be flown in by helicopter (or brought in via the river) for three days, or at most a week at a time. Thus, the environmental impact of the project would be reduced, with only a handful of buildings constructed for the site and no roads cut through the jungle because machinery, like workers, needs to be flown or shipped in.[33] But the company's concern is not only, or even primarily, environmental. As Humberto Gama, Eletronorte Works manager explains: "The idea is to get the men out of there. The employee goes there, works his shift and returns to his base, which would be in the nearest town."[34]

The *Corriente Continua* report explains that permanent housing and roads will not be constructed to "avoid attracting population hubs and building cities in the environs of the enterprise."[35] The first experiment with platform plants will be at the Tapajós complex, in the state of Pará. A huge project, the Tapajós complex will generate a capacity of 11,000 MW, similar to Itaipu.[36] But the impact of the project will not be greatly altered by the introduction of platform plants, as the real—if invisible—impact is on the social fabric of the affected local populations and aquatic life in the river.

Although it is not in the Amazon, the case of Rio Grande do Sul can serve as a reference because it is a region where the state has taken full advantage of hydroelectric potential. Passo Fundo University conducted a study on the social and economic impacts of the dams in the upper Uruguay River and concluded that indicators of economic and social development were down 40 percent, while environmental indicators fell 31 percent.[37]

Four dams have been built on the Uruguay River, and there are plans for ten more, not including those to be constructed on its tributaries. Leandro Scalabrin, lawyer for both the Movement of those Affected by Dams and the Landless Movement, said that in northern Rio Grande do Sul, the Uruguay is no longer a river, but merely "a set of artificial lakes."[38]

Nevertheless, the proposal to build platform plants can help solve some of the problems hydropower generates. First, by lessening environmental damage in the initial stages of the construction; and second, by minimizing the likelihood of workers' resistance, as occurred in Jirau and Santo Antônio.

A brief look at the Madeira River hydroelectric complex will help us refine this picture. It consists of four dams: two large plants, Jirau and Santo Antônio, upstream of the city of Porto Velho; the Ribeirão dam, situated in binational Bolivian-Brazilian waters; and the Cachuela Esperanza on the Beni River in Bolivian territory. The complex has a production capacity of 17,000 MW hydropower in total and its waterways are engineered for navigability, with locks built into the dams. This will complete a 4,200 km corridor for navigating the Madeira, Madre de Dios, and Beni rivers serving to integrate commerce in northern Brazil, Peru, and Bolivia, and opening a route for soybean export to Pacific ports.

The project is part of the IIRSA plan and also includes the construction of roads, airports, railways, pipelines, power lines, and fiber optic cables—all to facilitate the extraction of raw materials from the Amazon. Currently, navigation is possible on the Madeira River as far as Porto Velho from the Amazon estuary, but in the future, the Madre de Dios and Beni rivers will be navigable as far as Puerto Maldonado in Peru. From the Beni River, it is possible to navigate the Mamore River to the Central Interoceanic Hub. With navigable waterways in the states of Mato Grosso and Rondonia, it will be possible to increase soybean production from 3 to 20 million tons on 7 million hectares.[39]

This is a project with a history. In 1971, the military dictatorship identified the Jirau and Santo Antônio zones as possible sites for the construction of hydroelectric plants, and in 1983, Eletronorte made a feasibility study of the Madeira River basin. In 2001 and 2002, Furnas Centrais Elétricas and Norberto Odebrecht conducted feasibility and environmental impact studies of the zone. The companies noted the importance of the navigability of the rivers to facilitate transport of soybeans, and proposed to expand the port of Iticoatiara at the confluence of the Madeira and the Amazon, to facilitate cargo transport from Brazil, Peru, Bolivia, Colombia, and Ecuador.[40]

The projected energy production of the plants will be four or five times the electricity consumption of Bolivia. But what is really interesting about the dams is that Brazil will have the extra benefit of a more direct and speedy link with the markets of China and India. Brazilian construction companies Odebrecht and Furnas have the prospect of earning about $8.4 billion from the project.[41]

MAP 5: Dams on the Madeira and Beni rivers

(Santo Antonio and Jirau in construction, Guajará Mirim and Cahcuela Esperanza, projected.)

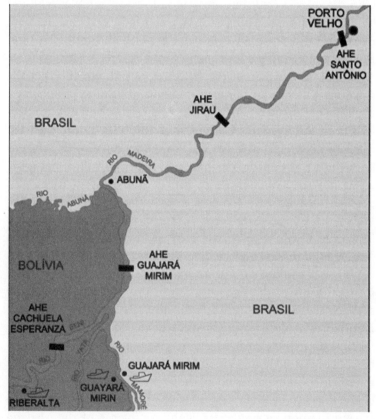

Source: Fobomade

The proposal to construct dams in Bolivia had led to a fierce battle, with environmentalists and NGOs on one side and the Brazilian Embassy, the Andean Development Corporation, the World Bank, and the Electric Industry Research Group at the Federal University of Rio de Janeiro on the other. In mid-2011, the Bolivian Deputy Foreign Minister, Juan Carlos Alurralde, expressed concern that the dams of Jirau and Santo Antônio would cause flooding in Bolivia and alter the flow of the Madeira, threatening other hydroelectric projects.[42] Besides the Cachuela Esperanza plant on the Beni River, which will produce 990 MW from 2019 onwards, the Bolivian government has planned a series of hydropower projects on the binational stretch of the Madeira with an potential capacity of approximately 3,000 MW.

Brazil is investing heavily in hydropower in Bolivia. According to the ambassador in La Paz, Marcel Fortuna Biato, it aims to develop the potential of the Bolivian rivers to a capacity of 40,000 MW, more than twenty times the current consumption.[43] Apart from the usual environmental concerns, the construction of the Bolivian dam would have at least two serious consequences. The town of Esperanza Cachuela has a population of 1,000, but would need to host some 18,000 outside workers needed for construction. Secondly, while dams built in Brazil are financed by the BNDES, those built in Bolivia receive no such funding, despite the fact that they will export energy to Brazil, so Bolivia must borrow, as Paraguay did in the construction of the Itaipu.[44]

Carlos Lessa, former president of BNDES, said that with the Madeira River Complex, "Brazil promotes its own version of the conquest of the Wild West in a jungle area neighboring Peru and Bolivia, with its mega-project embracing the dreams of Latin American integration."[45] Hydroelectric projects allow for "energy generation in significant quantities, and at low cost, for the consolidation of agribusiness development in the western region of Brazil and the Bolivian Amazon," and they reduce transportation costs of grain and other commodities.[46]

Brazilian companies will be the sole buyer of the energy produced by Bolivia, which means they can impose conditions of purchase, contracts, and price. Investments in these dams benefit Odebrecht and Furnas Centrais Elétricas, and the Tedesco Maggi group (the largest exporter of soybeans in Brazil), which has invested $100 million in the navigability of the Madeira River, "where it owns the largest fleet of barges and tugboats, with the ability to transport 210,000 tons per month."[47]

Taken in perspective, projects like the Madeira River complex are part of Brazil's geopolitical westward expansion and occupation of "empty" territories, to control strategic resources, such as Bolivian hydrocarbons, and confirms the impression that "Brazil's leaders seem to have reached the conclusion that increasing Brazilian competitiveness in the international market depends largely on the integration of South America."[48] One should add that integration comes with a double subordination: South American countries under Brazil, and for the whole region under the global market.

IIRSA: Integration through markets

At the regional summit of South American presidents, conducted between August 29 and September 1, 2000 in Brasilia, President Fernando Henrique Cardoso gave a speech outlining the differences between rich countries and the Free Trade Area of the Americas (FTAA). "The richest countries, the most powerful, are the ones with the most trade barriers that affect us, they want to go very fast, without realizing that we cannot, because we're going to fail."[49] In the same speech, he said that the FTAA would only be justified if it was a tool to overcome the socioeconomic unevenness of the Americas. At the meeting, attended by the twelve South American presidents and 350 Latin American entrepreneurs, Cardoso laid the foundation for the Initiative for the Integration of the Regional Infrastructure of South America (IIRSA), and said the purpose of his country was to "work together" with regional partners—leading without imposing—in order to "solve our internal problems, which are many."[50]

Cardoso's speech was almost identical to the one Lula would make years later and shows the continuity of Brazil's foreign policy regarding integration. However, it is clear that the Worker's Party has undertaken the initiative with more audacity, taking advantage of a changing context with the crisis of US global hegemony and the consequences of the attacks of September 11, 2001.

At the same meeting, the Inter-American Development Bank (IDB) presented—at the Brazilian government's request—the proposed *Action Plan for the Initiative for the Integration of the Regional Infrastructure of South America*, an ambitious plan for the implementation of physical projects and changes in legislation, rules and regulations to facilitate regional and global trade.[51] The IIRSA is a multistakeholder process aiming to develop and integrate transport infrastructure, energy, and telecommunications. It is re-organizing the landscape based on the development of land, air, and river transport infrastructure; implementing pipelines, waterways, sea and river ports, along with power lines and fiber optics cables. These projects are organized around ten principle hubs of integration and development, "corridors" of investment to increase commerce and create links with global markets. Andrés Barreda explains the concept of "corridors" as used in the IIRSA plans as an organic metaphor in which transport, energy, and communications networks are interconnected:

> In constructing the "global automaton," these networks allow the general metabolism of wealth feeding and draining the planet's economic tissue. Hence, following the logic that shapes biological organisms, historically tending to form themselves into arteries or central spines or integration corridors of transport, communications, industry, urban and rural life, as well as technical and social reproduction. They can be infrastructure corridors, resource corridors, or biological corridors of conservation.[52]

According to the geographer Carlos Walter Porto Gonçalves, the political and theoretical origin of the IIRSA and Plan Puebla Panama are found in two studies. The first was *Infrastructure for Sustainable Development and Integration of South America*, conducted by Eliezer Batista da Silva in 1996 for the Latin American development bank Corporación Andina de Fomento (CAF), Vale do Rio Doce, the Business Council for Sustainable Development Latin America, the Bank of America, and the Companhia Auxiliar de Empresas de Mineração.[53] The second study, in 1997, was the *Study about National Hubs of Integration and Development*, promoted by the BNDES, the Ministry of Planning, the ABN Amro bank, the US multinational Bechtel, Consorcio Brasiliana, and Booz Allen & Hamilton do Brasil Consultores. Reading the list of funders allows one to understand the interests behind the study. The concept of integration and development hubs privileges the notion of commerce flows over that of territories inhabited by indigenous peoples and nations.[54]

To carry out this megaproject it is necessary to remove physical, social, and political "barriers," which means harmonizing the national laws of the twelve countries involved and occupying the sparsely populated territories that are major raw material and biodiversity reserves.

A key aspect of the IIRSA, as noted by the IDB study *New Impetus for the Integration of Regional Infrastructure in South America*, presented in December 2000, is the idea that the main obstacles to physical integration, and therefore to the flow of goods, are the "formidable natural barriers such as the Andes, the Amazon rainforest and the Orinoco."[55] Former president of the BNDES, Carlos Lessa, also highlights this problem: "The Andes are certainly beautiful, but they're a terrible engineering problem."[56] That logic of seeing nature as a "barrier" or a "resource" is present in all aspects of the plan.

During a meeting organized by the IIRSA Technical Coordination Committee in Lima, in September 2003, three objectives were defined: to support market integration to improve intraregional trade; to support the consolidation of productive chains to achieve competitiveness in major global markets; and to reduce the "South American cost" by creating a logistics platform capable of insertion into the global economy. According to the principal studies available, one goal of this integration is to make the natural resources of South American countries available to the US and European markets.

Map 6: IIRSA Multimodal Hubs

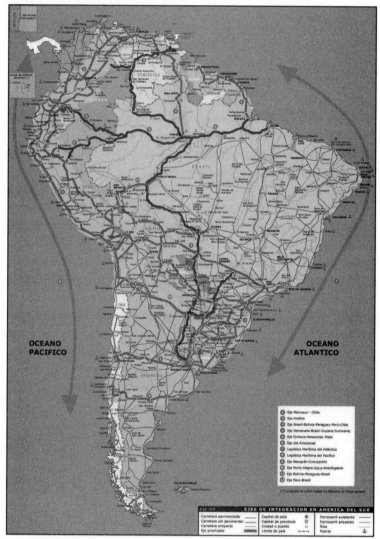

Source: Departamento Geografía, Univ. Federal de Río de Janeiro

These objectives become transparent on maps showing the integration and development hubs, which always cross the borders of several countries. The nine hubs are:

- Andean Hub (Venezuela-Colombia-Ecuador-Peru-Bolivia)
- Amazon Hub (Colombia-Ecuador-Peru-Brazil)
- Central Interoceanic Hub (Peru-Chile-Bolivia-Brazil -Paraguay)
- Capricorn Hub (Chile-Argentina-Paraguay-Brazil)
- Guianese Shield Hub (Venezuela-Brazil-Suriname-Guyana)
- Mercosur-Chile Hub (Brazil-Uruguay-Argentina-Chile)
- Southern Hub (Talcahuano-Concepción/Chile-Neuquén-Bahía Blanca/Argentina)
- Southern Amazon Hub (Peru-Brazil-Bolivia)
- Paraguay-Paraná Waterway Hub

In addition, there is a mega-project to join the Orinoco, Amazon, and La Plata, through a network of seventeen other rivers, allowing water transport between the Caribbean and the Rio de la Plata, which constitutes the tenth hub.

Each hub includes various projected construction works. For example, the Amazon Hub linking the Pacific and Atlantic incorporates three great ecosystems (coastal, Andean, and jungle), and will eventually link the Amazon and its tributaries to the ports of Tumaco (Colombia), Esmeraldas (Ecuador), and Paita (Peru). This means improving existing roads and building others. Furthermore, since it is a hub located in a dense network of river transport, the navigability of rivers needs to be ensured by dredging and straightening some sections, while river ports will need to be improved. These work projects and the ensuing traffic will have a significant impact on the Amazon ecosystem.

There is significant hydroelectric potential in this zone as well as large reserves of oil, monoculture and logging activities, fishing and fish farming. This hub will connect with three others (Andean, Central Interoceanic, Guiana Shield) and reduce the costs of transport from the Pacific countries to Europe, and from Brazil to Japan and China. In the Brazilian Amazon, the construction of two gas pipelines is being considered: from Coari to Manaus and from Urucu to Porto Velho, which will allow gas to be exported from key points through the Amazon and Peru-Brazil-Bolivia hubs. The first includes the port of Manaus, and the second includes Porto Velho (both in Brazil), which would be linked with the Peruvian ports of the Pacific in order to facilitate grain production in the region (which also is a center of soybean, corn, and wheat production), as well as Peruvian Camisea gas.

Most of the hubs are interconnected. Of the ten, four cover the Amazon region and five connect the Pacific and Atlantic oceans. Thus, all the natural wealth of the continent would be made available to international markets. The two main objectives of the IIRSA plan revolve around finding "the most appropriate routes for the transportation of goods" and making "the most important areas in terms of nonrenewable resources" available to the market.[57]

Initially investments were calculated at around $37 billion, but in reality, the amount is difficult to quantify given the diffusion of projects all over the vast region. In addition to significant contributions from the Brazilian BNDES, the entire IIRSA project will be funded by the IDB, the CAF, and the Financial Fund for the Development of the River Plate Basin (FONPLATA).[58]

An important part of these projects is already under way, although it isn't mentioned as part of the IIRSA. According to the CAF 2002 *Annual Report*, about 300 physical integration projects were identified around South America at that time.[59] By January 2011, almost a decade later, a total of 524 projects were counted.[60] Of that total, fifty-three of those projects were already completed and 176 were in progress. As can be seen, the number of projects has grown exponentially and more than half have not yet entered the construction phase.

Overcoming physical, legal, and social barriers in order to implement the IIRSA project will require redesigning local geography, state legislation, and social relations. In the logic of the IIRSA plan, the South American continent is reduced to five "islands" to be united: the Caribbean Platform, the Andean cornice, the Atlantic platform, the central Amazonian enclave, and the southern Amazon enclave. The integration and development hubs unify these "islands," breaking down what in technocratic language are referred to as natural "barriers."

Table 9: IIRSA Projects

(by hub, sector, and stage of progress: January 2011)

Hub	Projects	Transport	Energy	Communications	Concluded	Invest. Mill. US$
Andean	64	49	13	2	10	7,478.0
Capricorn	72	68	4	0	6	9,421.4
Waterways	95	85	7	3	5	6,677.3
Amazon	58	51	6	1	2	5,400.7
Guyana Shield	25	18	6	1	7	1,694.9
South	27	24	3	0	3	2,713.0
Inter. Central	55	51	2	2	6	5,518.1
Mercosur /Chile	107	90	17	0	13	35,836.1
Perú/Brasil/ Bolivia	23	17	6	0	1	21,402.3
TOTAL	524	451	64	9	53	96,111.6

Source: IIRSA

Connecting Pacific and Atlantic ports for commercial traffic reinvents the regional economy, reducing the importance of the Panama Canal. According to Barreda, Bolivia is the "strategic neck" of South America, through which five of the twelve corridors pass.[61]

Additionally, the South American region is, according to Barreda, one of the few in the world that combines the four strategic natural resources—hydrocarbons, minerals, biodiversity, and water. Note that this profound modification of geography (perhaps the most ambitious project is uniting the Orinoco, Amazon, and Paraná rivers) is not aimed at integrating the continent, but at creating a commercial network out to global markets. Thus, this is an "outward" focused integration—exogenous—rather than an "inward" one.

The hubs/corridors must also have certain characteristics: they must combine a modern telecommunications platform with the necessary infrastructure for intermodal transport. As Barreda points out, "for real-time connection, the Internet is essential. For actual connection, intermodality is essential."[62] Intermodality is based on the "container revolution." The system of transport for merchandise is the same for land, air, and river, and containers must be able to move from one medium to another seamlessly, which necessitates trucks and roads, airports and aircraft, rivers and barges, all capable of transporting the freight containers that have replaced the old system of storage and deposit. This process is linked to the rise of "global factories" operating under the *just in time* production strategy. This creates a kind of "global automaton" as large companies relocate and span the globe as a network. But this global automaton, this "industrial and productive integration, operates under new hierarchical, center-periphery, relationships with an industrial character," as exemplified by the *maquiladora* industry.[63] The IIRSA is the South American link that will integrate the continent into this process—but in a subordinate manner.

From the point of view of overcoming the regulatory barriers, the IIRSA has adopted the neoliberal strategy of deregulation and weakening of national states. Adapting national laws to the needs of global trade rules requires homogenization. In this manner, each region and each country loses its distinctive characteristics, and states lose their autonomy to multinationals and the governments of developed countries.

Winners and losers

Viewing the map of the IIRSA projects from the southern cone of the continent, one can identify nodal points not visible when viewed from the north. If we look from São Paulo—lair of the only existing bourgeoisie in South America—we see how the "axis of integration and development" is like a network of veins converging on the city or, if one prefers, the city is the starting point of the complex and interconnected spider web. We have already seen how the enormous infrastructure projects attempt to connect the two great oceans so that goods can flow through a network of interconnected rivers by navigable waterways, with connecting roads, ports, and airports, fueled by large hydroelectric dams. São Paulo is the sixth largest industrial zone in the world. Brazil is the leading global producer of beef and iron ore, and second in soy. The reason this impressive infrastructure has been built is so goods like these can be transported cheaply, safely, and quickly to Asia. We can assert that the IIRSA is a triumph of the South-South trade that is reshaping the map of the world.

This integration project affects each country and each region of the continent differently. Broadly speaking, we can define "winners and losers" in terms of benefit or damage resulting from the implementation of the IIRSA. One of the project's problems is how it widens the gaps between rich and poor countries, regions, and sectors within societies, integrating each into the world market unevenly, depending on the current "comparative advantage." To illustrate these differences let us consider two countries: Bolivia, the poorest on the continent, and Brazil, the most powerful.

Bolivia has the second largest hydrocarbon reserves on the continent after Venezuela, the largest reserves of lithium in the world, as well as large deposits of iron. It has a key geographical position and a territory rich in biodiversity that stretches from the Andean highlands to the Amazon jungle. The international bank plan "El Cambio para todos" (The Change for All) recommended that Bolivia become a "transit country for the subcontinent, and a distribution center of gas and other energy."[64] The country will be condemned to the construction of a new Core Road Network, which will connect its hydrocarbon reserves to world markets while leaving entire areas isolated. The country is crossed by five corridors: the Andean Hub, the Central Interoceanic hub, the Peru-Brazil hub, the Paraguay-Bolivia-Brazil hub, and the Orinoco-Amazon-Plata hub.

The Central Interoceanic Hub, linking the Brazilian port of Santos with Arica and Iquique in Chile, cuts through the middle of Bolivia, and is a crucial route for countries like Brazil and Chile, which have a bigger interest than Bolivia in promoting bi-oceanic trade. Thus Bolivia is the subject of external interventions that cut up its territory.

Brazil is in the opposite situation. This sort of exogenous integration allows Brazil "to advance their desire to achieve a dominant position in Latin America, a result of the strategy developed in the eighties to achieve regional leadership by incorporating neighboring countries into its zone of influence: first Argentina, Uruguay, Paraguay, Bolivia, and Chile, then other Andean Community countries, and finally all of South America, in order to strengthen its own economy and the FTAA."[65]

Brazil is in a position similar to first world countries when it comes to taking advantage of the IIRSA. In fact, Brazil's relationship with other South American countries is similar to the relations core countries have with peripheries—with the partial exception of Argentina. First, Brazil has the most to gain from Pacific access for its industrial production and agribusiness. Second, a substantial part of the infrastructure will be constructed by Brazilian companies. Third, the BNDES is one of the main financiers of IIRSA.

The nature of Brazil-Bolivia relations are transparently revealed in the project to build a road through the Isiboro Secure National Park and Indigenous Territory (TIPNIS). The area was declared a national park in 1965 and formally recognized as indigenous territory on September 24, 1990. This victory was a consequence of the indigenous march "for land, life, and dignity" in 1990, when Bolivian Amazon peoples came together organized around the CIDOB (Confederation of Indigenous Peoples of Eastern Bolivia, created in 1982). Three hundred Indians began a march from Trinidad in the Beni, in August 1990, and ended four days later at La Paz having swelled to 800 people. The march brought to the forefront dozens of indigenous peoples whose cultures and living conditions were invisible to most Bolivians, and with this groundbreaking march, ended "a long and complex process of building organizational links among communities and indigenous peoples who had previously resisted the expropriation of their lands and their exclusion from the state in isolation."[66]

The mobilization was a milestone for Bolivia's social movement. It came at the height of the neoliberal offensive and deep defeat of the popular movement. Its success lay in that it achieved significant state concessions, brought new actors to the stage, and put territorial demands on the table—namely the recognition of indigenous territories that were being overwhelmed by logging companies, as well as official recognition of traditional authorities. Acquiring the territory marked a watershed in the recent social history of Bolivia. From a symbolic point of view, the mobilization unified the peasants' movements and the indigenous from the lowlands.[67] The largest contingent of marchers, 190 out of 800, came from communities located in the Parque Isiboro Secure, inhabited since ancient times by Moxeño, Chimane, and Yuracaré peoples.

However, in one of life's little ironies, the very same people who struggled alongside these Indians went on to become their greatest foe in government. On May 7, 2011, President Evo Morales signed Law 112, approved by the Plurinational Legislative Assembly, authorizing a loan from Brazil's BNDES for the construction of the Villa Tunari-San Ignacio de Moxos Road. This IIRSA project would split the TIPNIS in half, without the constitutionally required authorization of the affected peoples. In recent years, coca growers have also taken over part of the park, felling trees while the state stood by. With the construction of the road, the park and indigenous territory will be destroyed, and their people will migrate or disappear. Roads facilitate colonization and will have a devastating impact on this region rich with fragile biodiversity, inhabited by people who remain unconnected to the market economy.

The TIPNIS encompasses both an Amazon national park and a living indigenous culture—two clear reasons it should be protected. Covering an area of 1,236,296 hectares, and 3,000 meters above sea level, it is home to rain forests with 5,700 to 3,500 millimeters of rainfall annually.[68] Located at the head of the Amazon, its forests regulate water coming down to the plains. Because of the intense rainfall, clear cutting the forest leads to significant land erosion. TIPNIS was a refuge for fauna and wildlife during the Pleistocene and is therefore a zone of endemic species, currently host to more than 500 species of birds and mammals.[69]

Three indigenous groupings distributed in sixty-four communities live there, numbering some 10,000 people in total.[70] The demographic pressure of colonization threatens part of the national park, since the new settlers—numbering about 15,000—are extracting timber and cultivating coca leaf. They are also armed, leading to clashes with indigenous peoples. As part of the reorganization of the state in February 2009, President Evo Morales gave indigenous Mojenos, Chimanes and Yuracarés collective title to 1,091,656 hectares of land, benefiting 7,000 inhabitants.[71] The land forms part of the so-called Native Community Lands (Tierra Comunitaria de Origen, TCO), collectively owned land recognized by the state in 1994 and according to Bolivian law, indivisible, imprescriptible, inalienable, and indefeasible, with the state as guarantor and protector.[72]

The 305 kilometer Villa Tunari-San Ignacio de Moxos Highway will traverse the departments of Cochabamba and Beni. Its construction was planned in the 1990s with lumber, ranching, and oil interests in mind. This road bisects the TIPNIS and is part of the IIRSA bi-oceanic corridor that runs parallel to the Sécure petroleum zone, for which the Repsol company acquired operating rights for thirty years. On September 22, 2006, Evo Morales enacted Law 3477 declaring the road a "national priority," and in August 2008, the Brazilian firm Constructora OAS won the contract in a questionable process, for $415 million, 80 percent funded by the BNDES.[73]

Other OAS interests in Bolivia include the 201 kilometer Potosi-Uyuni road, which allows access to the world's largest reserves of lithium, and the Potosi-Tarija road in the south, 410 kilometers long, with a loan from the Banco do Brazil.[74] Brazilian loans for infrastructure projects—which are already in its own national interests—come with the condition that Brazilian companies must build the projects funded by the loans.

The Bolivian Forum on Environment and Development (Fobomade) claims that "the plans for road infrastructure in Bolivia have little to do with the internal needs of communication and integration of the national territory," and that, since the colonial era, such projects were linked to the interests of foreign companies and, more recently, "the needs of transnational capital."[75] The British built the first railroads to export minerals and the United States started the Cochabamba-Santa Cruz road as part of their "March to the East." And now Brazil is promoting "the integration corridors" of the IIRSA.

Several analysts point out that the IIRSA is closely linked to the FTAA, to the point that they can be seen as two sides of the same coin. "The FTAA determines the administrative law and the IIRSA the infrastructure."[76] The Latin American Geopolitics Observatory argues that both the IIRSA and the Plan Puebla Panama (PPP, launched by Mexico's then-president, Vicente Fox) are part of the same project of subordination of the region to the global market controlled by the United States: "Two plans advertised as local initiatives with an autochthonous stamp, both have the curious merit of linking and reorganizing Latin American space from the southernmost zone all the way to Mexico."[77]

However, the IIRSA has a distinction: It is an integration project originating in the South, overseen largely by Southern elites, and benefiting the sectors most inserted in the international market.

While the original design of the IIRSA comes from international financial organizations subordinate to Northern governments and their multinationals, Brazil's three "progressive" government terms (Lula's two terms, and Rousseff's one) have adopted the objectives and specific projects of the plan to subordinate them to Brazil's strategic objectives. In other words, it plays into the hands of the new elite in power: the strange alliance between the São Paulo bourgeoisie, managers of capital, and the state apparatus.

The IIRSA is being implemented in silence. Even though there was extensive discussion on the FTAA and FTAs across the continent, the IIRSA-linked projects are taking place without any civil society/social movement participation, and without information from governments. This stealth suggests that its planners wish to avoid debate. Likewise, the projects are being constructed bit by bit, in parts that are linked at a later stage, a strategy that prevents the affected populations from properly assessing the complete impact, and facilitates sidestepping environmental laws. Although the IIRSA formally began operations in 2000, many of the projects were designed during the 1990s. The most disturbing aspect of this massive infrastructure network is that it will achieve the same goals as the FTAA—without the name and without debate—imposed vertically by the markets and the elites.

The first decade of the new century has witnessed a global and regional geopolitical reconfiguration. The shift means that Asia has become the center of the world economy, to the detriment of the United States and Europe. This is complemented by the new role of Brazil as regional hegemon. In 2001, Brazil's GDP was less than the rest of South America. But after the 2008 crisis, Brazil surpassed the rest of the region and currently has significant trade surplus with every South American country (except Bolivia, due to the importation of gas).[78]

The fulfillment of the IIRSA project represents a major shift in the regional balance of power. The concept of Latin America originated in the nineteenth century as a counter to imperialist America, but now we are witnessing a gradual shift that places the notion of an "America of the South" center stage, as Porto Gonçalves correctly points out. At the start of the Lula government, South America became "a new geopolitical space" coinciding with the hegemonic crises of the United States.[79] This shift discards the anti-imperialist meaning that the concept of Latin America once had. The result is worrisome: South America is the space in which big Brazilian multinationals expand, financed by the BNDES, and supported by Brasilia, while accepting US hegemony in Central America and the Caribbean. This America of the South is a strategic concept coined by the Superior War School a half a century ago and revived by the Lula government.

This political shift goes hand in hand with the emergence of a new generation of struggles and social movements. The conflicts that we have highlighted in this chapter (at the Jirau and Santo Antonio dams on the Madeira River, the Inambari dam in Peru, and around the construction of the highway through the TIPNIS in Bolivia), show a new geography of social struggles occurring along the IIRSA corridors. This conflict goes beyond the framework of the nation-state, and situates itself where capital flows affect people and the environment. A survey conducted by Fluminense Federal University's Laboratory for the Study of Social Movements and Territorialities reveals the nature of the population located around the IIRSA hubs. There are 1,347 territorialized populations that include: 664 indigenous communities, 247 rural communities, 146 of African descent, 139 communities of traditional populations (fishermen, riverbank communities), sixty social organizations (homeless, unemployed), and fifty-nine environmental organizations.[80]

For such communities, the IIRSA is an neocolonial initiative, a vertical and external imposition that has nothing to do with their interests and that destroys them as communities. This new colonialism affects Brazilian grassroots communities as much as those in other countries in the region and solely benefits a financial and industrial power in which the Brazilian/São Paulo business clique is central.

8
Relations with Peripheral Countries

"Brazil must not dwell on what it has already accomplished; its hegemony must reach the Pacific."
—*Baron of Río Branco*

At seventy years of age, the entrepreneur Ernesto da Silva Filho Corrêa is as unknown as he is successful. In 2002, he sold his 15,000 hectare estate in Hulha Negra, Rio Grande do Sul, crossed the border, and bought 110,000 hectares in Uruguay, as well as the PUL livestock firm in the city of Cerro Largo. Since then he has lived between Punta del Este and his home near Lascano, in the department of Rocha, Uruguay. From there, he conducts his business—Paramount footwear company in China, the largest exporter of shoes in the world, the InterCity Hotel chain that has fourteen establishments in several Brazilian states, and the Embratec Good Card credit card with more than 1 million users.[1]

In 2011, he sold PUL for $65 million to the Brazilian group Minerva, bought 49 percent of the newspaper *El Observador* (continuing to invest in it, it is assumed, in order to become the majority shareholder), and announced the construction of a cement plant. Since Brazil is a major consumer of cement for construction works for the 2014 World Cup and the 2016 Rio

Olympic Games, Corrêa intends to produce 500,000 tons per year in Uruguay for export to Brazil.[2]

Corrêa's trajectory to become the largest Brazilian businessman in Uruguay and the largest individual landowner came, ironically, as a result of social movements in Brazil. His Rio Grande do Sul estate was occupied by the landless movement, and this gave him the "momentum" to look beyond national borders for environments more conducive for capital accumulation. And so he arrived in Uruguay. This then, is a cautionary tale.

Ernesto Corrêa does not give interviews, nor do records exist to verify the size of his business interests in Brazil, China, and Uruguay. It is known that he was born in Campo Bom, fifty-four kilometers from Porto Alegre, in 1931, and began his business career exporting shoes. In the early 1990s, he founded Paramount Asia in the Chinese city of Dongguam to take advantage of Chinese incentives to create export platforms to the United States. The *Veja* magazine says that Corrêa brought 800 of his manufacturing specialists to China.[3] Overseen by his son Richard, sales rose to $1 billion annually, and the company became the world's largest footwear exporter.[4]

Corrêa decided to invest in livestock as a way to diversify his businesses. He bought Ana Paula Agro, a property of 14,500 hectares in Campanha Gaúcha, in the state of Rio Grande do Sul, a Brazilian ranching region bordering Uruguay. The ranch had 15,000 head of Hereford and Aberdeen Angus cattle, and its high-quality product was a niche in the market for unique cuts.

On May 3, 2002, about 800 members of the Landless Movement (MST) from several nearby settlements occupied the Ana Paula ranch to pressure the state's governor, Olivio Dutra (PT), to hand over land to the peasants. The estate was occupied for fourteen days, and the action had a huge impact, a moment that "redefined the role of land struggle in the recent gaucho agrarian history, garnering a lot of state and national media, and intensifying the mobilization of ranchers to combat MST actions."[5]

The reaction of the landowners was overwhelming. The Rio Grande do Sul Federation of Agriculture (FARSUL) mobilized its affiliates from around the region to hold a vigil at the gate of the occupied farm. The director of the Ana Paula Ranch, Martim Teixeira da Luz claimed that every year about three hundred thoroughbred animals were stolen. Speaking with journalist Diego Casagrande, he could barely veil his hatred for the landless movement:

> There are unproductive MST settlements surrounding the farm, a clear indication of the source of the robberies. For that reason, the Ana Paula owners decided to create a twenty-kilometer buffer area to contain the settlements. We will stop producing meat on some 6,000 hectares for reforestation. It is difficult dealing with terrorists.[6]

The director of the *hacienda* portrays a situation in which a property is "surrounded" by settlements formed by MST activists, who at that time had the support of the state government.

The MST emerged in the late 1970s in the northern region of Rio Grande do Sul, a result of the expulsion of family farmers caught up in the modernization of agriculture. The region had originally been colonized by German and Italian immigrants who practiced subsistence farming on small holdings. With the mechanization of agriculture and the construction of dams along the Uruguay River and its tributaries, many peasants became landless in an area known for strong resistance to the military dictatorship.

The occupation of the Macali property in 1979 in the municipality of Ronda Alta, and the large Encruzilhada Natalino landless camp in 1981, marked the birth of the MST, and the first settlement won by the movement was located in the bordering state of Santa Catarina.[7] Another milestone in the movement was the 1985 occupation of Anoni *hacienda* in the same region, settled by 1,500 families.

Over the years, the struggle for land had been limited to the north of the country, with a gradual geographical shift first toward the central region, and then south, where large estates predominated. These were lands taken over during the colonial era by Portuguese forces, and land titles were handed out by the crown to loyal soldiers as a way of defending the southern border. Beginning in the mid-1990s, the MST began to take root in the Campanha Gaúcha region.[8] Unlike the northern part of the state where the movement was born, ranching cattle and sheep in the south of the country was characterized by low productivity and low population. Large estates predominated, and small holdings were few and far between.

In the 1980s, the Campanha Gaúcha region underwent a process of restructuring, investment flight, emigration, and impoverishment. In the 1990s, under pressure from the MST to meet land reform demands, the State Institute of Colonization and Agrarian Reform (INCRA) approached unproductive properties with the plan of integrating them in the land reform program.[9] By 2006, there were sixty-one settlements in the southern region covering almost 150,000 hectares.[10]

The massive influx of peasants from other regions brought new ways of working the land, the introduction of new crops, and the creation of peasant communities. First of all, there was a strong territorial and demographic impact. In the Hulha Negra municipality, where the Ana Paula property is located, twenty-five settlements occupied 21,997 hectares, accounting for 26.7 percent of the total area of the municipality. Of the 6,030 inhabitants in 2006, about half (1,016 families) belonged to MST settlements.[11] In neighboring municipalities, it was similar—settlements were almost contiguous, as denounced by the director of Ana Paula, forming a kind of peasant stain on the map of disputed *latifunda* territory.

Many property owners who fell into debt in the 1990s agreed to sell their land to the state, and with the proceeds they acquired land in central Rio Grande do Sul and in Uruguay, where the price was significantly lower. "The spatial hegemony of regional landowners began to be questioned with the first occupations of land near the town of Bagé."[12] The MST pressed the state and the INCRA to accelerate their assessment of which big estates would be included in the agrarian reform.[13] The occupation of the Ana

Paula Ranch became the major focus of the land conflict in Rio Grande do Sur, with an intense legal and political battle between the MST and the landowners organization, FARSUL. In this context of intense social conflict, Ernesto da Silva Filho Corrêa, owner of the Ana Paula Ranch, decided to move across the border.

In early 2003, less than a year after the occupation of Ana Paula, the PUL cooperative in Cerro Largo, Uruguay, voted by a wide margin to capitalize 75 percent of the company, with $7 million invested by Corrêa.[14] The PUL was the largest Uruguayan meat exporter in 2002, with 600 workers. The cooperative purchased 100,000 hectares between 2002 and 2003, which proved lucrative, since by 2009 the average price of land in Uruguay had increased sixfold, from $500 to $3,000 per hectare on average.[15]

The purchase of PUL by Corrêa sparked a race among major Brazilian companies taking advantage of the 2002 crisis to seize a succulent slice of Uruguayan meat industry. The Bertin group bought Canelones Meats, Marfrig bought Tacuarembó, San Jose, Colonia, and La Caballada in Salto, alongside multiple purchases in Argentina and Chile. In 2007, Marfrig alone cornered 30 percent of the Uruguayan slaughter industry and the country's meat exports. Overall, Brazilian investors controlled 43 percent of meat exports, Uruguay's most important line of commercial export.[16]

In 2004, Petrobras acquired a 51 percent share of Gaseba (Gaz de France) and, with the purchase of eighty-nine Shell service stations in December 2005, it dominated 22 percent of the fuel market. The Rio Grande do Sul-based Camil group controls half the harvest and export of rice, and the multinational Ambev monopolizes 98 percent of Uruguayan beer.[17] Of the top ten exporting firms in Uruguay, five are Brazilian (a rice firm and four meat), one is Finnish, one American, one Argentinian, and only two from Uruguay. The concentration and passage to foreign hands of land, meat processing, rice and beer production, and export leaves Uruguay very vulnerable to Brazil. Although there has been no direct conflict to date with Brazilian corporations, the Uruguayan authorities have expressed their fears of monopoly control and price fixing that could have negative effects on Uruguayan suppliers.

The expansion of Brazilian capital in the region is so powerful it is redesigning big business and property in many South American countries. Its methods are varied. In countries like Uruguay, it manifests itself in the control of agribusiness and land ownership; in Paraguay, it does so through the bulk purchase of land for soybean cultivation and control of hydropower; in Bolivia, it monopolizes hydrocarbons and has control of agricultural production in the Santa Cruz region. In Argentina, it comes in the form of investments in industry and petroleum. And in all countries it takes on responsibility for major infrastructure projects, where no local firms can compete with the giant Brazilian construction firms.

So far we have looked at Brazil's external projection from a Brazilian perspective. Now we will take a look from the perspective of the countries at the receiving end of Brazilian investments or its construction megaprojects.

Paraguay, the weaker neighbor

On October 17, 2008, 10,000 Brazilian troops began Operation Southern Border II military maneuvers on the border with Paraguay, using planes, tanks, ships, and live artillery. The Asunción press reported that the military maneuvers and exercises included simulations of the occupation of the Itaipu dam and the rescue of Brazilian citizens. A few days earlier, President Fernando Lugo had complained to the OAS Permanent Assembly that Brazil was conducting the operation as a form of leverage in negotiations over Itaipu, because Paraguay was in the process of reviewing the agreement between the two countries: "No agreement is sustainable when it enshrines inequality. It is not an ethical agreement when it creates disparities between the two parties involved."[18] Other media in the region held the view that the operation was a reaction to Lugo's decision to ban land sales to *brasiguayos* (Brazilian-Paraguayans).[19]

The facts confirmed that it was indeed deliberate, and dual, pressure. Statements from Brazilian General José Elito Carvalho

Siqueira, head of the Southern Military Command, left no doubt: "The time for hiding things is over. Today we have to demonstrate that we are a leader, and it is important that our neighbors understand this. We cannot avoid exercising and demonstrating that we are strong, that we are present, and we have the capacity to confront any threat."[20] With regard to the security of Itaipu—which supplies energy for the São Paulo hub—the General said that it was a military issue should the dam be occupied, even by "a protesting social movement," a clear reference to the Paraguayan peasant movement. In turn, Kaiser Konrad, editor of *Defesanet*, wrote (based on an interview with General Carvalho), "Operation Southern Border II attempts to send the message to the Lugo government that the Brazilian military is aware of the situation confronting the *brasiguayos*, and that they face land invasions and threats to their legally acquired lands."[21] The same day Foreign Minister Celso Amorim, who had followed the operation in person with General Carvalho, bluntly asked the Paraguayan government to "control excesses" against *brasiguayos*.[22]

Lugo won the April 20, 2008, election and became president on August 15. For the first time in history a man of the left was president of Paraguay defeating the mighty Colorado Party that had ruled for sixty years. Just as Lula worked his reputation as a laborer and trade unionist, Lugo did the same as a Bishop who had supported the peasants' struggle for land reform. During the election campaign, he promised to recover energy sovereignty and give land to the peasants. The climate of popular euphoria as he took office prompted a wave of land occupations, especially in the border departments of Itapua, Alto Parana, San Pedro, Concepción, and Canindeyú Amambay. These rich prairies carpeted with soybeans had once been strongholds of family farming and of the powerful Paraguayan peasant tradition, a sector that supported Lugo's candidacy. But these lands were now owned by Brazilians.

The most well known *brasiguayo* is Tranquilo Favero, the largest single producer of soybeans in Paraguay, owner of at least 40,000 hectares, 40,000 cattle, and direct employer of 1,500 workers.[23]

Favero was born in Paraná, Brazil and settled in Paraguay in 1968 during the dictatorship, a time when Paraguayan land was worth ten times less than Brazilian land. Most of his land holdings are in the states bordering Brazil, and they have been occupied at various times by the peasant movements. In October 2008, five weeks after Lugo took office, about 4,000 peasants mobilized in front of one of Tranquilo Favero's properties, tore down fences, and threatened to burn down one of his thirty silos.[24]

Brazilian farmers began to become a presence in the Paraguayan countryside in the 1960s. Statistics vary as no conclusive data exists. However, researcher Mark Glauser made a thorough

MAP 7: Areas in Paraguay occupied by Brazilians

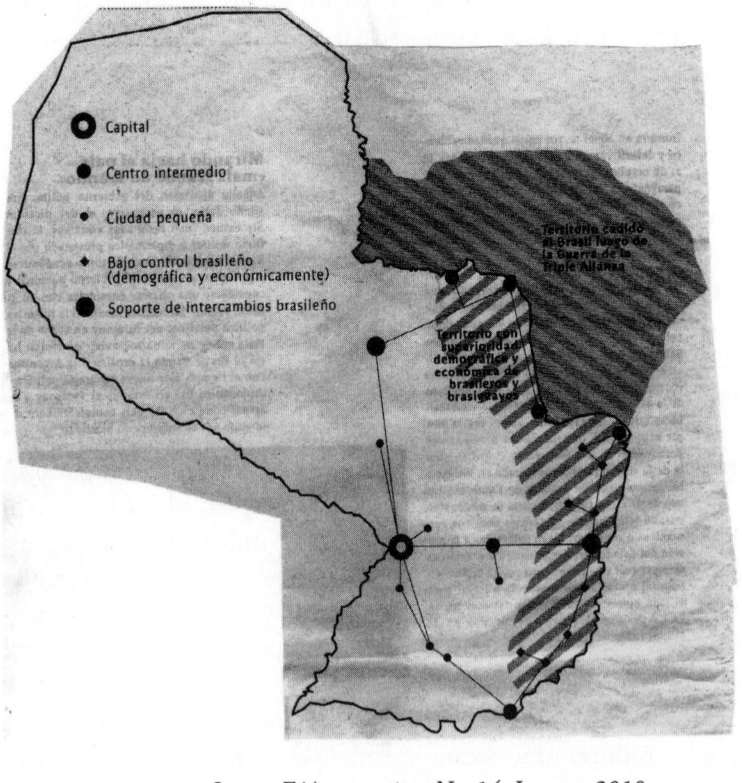

Source: E'A magazine, No. 14, January 2010.

study based on the 2008 Census of Agriculture, coming to the conclusion that nearly five million hectares of Paraguayan land are in Brazilian hands.[25] In terms of population, 326,000 Portuguese speakers were recorded in the 2002 Census, a possible indicator of the number of Brazilians living in Paraguay.[26] Several studies claim that *brasiguayos* are responsible for the production of 90 percent of Paraguayan soy, and that 55 percent of the arable land belongs to them.[27]

Like many Paraguayan investigators, Glauser says that the momentum for Brazilian colonization came with the Itaipu Treaty, signed by the dictators Stroessner and Garrastazu Medici in 1973, and the Cooperation Treaty of 1975 that "supported Brazilian investments in Paraguay and gave Brazil control of different sectors such as commercial agriculture, livestock, banks, money exchange, mills, etc."[28] With the mechanization of agriculture in Brazil, the influx of Brazilian settlers that began in the 1960s accelerated sharply between 1970 and 1985. Most were medium-sized producers, with an average of about 500 hectares each, and they brought their laborers from Brazil with them. By the late 1990s, the biggest settlers began to form large estates at the expense of the local Paraguayan population.[29]

The Stroessner dictatorship played its part, seizing over 12 million hectares of Paraguayan land, much of which ended up in the hands of foreigners. Glauser estimated 32.7 percent of Brazilian-held land is "ill-gotten lands."[30] That process continued with the return of democratic rule: between 1989 and 2003, almost 1 million hectares were awarded to agribusiness in an irregular manner. In the departments bordering Brazil—Alto Paraná, Canindeyú, and Amambay—a significant part of the territory is dominated by Brazilians, who have also made inroads in the central department of Concepción, buying up thousands of hectares for soybean crops. In the departments of Alto Paraná and Canindeyú, bordering Parana and Mato Grosso in Brazil, *brasiguayos* own 40 percent of the area and control 80 percent of the soybean crop, although Glauser estimates only half the properties are officially registered and the real figures may be even higher. In some areas,

Portuguese is the main language spoken and the most common currency is the Brazilian *real*.

In the north of the department of Alto Paraguay, Brazilian landowners have bought vast tracts of land for livestock farming, "directly feeding the meatpacking industry in the state of Mato Grosso do Sul," crossing a border where smuggling is ubiquitous.[31]

Brazilians own 13 percent of the area of Paraguay and just over 20 percent of all arable land, comprising the best land for agriculture and livestock. A good example is the production of soybeans, the main export product. Paraguay has become the fourth largest exporter of soybeans in the world. The harvest for 2011/2012 reached 9 million tons, growing at a rate of 20 percent annually.[32] These figures give some idea of the economic power of Brazilian landowners in Paraguay.

Their location on the border has a huge social and economic impact. In border districts like Nueva Esperanza and Katueté in Canindeyú, some 58 percent and 83 percent of landowners, respectively, are Brazilian.[33] This leads to smuggling and a general weakening of the border security essential to national sovereignty. This process of territorial occupation blurs boundaries, always in favor of the stronger nation, and decreases the tools and skills with which a smaller nation might defend and control their wealth.

This asymmetry is very visible in the energy sector. The binational Itaipu dam has an installed capacity of 14,000 MW, half of which should go to Paraguay as established by the Treaty of Itaipu. However, in reality, the country consumes only 5 percent of the energy produced by the dam and must export 95 percent to Brazil at cost. According to the treaty, Paraguay receives about $120 million a year by selling energy, well below the international price and replacement cost.[34]

The Itaipu dam was negative for Paraguay for several reasons:

- The country did not need that energy. Even today it only consumes 16 percent of Itaipu and Yacyretá's (the other binational dam, shared with Argentina) installed capacity. Brazil and Argentina had a greater need for the energy.
- It leaves Paraguay in debt. The estimated cost of the dam

was $2 billion but it ended up being $20 billion, ten times more, due to overbilling by Brazilian companies, corruption, and usury imposed by Eletrobras, whose interest rate was three times higher than that set by Libor, the main international reference.[35] In 2008, Paraguay's debt reached $20 billion after it had already repaid $32 billion. Scheduled payments until 2023 will be $65 billion, or 32 times the initial estimated cost.

- Paraguay cannot freely dispose of its energy and is obliged to sell Brazil what it does not consume.
- Paraguay receives a below-market price for energy sold to Brazil. Specialist and Paraguayan engineer Ricardo Canese estimates that the country loses between $3 and $4 billion annually by subsidizing energy to Brazil, and to a lesser extent Argentina (because Yacyretá has an installed capacity of 3,100 MW, 22 percent of Itaipu). Paraguay loses out on a sum that represents approximately 25 percent of its GDP.

Lugo took office with the express desire of renegotiating the Itaipu deal. He did not intend to go as far as the Canese estimates, pushing instead for Paraguay to receive an additional $2 billion annually. The negotiations were long and complex, and Lugo failed to revise the Itaipu Treaty. On July 25, 2009, he and Lula signed a compensation increase for Paraguay of only $120–$360 million, effective May 14, 2011.[36]

Bolivia, gas, and soybeans

The popular uprising against rising fuel prices (the *gasolinazo*)—imposed on December 26, 2010, by Decree 748—exposed the shortcomings of hydrocarbon "nationalization" introduced by Evo Morales on May 1, 2006. Six years after electing the first indigenous president in Bolivia's history and after nearly five years of "nationalization," the population took to the streets of major cities demanding reasons for the increase in price of gasoline by 72 percent, 82 percent for diesel.

The *gasolinazo* was an economic blow to the popular sectors, and in particular to the poorest people who had offered almost seamless support for the Morales administration. Despite the Christmas holidays, protest began immediately in the main bastions of "*Evismo.*" Huge demonstrations took place in mining areas where government support is traditionally high. In El Alto, where Morales garnered 81 percent of the vote, a crowd that included the Federation of Neighborhood Councils (FEJUVE, a major force in the 2003 uprising against Gonzalo Sánchez de Lozada), and the Regional Worker Center, attacked the headquarters of organizations that supported Decree 748. They also attacked the city government and headquarters of various groups affiliated with the official Movement Towards Socialism (MAS).[37]

Protesters burned tollbooths on the El Alto, La Paz toll road and burned a Venezuelan flag and portraits of Evo. In La Paz, 30,000 people demonstrated and attacked police trying to prevent the crowd from entering the Plaza Murillo, the seat of the government. On December 31, Evo attended an assembly of coca growers in the Chapare region to seek support, but instead they asked him to cancel the fuel price hike. In a message to the nation two hours before the end of the year, the president revoked Decree 748.

The brutal rise in fuel prices opened a debate on the consequences of the 2006 nationalization and the true current state of the hydrocarbons industry, the main wealth of the country. The government claimed the economy was losing $380 million annually from subsidies, $150 million of that from contraband. Former oil minister during the early years of the Evo government, Andres Soliz Rada, a supporter of the nationalization, said that "The *gasolinazo* has generated a feeling that the petroleum companies have regained domination of the country," neutralizing and even reversing the effect of the hydrocarbon nationalization.[38]

Former Vice Minister of Lands, Alejandro Almaraz criticized the $1.5 billion that the state corporation Yacimientos Petroliferos Fiscales Bolivianos (YPFB) committed to pay oil companies for supposed losses on investments, even though these companies continue to own and benefit from those investments. He also criticized "the $700 million we give away to Brazil every year in gas and other petroleum products, which we sell them in the absence of the famous and long-promised refinery that would cost just $150 million dollars."[39] Almaraz added that most of the new blocks of available oil reserves have been set aside for the same transnationals "that already have more than 80 percent of our remaining hydrocarbons in their power."[40] In other words, Petrobras, Repsol, and Total. They stand to be the main beneficiaries of the increase in domestic prices, a requirement for them to invest in exploration for new wells.

The debate around gas and oil continues. What seems beyond doubt is that the interests of Brazil in Bolivia continue to expand with the steady growth of both Petrobras and soybean production overseen by Brazilian firms based in the department of Santa Cruz.

A report by the *Folha de São Paulo* newspaper established that, in 2005, the year that Evo took office, Brazil controlled about 18 percent of Bolivia's GDP.[41] The report further stated that Brazilian ranchers—about 200 families—controlled 35 percent of soybean production, and the Banco do Brasil in Bolivia made $700 million profit in 2004, the highest in the region.

Under the MAS government, Brazil has strengthened its grip on the two areas where it has a strong presence: hydrocarbons and soybeans. The Terra Foundation estimated that the Brazilian control of soybean production had risen to 40 percent by 2010 (compared to the above-mentioned 35 percent in 2005 and 29 percent ten years before that).[42] Meanwhile, in Santa Cruz, the department bordering Brazil, soybeans and other oilseeds occupy almost 1 million hectares, 40 percent of which are held by Brazilian ranchers, and this doesn't include Brazilian-owned land dedicated to livestock. The total amount held by Brazilians is around 700,000 acres of the best land.

There is a similar predicament in the hydrocarbons industry: gas is Bolivia's main export (followed by mining and soybeans) and the Petrobras share in the industry rose to almost 60 percent in 2010 (compared to 51 percent in 2005), according to a report from the Ministry of Hydrocarbons.[43] Between Petrobras Bolivia and Petrobras Energía, Brazil controls 63.8 percent of gas production and 55.8 percent of petroleum in Bolivia.[44] This suggests that Brazilian control of Bolivia's GDP has increased from the 18 percent it held in 2005, and will keep increasing if the planned dams and the IIRSA public works go ahead.

It is interesting to note that despite the "nationalization" of the natural gas industry, foreign companies control 80 percent of gas production and a similar percentage of petroleum. How this came about deserves a brief explanation. The third nationalization of hydrocarbons in Bolivia was mandated by Supreme Decree 28701, May 1, 2006 (the previous ones were in 1937 and 1969). This was done without actually expropriating any foreign company. Instead, the Bolivian state drew up new contracts with the companies: 82 percent in royalties and taxes to the state and the remaining 18 percent to the companies. The decree provides that YPFB defines the conditions, volumes, and prices for the domestic and export markets, and controls at least 51 percent of the shares in the following companies: Chaco, Andina, Transredes, Petrobras Bolivia Refinacion, and Compania Logistica de Hidrocarburos de Bolivia.[45]

None of the foreign companies sued the state and all signed new contracts. According to Soliz Rada nationalization must be gradual and should not begin with "the expulsion of the companies: production would stop if that happened, disrupting the supply to the domestic market, as YPFB lacks the capability for an immediate takeover."[46] The government decided to conduct independent audits of the foreign companies and found major discrepancies between the actual and declared totals, but decided not to act on this, with the State refusing to put anyone on trial. Worse still, according to Soliz Rada, the government began contract negotiations with Petrobras behind his back, precipitating his resignation as minister in September 2006.

> Evo and Alvaro Garcia believed that nationalization was possible only by surrendering to Petrobras. Grave error. The only way to do it was to negotiate from the position of strength we had: the powerful São Paulo industrial complex's dependence on Bolivian gas, without which

it could not manage. The strategic advantage was lost a year later, when Brazil achieved self-sufficiency in gas.[47]

Five years after the "nationalization," Bolivia still does not export value-added gas but imports liquefied petroleum gas (LPG), gasoline, and diesel. The Bolivian policy of favoring Petrobras is reflected in the signing of the fourth addendum to the contract for gas exports to Brazil, in December 2009, which commits Bolivia to selling wet, or rich, gas rather than dry gas. Wet gas, at 9,400 kilocalories per cubic meter, has a higher calorific value than dry (8,900 Kcal/m), and includes gases such as methane, butane, and propane, which are used as raw material for the petrochemical industry. Now these gases are separated in Brazil with annual profits of a billion dollars.[48] In agreeing to deliver wet gas until 2012, Bolivia has abandoned the construction of a proposed refinery in Puerto Suarez.

Petrobras wins, as both Brazil and Argentina have plants that separate Bolivian gas, LPG, and other compounds, which means Bolivia buys LPG from Argentina.[49] The Brazilian company is preparing to construct the first Latin American urea and ammonia factory in Minas Gerais. It will do this with Bolivian gas brought in via a 250 km Gasbol pipeline that will transport the gas to the "Mining Triangle," where the Brazil's largest phosphate reserves and biggest fertilizer mixing plants are found. The Uberaba nitrogen fertilizer factory will be operational in 2015, in addition to another at Tres Lagoas in the neighboring state of Mato Grosso do Sul. The estimated $2.7 billion invested for this gas project will allow Brazil to stop importing urea and ammonia by 2020.[50]

The value chain from natural gas to fertilizer production reveals an extraordinary price increase. One ton of natural gas was priced at $200 million in early 2011, but its price rises to $700 million when processed, and leaps to $3 billion when converted into plastic.[51] Bolivia needs to enter into this chain to start reversing their dependency.

An editorial in the *Petropress Journal* concludes that "in the hydrocarbons sector Petrobras is the boss...a situation similar to the tin barons."[52] Analysts of various persuasions agree that Petrobras's position in Bolivia has not been changed by the "nationalization" of hydrocarbons. Carlos Arze of the Center for the Study of Labor and Agrarian Development (CEDLA), recalls that the Brazilian company was a major player in the 1996 neoliberal reforms in the Bolivian oil sector, and that, beyond the purchase of the two refineries, the Bolivian state has in no way regained its ability to control the industry.[53] Mirko Orgaz points out that Brazil pays $5.62 per thousand cubic feet, a price that would be doubled if the caloric value was included: "Brazil sells that same volume of gas for $23, excellent business for Petrobras, to the detriment of the YPFB and the Bolivian state."[54]

No doubt Brazil has excessive power in Bolivia. It had it before Evo and maintains it still. Petrobras first invested in Bolivia in 1995, during the neoliberal period, and benefited from the exceptional operating concessions offered by the first administration of Gonzalo Sanchez de Lozada (1993–1997) as part of a bid to supply Brazil's southern and southeastern states, including none other than the industry of São Paulo. Petrobras has since invested $1.6 billion in Bolivia, constructed the pipeline carrying gas to a wide region of Brazil—the most important energy infrastructure

MAP 8: Brazilian petrochemical processing of Bolivian gas

Source: HidrocarburosBolivia.com

in Latin America—and came to control the main fields and refineries, ultimately accounting for about 20 percent of Bolivia's GDP and 24 percent of state tax revenues.[55] Furthermore, Brazil purchases 68 percent of Bolivia's extractable gas.

It is a case of too much power in a small country with a weak state. The nationalization of hydrocarbons should have been a remedy for "Bolivian technical and financial dependence and [helped to] autonomously develop the sector," while Brazil oversees a long-term plan to capture Amazonian power.[56]

Ecuador against Brazilian companies

With the expulsion of the Norberto Odebrecht construction company by Rafael Correa's administration in October 2008, Brazil suffered its biggest setback in the region. Two years later, Petrobras voluntarily withdrew from Ecuador, refusing to sign new oil deals proposed by the state. The setback was so great that the efforts being made by Dilma Rousseff's administration to reposition itself in relation to Ecuador have not yet yielded results. China is beginning to fill the role previously occupied first by the United States and then Brazil.

For Lula, who has close relations with Odebrecht, the situation was a personal defeat, all the more so because it is one of Brazil's most important multinationals. The main reason for the expulsion was Oderbrecht's faulty construction of the San Francisco dam, Ecuador's second largest dam with 230 MW of installed capacity, which was to provide 12 percent of the country's electricity. The dam was meant to play a strategic role in the development of Ecuador, but serious technical flaws in the turbines and the tunnel meant it shut down just a year after it was opened.

The brief history of Odebrecht in Ecuador is blighted with technical, legal, and financial irregularities. It arrived in 1987 to oversee work diverting water in the Santa Elena peninsula to regulate and control the enormous flow of the Guayas rivers basin all the way to the ocean estuary. The Brazilian construction company then oversaw four other projects in Ecuador up to 2008: the Baba

River, the Tocachi-Pilatón dam, the Carrizal-Chone irrigation system, and the Tena airport.

The Commission for Public Credit Audit (CAIC) report released in November 2008, authored by members of social organizations and the government, revealed the true extent of Ecuador's national debt between 1976 and 2006. According to the report, debt in 1970 was $240 million and by 2007 it had reached $17.4 billion. The report concluded the country's debt "has been a tool to plunder resources and for submission to policies imposed by multilateral organizations."[57]

Odebrecht's first project in Ecuador, the construction of the Santa Elena channel, cost a total of $1.5 billion, 180 percent above the original budget.[58] Similar problems existed with the San Francisco dam, which was financed by the BNDES with a loan of $243 million in March 2000. The contract was signed between Odebrecht and Hidropastaza with a "turn-key" clause that allowed the builder to make changes without state approval. In the following years, changes were made in ten illegal addendums "which legally shielded the construction consortium from liability for future damages," and raised the costs of the dam to $357 million, but the total loss to the state for work not performed exceeded $123 million.[59]

Odebrecht installed different turbines than originally agreed upon; they broke down due to excess sediment from landslides in the eleven-kilometer tunnel carrying the waters of the Pastaza River. Furthermore, the tunnel coating was not adequate.[60] No less than 253 problems were identified in the dam within days of its inauguration. Basically, it did not function, but the State still had to pay its debt to the BNDES until 2018, bringing the total cost of the failed project, plus interest, to $600 million.[61]

The debt is a separate issue. The BNDES loans are "conditional upon the use of Brazilian goods and services, since loan funds are paid directly to the construction company."[62] In other words, Ecuador never had access to a loan that it is now required to pay back, for a dam that does not function. No wonder then that the Correa government decided to expel Odebrecht on September 23, 2008, and cancel the four projects in progress, worth about

$670 million, which were eventually taken over and completed by the state in conjunction with private companies.

President Lula and Foreign Minister Celso Amorim defended Odebrecht and tried to minimize the problems. A week after the expulsion, the Second Bilateral Summit on energy issues between Brazil and Venezuela took place in Manaus. In defense of Odebrecht, President Chávez said "this company is a friend of Venezuela," advancing money to the government when it had difficulties.[63] Lula's strategy was to lower the decibel level of the controversy, and give a little time for negotiations to overcome the crisis, while focusing on a much more important project—the IIRSA Manta-Manaus-Belem hub, linking the Pacific with the Atlantic via the Amazon River, a waterway of nearly 3,000 kilometers. This project had an initial cost of $1.8 billion, and Odebrecht was a likely candidate for the job.[64] Nevertheless, Correa did not back down.

If one wonders why Lula would defend Odebrecht with such determination, it is useful to recall that for many years the construction giant was one of the main donors to the PT's electoral campaigns. A study by two political scientists at the University of California estimated that in the thirty-three months following the election, donor companies received contracts worth 8.5 times the size of their original campaign contributions.[65]

Petrobras also had innumerable problems working in Ecuador, and finally left the country in 2010. It first entered Ecuador in 2002 as part of the takeover of Argentina's Perez Companc petroleum company, which operated Ecuador's oil Blocks 18 and 31. Since the sale happened without any public bidding, it was illegal, part of a framework of corruption revealed by the 2007 report by the Special Commission overseen by Alberto Acosta, a Minister in Correa's administration.[66]

When Ecuador introduced new service contracts in July 2010 as part of its push to increase state revenue from the oil sector, Petrobras decided not to sign, even though Ecuador only represented one percent of its total global production. In mid-2011 it was negotiating the sale of its assets to Ecuador for a price of $343 million, with Ecuador only willing to pay $168 million. Brazil and Ecuador's Foreign Minister's have participated in negotiations.[67] Gradually Ecuador has been regaining control of the oil industry at the expense of private companies. In the first half of 2011, the state-run Petroecuador and Petroamazonas controlled 73 percent of oil output while private control had fallen to 27 percent.[68]

However, this is not the last word. The 2007 announcement of the Yasuní-ITT project at the United Nations General Assembly involved a commitment to leave the unexploited reserves of 846 million barrels of oil in the ITT (Ishpingo-Tambococha-Tiputini) field unexploited. The oilfield is located in the Yasuni National Park in the Amazon, and is equivalent to 20 percent of Ecuador's current reserves. The idea is that, through a capital fund managed by UNDP, the international community would contribute at least $3.6 billion—or 50 percent of what the state would receive if they opted for oil exploration—and thereby avoid the emission of 407 million tons of CO_2.[69]

The first goal was to raise $100 million by December 2011. Odebrecht contributed $130,000, a figure higher than several states. Brazil has supported the initiative, hoping to renew good relations with Ecuador and open the doors again for its corporations. Meanwhile, due to the Chinese presence, Ecuador is growing at a faster rate than the rest of the region, giving it a strategic importance as a gateway to South America.[70] According to Ecuador's ambassador in Beijing, China spent $6.5 billion in Ecuador in 2011, mainly on hydropower and copper mines, and could invest in the huge Pacific refinery that is budgeted at $12 billion.[71] The key focus will be on implementing the Manta-Manaos-Belem hub, which will transform the intra- and extra-regional trade map.

The entry and exit of two major Brazilian multinationals in Ecuador occurred in the midst of a unique situation marked by the profound political changes brought about by social movements. Since 1990, Ecuador has undergone a deep crisis with the emergence of an indigenous movement whose political and social demands have put the traditional political class on the defensive.

This crisis reached a climax between 1999 and 2006—from the financial and banking crisis that led to the end of dollarization to the expulsion of the American OXY company and the breakdown of Free Trade Agreement negotiations—reconfiguring the country in the process.[72]

Those years coincide with a cycle of phenomenal indigenous and popular struggles that toppled two governments (Jamil Mahuad in 2000 and Lucio Gutiérrez in 2005), delegitimized the ruling class, and opened the door to the electoral victory of Rafael Correa in November 2006. Major indigenous uprisings took place, like the one in 2000 that led to the formation of "popular parliaments" in the provinces.

The crisis led to a change in the ruling classes, with hegemony moving from the financial capital of Guayaquil (Filanbanco and Banco Pacifico) to Quito (Pichincha, Produbanco).[73] The pressure on the state from below was unrelenting. The uprising of 2000 gave birth to local organs of popular power, which were joined by the *forajidos* (outlaws) in 2005 to end the Gutiérrez administration. In March and April 2006, the Ecuadoran indigenous movement paralyzed the country for three weeks, at one point taking over Quito.[74]

Petrobras arrived during this period of political, social, and economic turmoil. Initially, Brazilian interests were aligned with the government of Gutiérrez and Brazil expressed displeasure at his removal, offering him shelter in their embassy in Quito, from which he could apply for asylum in Brazil. In the year and a half of Alfredo Palacios's government, OXY left and the FTA talks ruptured, so that when Correa entered the government in early 2007, the change was complete.

Brazil used its best diplomacy to approach Correa's new government. This seemed to succeed at first, but the Odebrecht crisis and increased popular sensitivity against turning Ecuador into a new Brazilian backyard disrupted relations. Meanwhile, Ecuador sought other regional alliances. Their approaches to Venezuela and Petróleos de Venezuela (PDVSA) failed to achieve results, although they consolidated an alliance with China. In terms of future development plans, Brazil has many interests in Ecuador with the Manaos-Manta hub, including the port, the refinery and the airport in Manta, the Tena airport in the Ecuadorian jungle, the Guayaquil-Quito Highway, and hydroelectric projects. Nevertheless Ecuador is fully aware of the risk of being a toll-road in a macro agreement between China and Brazil, or taking part in a game where it can only play a secondary role.

"Strategic alliances": Argentina and Venezuela

In Chapter 3, we saw how Brazil decided to build a strategic alliance with Argentina as a means to get the whole region behind its integration project and strengthen its hegemony. In the 2000s, Brazil also prioritized establishing a strong alliance with Venezuela with a long-term commitment to strengthening the Boliviariano process.

In the wake of the 2001 Argentina crisis that destroyed much of the country's productive capacity, a few Brazilian multinationals were left in control of some important industries. Petrobras bought Perez Companc, Argentina's largest oil company, JBS Swift controlled Friboi Armour and therefore a significant portion of the meat industry; Camargo Corrêa bought the Loma Negra cement company; and Ambev took Quilmes. These four purchases give an idea of the importance Brazilian businesses acquired in the country.

Brazil established a strong strategic alliance with Argentina, but relations were never easy, largely due to Argentinian instability, and its succession of economic crises and political changes. The 1990s saw the dismantling of the state and a significant portion of the industrial apparatus, which was closed down or taken over by foreign interests. A 2005 study by the INDEC (National Institute of Statistics and Census) emphasizes how foreign capital that year controlled 80.2 percent of the value of production, in comparison to 1993 when it had accounted for 50.5 percent. Furthermore, foreign capital contracted 57.6 percent of the workers in 2005 compared to 36.4 percent in 1993.[75]

The combination of crisis, slow growth, and an unstable and hostile context, meant that many national companies "disappeared or were acquired by foreign corporations."[76] Foreign investment came mainly from Spain, the USA, France, Netherlands, Italy, and Germany, and to a lesser extent, Chile and Brazil.

Until the 2001 crisis, Brazilian investments in Argentina were minor and concentrated mainly in oil and gas. Given its size, the entry of Petrobras was felt throughout the productive chain— in extraction, refining, and marketing of petroleum, and in gas, chemical, petrochemical and electric energy. But to the extent that Argentina had a mature and significant industry, with extensive technological development and production chains in various sectors, Brazilian investment reflected that reality, a reality very different from other countries in the region, where Brazilian capital focused on primary natural resources or manufacturing.

In 1998, Petrobras invested $715 million in Mega to provide liquid gas (LPG) to the Brazilian market, and in 2000 it reached an agreement with Repsol to exchange assets of $500 million in order to take over the EG3 distribution and refining company, through which it now controls 12 percent of the fuel market in Argentina.[77] The most important acquisition was Pecom Energy (Perez Companc, which was renamed Petrobras Energía) in 2002, the largest independent oil company in the region with operations in several countries—a purchase that cost Petrobras $1.03 billion. With this purchase, it took a leap forward: the company could now refine 36,000 barrels per day in Argentina, incorporate 102 new service stations, and extend its pipeline network abroad to 7,400 km.

In 2004, Petrobras drilled wells in the south, in the province of Santa Cruz, and acquired new businesses—a company producing ethanol and an ammonium thiosulfate plant. That year, it also became involved in importing gas from Bolivia. In 2006, it began deep-water exploration in the Argentinian Sea, 250 kilometers off Mar del Plata, and in 2007, for that very purpose, it partnered with Enarsa and Repsol-YPF. In the 1995–2006 period, Petrobras was the leading Brazilian investor in Argentina with almost $3 billion.[78]

However, the Argentine government reined in Petrobras and stopped the transaction when it tried to sell Transener—regarded as strategic to the country—to a US company. Petrobras also reduced its presence in areas where the state intervened with price controls and tariffs, such as the production and marketing of fuels and electricity distribution. By early 2011, the Brazilian company had sold 360 service stations and its refinery in San Lorenzo, Santa Fe to an Argentine group that arose under the governments of Nestor Kirchner and Cristina Fernández.[79] Overall, Petrobras tends to focus its Argentinian business in less regulated industries such as oil and gas production.

According to Petrobras itself, by late 2011 it had investments in seventeen companies in Argentina. It has majority ownership and operational control in six of them: Atalaya Energy and Canadian Hunter, both engaged in the exploration and production of petroleum and gas; EG3, dedicated to refining and distribution; World Energy, Enecor, and Petrobras International Energy in the area of gas and energy. It has joint control in four others—including a 27.33 percent interest in Edesur and 27.65 percent in Transportadora de Gas del Sur—and a minority stake in seven other companies, including refineries and gas and petrol exploration.[80]

The well-developed nature of the Argentinian economy has led a prominent deployment of Brazilian capital throughout its domestic industry:

- In 2005, Camargo Corrêa spent $1 billion to acquire Loma Negra, Argentina's primary cement producer and a strategic company in the country, which allowed it to take over nine factories and six concrete plants, and to control 46 percent of the Argentine market. More than half of Carmargo Corrêa cement production now comes from Argentina. In 2007, it increased its textile business with the purchase of Alpargatas—owner of Topper, Flecha, and Pampero—becoming one of the most important textile companies in the country.
- The multinational Ambev bought Quilmes, Argentina's leading brewer, for $500 million, taking over its malt plant, five other factories, and besides Quilmes's foreign assets, giving it control of the regional beer market.

• Friboi bought Swift in Argentina for $200 million, representing a quarter of Friboi's total production, and access to one of the largest markets.

The steelmaker Gerdau purchased Sipar and Sipsa in the late 1990s and Belgo Mineira purchased Acindar (steel) in several stages, so that now 97 percent of the Argentine steel market is in Brazilian hands: 55 percent Acindar-Belgo Mineira and 42 percent Sipar-Gerdau.[81]

Other major Brazilian companies such as Agrale, Coteminas, Natura, and Random have entered the Argentinian market with force. But the presence of "green and yellow capital" is not confined to large companies. It has also continued to grow throughout the first decade of the century, beyond the opportunities afforded by the 2001 crisis. Between 2002 and 2010, the number of Brazilian companies established in Argentina grew from sixty to 250, ranging from Vale and Banco do Brasil, which purchased Banco Patagonia, to the battery manufacturer Moura, the Eurofarma laboratory, and various computer companies. In 2010, Brazil led investments in Argentina with $5.3 billion, surpassing both China and its own $4 billion worth of investments in 2009.[82]

The character of Brazilian investments has been changing in recent years. Between 2002 and 2003 "they were addressed mainly to mergers and acquisitions," taking advantage of the crisis and Argentinian business debt. In the following years, however, it began making "investments in new projects, designed to increase production capacity."[83] One of the best examples is Gerdau, which in 2008 invested $524 million in a new plant with 3,000 workers to produce one million tons of rolled steel for both the domestic and export markets.[84]

Clearly, Brazil has a huge interest in maintaining a strategic alliance with Argentina and has taken steps to do so, creating joint working groups and establishing agreements that benefit both parties, as well as overcoming commercial conflicts in the automotive industry. Nevertheless, it is not an alliance of equals, since Brazilian capital controls strategic sectors like steel, and has a strong presence in energy and petroleum. Still, the diversity of Brazilian investments in Argentina should be noted, in contrast to other countries, where they are focused on raw materials and hydrocarbons. It should also be noted that Argentina has a certain capacity to place conditions on some of those investments.

In regards to Venezuela, Brazil fortified its relations in 2011. On June 6, Dilma Rousseff received a visit from Hugo Chávez and reaffirmed the strategic alliance between Brazil and Venezuela. In addition to signing agreements to deepen cooperation in areas such as petroleum, science, and technology, Rousseff said that the alliance between Petrobras and PDVSA (the two state petroleum companies) would continue. Apart from oil, the priority is fixed on the border zone, which in the opinion of the Brazilian president "merits policy and initiatives for the interconnection of our systems, whether it be electricity, television, highways, or the integration of the productive chains."[85] Both countries have been consistent in promoting binational integration with the Amazon-Orinoco hub. The Zona Franca in Manaus (Brazil), with its 450 industries, some high-tech, is the driving force behind the development of complementary production chains in both countries.[86]

The Brazil-Venezuela Strategic Partnership was signed in February 2005 by Lula and Chávez. Between 2007 and 2010 quarterly presidential meetings were held to further agreements and design strategies. In 2010, the Institute of Applied Economic Research (IPEA) was established in Caracas to contribute to the formulation of joint integration projects. The Brazilian Agricultural Research Corporation (Embrapa) and Caixa Econômica Federal were later established to facilitate the process.

One of the most important decisions was to shift priorities from the Guyana Shield hub to the Amazon-Orinoco hub within the IIRSA in order to implement "comprehensive development" projects, to convert it into "the Brazilian South-South cooperation paradigm," according to the IPEA.[87] Plans include integrating land, river, and air transport systems, electrical integration, and the possible construction of the Southern Gas Pipeline to connect Venezuela, Brazil, and Argentina.

Concrete plans are in place for connecting the Amazon and Orinoco rivers as well as the formation of a common economic zone in northern Brazil and southern Venezuela, an area of "geostrategic importance" as defined by an IPEA report in May 2011. The analysis highlights the geopolitical importance of the region, because of "the quantity and quality of resources," which includes biodiversity, watersheds, energy, iron ore, "and others" that are "awakening diverse interests."[88]

The IPEA notes that the Amazon-Orinoco hub "creates a new frontier for rapprochement for Brazil with the countries of the Caribbean basin in the context of its foreign policy towards regional integration, expanding its area of South American operations to other Latin American and Caribbean regions."[89]

The alliance between the two countries can be read in various ways. Venezuela is first in petroleum reserves in the world, third in bauxite, fourth in gold, sixth in natural gas, and tenth in iron. The Brazilian state of Roraima, bordering Venezuela, contains the largest gold, niobium, and tin reserves in the world, along with important deposits of thorium, cobalt, molybdenum, diamonds, and titanium, according to Brazil's Ministry of Mines and Energy. Most importantly, this region contains the largest uranium reserves in the world, shared by Brazil, Venezuela, and Guyana Essequibo (a disputed area between Venezuela and the Republic of Guyana). Canadian companies have been exploiting uranium deposits in the region since 2009, something that is looked upon unfavorably by Caracas and Brasilia.

For both countries, "occupying" the border zone is a response to Plan Colombia (that is, the Southern Command) whose zone of "natural" expansion is precisely the Amazon—particularly the Amazon and Orinoco river basins—as well as the Andean region. But it is also a way to strengthen a country like Venezuela, whose stability is in the interests of Brazil as much as its instability benefits the Southern Command. Brazil is promoting Venezuelan industrial development through the coordination of the productive chains in both countries in order to help reduce Venezuela's dependency on oil exports, as well as its importation of 70 percent of the food it consumes and a large portion of its industrialized products.

Beyond the role played by the government of Hugo Chávez, the integration of the border region will play a decisive role in the consolidation of the Bolivarian process. Brazil's dual alliances with Argentina and Venezuela have enough power to neutralize any external force and to attract other South American countries. At this point, it is worth emphasizing the differences between the Brazilian trajectory—evolving through a framework of peace and consensus—and other hegemonic powers that scaled the summit through wars and invasions.

Is Brazil creating its own "backyard"?

The power vacuum left by waning US influence in South America has been filled by new global world powers, as well as a local power with the ambition of becoming a global player. As recently as the 1990s it was European capital—Spanish and French—that was most dynamic in South America, buying up privatized state-owned enterprises. More recently, China has tried to move into the economic void, importing oil and gas, and investing in mining.

For some time, Brazil has set out to expand its influence using the South American region as its springboard, a fact that has been the subject of various analyses and studies. However, lately this expansionist policy has generated serious conflicts, like those previously mentioned in Ecuador, Bolivia, and Paraguay. Sometimes the conflict goes beyond the scope of interstate relations and is fueled by social movements denouncing Brazil's meddling in their country's affairs. This can be separated into two issues: the role of capital and that of the state.

The growing opposition to Brazilian companies, as in Bolivia over the role of the OAS in the construction of the road through the TIPNIS, in Ecuador with Odebrecht, and over soy production in Paraguay, is perhaps the price Brazil pays for its trade and economic expansion. However, the expansion of capital does not mean, as we shall see in the next chapter, that all this is simply a case of "imperialism."

In some of these conflicts, Brazil has mobilized troops to defend its interests, as it did on the Paraguayan border, and has unleashed all their experienced diplomacy in powerful lobbying efforts. On October 2, Lula enacted Decree 6.952, which regulates the National Mobilization System dedicated to confronting "foreign aggression." The decree defines "foreign aggression" as "threats or injurious acts that harm national sovereignty, territorial integrity, the Brazilian people, or national institutions, even when *they do not constitute an invasion of national territory*."[90]

The ambiguity of the description of "threats" is worrisome, especially given the disparity between Brazil and its neighbors. So far, Brazil has not acted militarily against any regional countries, with the exception of the invasion of Haiti under the United Nations umbrella. But there are other forms of pressure and intervention, like economic sanctions, capable of putting the brakes on any economy dependent on a single export commodity.

Furthermore, it should be noted that Brazil has throughout its history practiced a vigorous expansionism and was under military rule between 1964 and 1985, supported by the political and business elites. The original expansion westward, reaching the foothills of the Andes and the Río de la Plata, was led by São Paulo colonists who organized large expeditions into the interior seeking slaves, gold, and precious gems. The *bandeirantes*—poor settlers seeking a way to improve their situation—gave shape to the boundaries of what was, from 1822, an independent Brazil. The expansion continued with the creation of the republic, to the point that, between 1859 and 1950, Brazil's "Amazon territory" doubled, at the expense of its neighbors (Bolivia, Peru, Colombia, Paraguay, and Venezuela). The Triple Alliance War (1865–1870) against Paraguay, and the forcible annexation of the state of Acre in 1904, are notable milestones in Brazilian expansionism.

The case of Acre is only the most recent historical example of "marching west." It was with the military coup of 1964, that the conquest of the Amazon became state policy, along with what military strategist General Golbery do Couto e Silva called "the revitalization of borders."[91] The 1946 Constitution obliged the federal government to spend 3 percent of tax revenue on the Amazon for twenty years. This effort resulted, in part, in the 1960 replacement of Rio de Janeiro with Brasilia as the capital city in the central region at the edge of the Amazon basin. In 1966, Manaus was declared a free-trade zone to establish a commercial and industrial pole in the Western Amazon. And in 1970, the National Integration Plan planned the construction of two major highways, including the Trans-Amazon, as part of a vast colonization plan.

Decree 6952 seems part of a long tradition, revived and systematized during the military regime, with an ideological foothold in the Superior War School and influence extending up to the present day. General do Couto e Silva implored his nation to never forget that "Brazil is an empire, a large, compact empire with extensive shoreline and an extensive continental border."

The policy of "revitalizing the borders" and "filling empty demographic gaps" remains one of the central premises of the *National Defense Strategy*, although it employs a different language. Paulo Schilling argues that even after the Brazilian military dictatorship, expansionism has continued but "now the projects are developed in a clandestine manner," referring to the North Calha border project implemented in the 1980s to strengthen control over that area.[92] He considers that Brazil's projection "beyond its borders," as General do Couto e Silva emphasized, goes hand in hand with his theory of "privileged satellites," or countries with such a degree of asymmetry to Brazil that they have little choice but to follow the regional power. In that sense, Uruguayan President José Mujica made sense when he said Uruguay must "travel on Brazil's running board."[93]

An editorial column in *Defesanet* states that the approval of the decree constituted a clear message to neighboring countries: "Any act of aggression or persecution of Brazilian citizens residing in Paraguay (*brasiguayos*), in the Pando region of Bolivia, as well as new threats to cut gas lines or take over Brazilian installations and companies operating in other countries are now characterized as external aggression and a military response from Brazil will be legally sanctioned."[94]

Every time a political crisis occurs in countries close to Brazil, the diplomats swing into action, forcefully. One clear example was Lula's efforts to defend the interests of Petrobras in Bolivia, on the eve of a 2004 referendum on hydrocarbons. Lula signed a statement with Bolivian President Carlos Mesa—nine days before the referendum—that the two leaders hoped "the results of the referendum on Bolivia's energy policy and the future new law for the country's hydrocarbon industry would ensure the continuity of bilateral cooperation."[95] This was a strong sign of support for Mesa and a bucket of cold water for the social movement, some of which had called for a boycott of the referendum.

In crisis situations in Bolivia, Brazilian diplomacy intervened through Lula's international adviser, Marco Aurelio Garcia, "to assess the situation via dialogue with the various political forces."[96] Something similar happened in Ecuador. On July 7, 2005, Ecuador's Minister of Environment ordered a freeze on Petrobras public works in Yasuni National Park. On July 26, Lula sent a letter to the president of Ecuador: "I wish to express to Your Excellency my concern about the government's recent decision to suspend the activities of Petrobras in Block 31, a fact that threatens the very future of the project."[97] Two weeks later, on August 16, Brazilian Foreign Minister Celso Amorim traveled to Quito to "discuss issues of regional integration and the presence of Petrobras in the Ecuadorian Amazon."[98]

Furthermore, in 2005, the Brazilian Intelligence Agency (ABIN) opened four offices in South America: in Venezuela, Colombia, Paraguay, and Bolivia (previously it only had offices in Washington and Buenos Aires). According to Brazilian analysts, "This decision to expand the regional scope of the Brazilian intelligence agency is a kind of 'imitation' of the CIA." The director of the agency said that the expansion of Brazilian intelligence sought to "exchange information on terrorism, drug trafficking, security, and economic issues," revealing the extent of intelligence service intervention.[99]

The issue transcends the Lula government. It is basically an emerging power affirming that its borders extend to wherever its national interests lie. In her visit to Paraguay in July 2011, President Rousseff demanded that Lugo ensure the safety of Brazilian settlers in the face of a recent wave of land invasions, and the Foreign Ministry at Itamaraty questioned a Paraguayan court decision to pardon the occupiers.[100]

All great powers were built up in this way, with an attitude that has always been known as "imperialism." Maybe that's why many South Americans feel that Brazil is creating its own "backyard."

9

Toward a New Center and New Peripheries

"The Brazilian industrial bourgeoisie was gradually won over by the geopolitical theory of the military men at the Superior War School, where many of their representatives studied."
—*Paulo Schilling*

When Marini formulated the theory of sub-imperialism four decades ago, US hegemony had not yet begun to decline and the capitalist system had not entered into global crisis. In 1969, year of the first edition of *Sub-Development and Revolution,* the system had not yet shown the signs of decay that were visible by 1973. Analysts from diverse schools of thought support historian Fernand Braudel's thesis that in the early 1970s the economic system led by the United States began a process of financialization as a means of maintaining hegemony.[1]

The transformation of the system occurred around the same time Marini was writing his thesis. Threatened on several fronts, the empire moved back and forth. The years from the Cuban Revolution (1959) to defeat in Vietnam (1975) and the Iranian Revolution (1979) were characterized by massive rebellions not only in the third world but also in developed countries, most notably civil rights and peace movements in the United States and workers' struggles in Europe. For the first time in the five-century history of capitalism, social conflict from below preceded and configured the crisis of US hegemony, the intensification of competition between companies, and rivalry between states.[2]

Competition from Europe and Japan, the numerous social conflicts in the first world, and rivalry between third world countries and the United States led the ruling class of the superpower to change course. The decision to redirect the economy from accumulation to the financial sphere implied abandoning the welfare state, or that is to say, the claim of attempting to integrate classes. This remarkable counterattack was reflected in the Washington Consensus, which gave birth to the neoliberal model. But when Marini wrote his thesis, the ruling classes of the world and the Latin American region were still reacting to the first effects of the riots and revolutions. The 1964 coup in Brazil was the first major action taken by these classes against "those from below" in the region. Although changes were beginning to take shape, the rudder was still firmly in the hands of the empire and United States hegemony was, as Marini wrote in 1977, still "invincible."[3]

It would take two long decades more before this hegemony began to crumble, confronted in the 1990s with a strong movement from below that powerfully mobilized to delegitimize the neoliberal model. Between 1989's *Caracazo* and the second Gas War in Bolivia in 2005, waves of protests across the region managed to bring down a dozen conservative governments and allies of Washington. Towards the second half of the first decade of the twenty-first century, eight South American governments were defined as progressive or left, and distanced themselves from US policies.

The first of the three arguments woven into Marini's sub-imperialism thesis changed drastically to the point that by 2011 only Colombia still acted as a gendarme for the United States, a role that had belonged entirely to Brazil in 1964. But changes on the regional and global stage went much further. Shortly after Lula took power in Brazil (2003), the BRIC grouping (Brazil, Russia, India, and China, and later South Africa) began to form, an acronym that embodies the rising power of emerging countries moving to displace the old powers. Between 2009 and 2011, there were some notable changes: China overtook the US as Brazil's largest trading partner, a position the US had held since early in the twentieth century; China overtook Japan as the country with the second largest GDP in the world, and by 2020 it could possibly dethrone the US as the world's leading economic power (although the IMF predicts it could happen even sooner, in 2016).[4]

It is evident that US hegemony has eroded to unimaginable levels since the economic and financial crisis of 2008. That decline, hastened by failed wars in Iraq and Afghanistan, opened up room for the construction of different regional realities. The creation of UNASUR and the South American Defense Council has powered the region's political disengagement from the United States. Through the IIRSA and the BNDES, a regional dynamic is being generated that could lead to the creation of a regional trading currency and a new financial architecture endorsed by the Bank of the South (created in 2009 as a development bank). Within just a few short years, the region has gained clout and personality on the world stage.

Neither gendarme nor dependent

If the world and the region changed dramatically, Brazil also underwent profound mutations. The first was of a demographic nature. In 1960, it had seventy million people—more than half living in rural areas—with a high population growth rate, close to 3 percent annually.[5] By 1970, Brazil had 93 million inhabitants, and 56 percent lived in cities. The vast majority were poor or very poor and the level of inequality was enormous. By the end of the twentieth century Brazil still had 50 million people living in poverty.[6]

Today, the situation is completely different. Over 80 percent of Brazilians live in cities and less than 20 percent in the countryside. Poverty has declined dramatically, but the turning point is that Brazil became a middle-class country.[7] When Marini wrote his thesis on sub-imperialism, Brazil was an ocean of poor below and an ostentatious rich bourgeoisie above, with a dwindling middle class.

Secondly, take into account Marini's emphasis that Brazil was a "medium-sized center of accumulation," which, as a dependent country, had accepted a "junior partner" status.[8] If we compare the economic situation of the country between the 1960s and the first years of this century, the contrast is quite enormous.

Perhaps the most notable difference is the autonomy gained in capital accumulation and export dynamism, which reveals the changes in the structure of production. Between 1964 and 1969 commodity exports made up 80 percent of the total, while manufacturing accounted for about 10 percent. Between 2002 and 2008 commodities ranged between 28 percent and 37 percent of total exports, but manufacturing climbed from 47 percent to 55 percent, despite the "deindustrialization" caused by competition from China.[9] Manufacturing exports reached the 55 percent mark in 2005, compared to 6 percent in 1964.

Capital flows truly underwent a revolution. The 1960s closed with a foreign investment income of $221 million in 1969. It jumped to $67 billion in 2011. International reserves exceed debt: they reached $350 billion in 2011, while debt stands at $297 billion.[10] In the 1960s, reserves accounted for only 10 percent of the external debt.[11]

Since the global crisis erupted in 2008, Brazil has become one of the most attractive destinations for direct foreign investment, reaching fifth place in 2010, with $48 billion, behind only the US, China, Hong Kong, and Belgium.[12] In addition to raising funds, Brazil has consistently accumulated capital, particularly in the last decade. The country's pension funds assets had the best global growth rate in the first decade of the century: between 2000 and 2010 their total assets rose from 12 percent to 17 percent of GDP.[13]

Previ, the largest Brazilian pension fund, rose to 24th place in world rankings from 42nd place only two years earlier.[14] The exponential growth of Previ's equity—80 percent over three years—is not an isolated case. Petros increased its assets by more than 40 percent between 2007 and 2010, rising from 173rd to 105th worldwide. And Funcef rose from 177th to 131st.

The third major change involves important Brazilian investments abroad, particularly in South America. The BNDES has become the largest development bank in the world and plays a decisive role in the economy. In December 2010, Brazilian direct investment abroad totaled $190 billion, a figure that exceeds the annual joint GDP of Ecuador, Uruguay, Bolivia, and Paraguay.[15] According to the Central Bank, Brazilian direct investments were $49.7 billion in 2001, which means they quadrupled in one decade.[16] One major recipient of BNDES support is the Brazilian construction industry. Between 2001 and 2010, funding for works abroad grew by 1,185 percent.[17] Between 2011 and 2014, the BNDES plans to invest $1.9 billion in Brazil, representing an increase of over 60 percent compared to 2009.[18] In part due to this generous funding, Brazilian construction companies expanded operations across five continents: Andrade Gutierrez in thirty-seven countries, Odebrecht in nineteen, OAS in eighteen, Queiroz Galvao in ten, and Camargo Corrêa in six.[19]

A substantial part of the BNDES disbursements focused on expansion in Latin America. In 2009, Odebrecht received $600 million from the development bank, 80 percent for contracts in Argentina, Dominican Republic, and Angola. The BNDES took lessons from World Bank and IDB operations, among others, learning how this kind of funding promotes the export of Brazilian goods and services, which account for between 50 and 80 percent of the value of the work funded. As the president of Odebrecht Latin America and Angola, Luiz Antonio Mameri, pointed out: "There is a misinterpretation that Brazil finances works in another country when actually it finances Brazilian goods and services, thus generating taxes and moving our economy."[20]

Brazil is the largest foreign investor in Argentina, with investment totaling $11.1 billion in 2011, 25 percent in the industrial sector, 18 percent in oil, and 11 percent in gas and mining, data that indicates the depth and diversity of the Brazilian presence.[21] The Vale mining company plans to invest $5 billion in Mendoza, Neuquén, and Rio Negro for extraction of potassium, a project that includes the construction of a port and a railway. This represents a broad range of investments in a moderately indus-trialized country, investments once reserved only for the major capitalist powers. Incursions into the Argentinean market are, according to the state media agency *Portal Brasil*, driven by the same things that motivated US and European capital in previous eras—energy prices seven times lower than in Brazil, the search for new markets, and the possibility of producing with lower costs in Argentina to sell in the Brazilian market.[22]

The other side of the coin is capital repatriation by Brazilian multinationals. Between 2007 and August 2011, $107 billion was repatriated, the sort of movement that has been recorded consistently since 2006.[23] This is a real novelty for the Brazilian economy, unthinkable in the 1960s and 1970s. So, in assessing Marini's thesis, we can assert that Brazilian capitalism today is no longer dependent, the country is no longer a medium-sized center of accumulation and no longer plays a role of "sub-power." The term "sub," so important at the time in order to understand the 1964 coup and Brazil's role in the region, has become obsolete. As noted by intellectual and activist Virginia Fontes:

> The concept forged by Marini does not take into account the substantive changes to the concentration of capital in Brazil, the reconfiguration of the state to favor it, the role that capital/imperialist expansion comes to exercise in all social relations within the country, nor the inter-imperialist tensions that arose in the international context after the fall of the Soviet Union and the emergence of China's capital/imperialist expansion.[24]

Ongoing debates

Most analysts and critical intellectuals have chosen to continue using the term "sub-imperialism" to describe Brazil's expansionist tendencies. However, that is beginning to give way to another orientation that sees, for different reasons, Brazil's rise to global power as being of an imperialist character. The more compre-hensive and profound studies in recent years come to different conclusions: Mathias Luce Seibel defends the validity of the Marini thesis; Fontes argues that, in today's world, all capital is "capital-imperialism"; and finally, João Bernardo subscribes, from a different perspective, to the idea that Brazil's current expansion is of an imperialist nature.[25] All three merit some brief comments.

Luce wrote his master's thesis before the global crisis of 2008. He puts special emphasis on Marini's concept of "antagonistic cooperation" and the dependent nature of Brazilian capitalism, which prevents autonomous development. One difference between imperialism and sub-imperialism, he notes, is that sub-imperialists are merely importers of capital; they are not in a condition to export it, which is "a determining factor."[26]

To support his thesis, he emphasizes what he sees as the denationalization of the Brazilian economy in the interests of major foreign capital, and Brazil's regressive integration into the world market as an exporter of commodities to China and other Asian countries. The fact that Lula's government has opted for the IIRSA and free trade does not contradict the hegemonic model, says Luce, but on the contrary "addresses the expectations of big capital, which finds an enabling environment in the region for installing export platforms for its products, such as automobile assembly."[27]

The dependency is centered in agribusiness, with companies like Cargill and Monsanto using Brazil to expand into Paraguay and Bolivia. With the growth of the biofuels industry, the role of sub-imperialism would appear to be even greater: "The availability of Brazilian territory to transform ethanol into an international commodity would cause, in turn, increasingly regressive economic specialization."[28] Although regional integration benefits the Brazilian bourgeoisie, Luce argues that the ultimate beneficiary is US capital, and notes the growth of US investments in the region as proof. No data exist, however, to support this assessment. On the contrary, since the mid-2000s, US capital is being displaced by Brazilian and Chinese capital. In reality, agribusiness is one of the few sectors not controlled by Brazilian multinationals.

A second point relates to the claim that Brazil serves US interests in stabilizing the region. For Luce, the US needs "to be able to

depend on countries like Brazil, who accept the role of interme-
diaries preserving imperialist interests on the continent, in return
for some concessions."[29] This would explain the role that Brazil
played in the internal crisis in Bolivia in 2009, and especially
through the UN military mission in Haiti (MINUSTAH). By
taking over leadership and employing troops on the ground, Brazil helped the US, which was otherwise busy and over-extended
in Iraq. He argues that Brazil's interests coincide with US strategy
in South America through a "pyramidal hierarchical integration"
that allows some leeway without veering from the idea of a key
nation in the region. Here Luce's analysis reflects Marini's concept
of "gendarme," while acknowledging that the role is not currently
exercised by military means but through consensus. In his rescue
and upgrade of the concept of sub-imperialism, he emphasizes
continuities, while introducing new trends:

> But unlike the period studied by Marini, correspond-
> ing to the Brazilian dictatorship from 1960 to 1970,
> when sub-imperialism was strongly influenced by a mil-
> itarism that pushed the internal dynamics of the phe-
> nomenon into the realm of coercion, sub-imperialism
> now responds to the opposite dynamic of the coercion/
> consensus relationship. Under the Lula government,
> Brazilian sub-imperialism, within its appropriate scale
> of South American regionalism, is developed by con-
> sensus. The novelty of this dynamic, which leaves cor-
> porations and the state with the same leading roles, can
> be defined in the various policies that claim to be reduc-
> ing the asymmetries within the subcontinent. It could
> therefore be seen as a new kind of sub-imperialism—a
> social-liberal sub-imperialism.[30]

In contrast, Fontes focuses on changes rather than continuities.
Her analysis revolves around the concept of "capital-imperialism,"
which she says characterizes the movement of capital after the
Second World War, a capitalism altered through the dominance
of monetary capital, the supremacy of property rights, and an

overwhelming expropriating momentum. In this new phase, capital expands in an imperialist manner because it expropriates entire populations, combining a double domination, internal and external, which reduces democracy to an "authoritarian-electoral model, similar to shareholders' meetings."[31]

In her opinion, the driving force of the process of financialization was pension funds that generated an unprecedented degree of accumulation, a "pharaonic resource concentration" beyond the traditional division between financial and industrial capital, to a point that necessitated the deregulation of the traditional conglomerates that hindered the circulation and subsequent accumulation of capital at an unprecedented scale. In other words, Fontes asserts that the old structures of capitalism slowed the continuity of accumulation, and this led to the implementation of the neoliberal model. She argues that imperialism can no longer be viewed as something external that penetrates a country, but as a new kind of capitalism, which she defines as "tentacular and totalitarian" capital-imperialism that can only exist by expanding and devouring new spaces, supported by military force.[32]

Fontes's argument is powerful, rigorous, and has the virtue of polemicizing Marini. Put another way, it resolutely upgrades Marini's legacy with which it shares a single theoretical link: the hypothesis that the Brazilian bourgeoisie and Brazilian capitalism are dependent, or subordinate. If I had to point out some controversial aspect in her work, it is that capital-imperialism appears be *de-subjectified*, like a machine without a pilot, as if the accumulation cycle itself was capable by itself of shaping societies. However, when she periodizes social conflicts in Brazil, Fontes places the class struggle as the key to the intensifying processes of capital accumulation. This leads to the claim that the "frantic race to accumulate," which is more important than the production of goods, is necessary for the continued existence of the bourgeoisie, a race from which capital cannot be distracted for a moment at the risk of disappearing.[33]

Fontes says Brazilian imperialism offers some protection to a group of Latin American countries against the devastation that

242 • *The New Brazil*

accompanies North American capital-imperialism. These "subtle contradictions" offer some relief to countries seeking to avoid US control. She points out that social movements "need to build more cautious relationships with the popular governments of South America."[34] She accepts that this relationship implies the penetration of Brazilian capital, which will always cause problems for social movements, but she hints that it may be a way to work within the new balance of power. At times, she suggests that the main task at hand is to work toward exiting US hegemony.

One of Brazil's most creative and critical writers, João Bernardo, wrote a series of articles, published on the *Passapalavra* website throughout 2011, which outline his analysis of the country's imperialist character. He says that in recent decades, "the Brazilian economy has internally accumulated elements of strength, reinforced during the first Lula government, which now give it potential for expanding beyond its borders."[35] With an abundance of data, he states that Brazil has been capable, since the mid-twentieth century, of forming solid business groups that can compete abroad with high levels of productivity and a great capacity to enter a cycle of sustained growth, despite obvious weaknesses.

In contrast to the "economic miracle" during the military dictatorship, which was disrupted by the 1980s global crisis, the country emerging under Lula was strengthened to the point that the 2008 crisis "came at the right time for Brazilian capitalism, which was internally prepared to respond."[36] In his view, Brazil is one of the few countries where the state is fully capable of intervening in the economy by means of a *techno-bureaucracy* that "circulates between the administrations of companies, universities, and ministry consultancies, forming a stronger ruling-class core" and that is able to ensure growth.[37] We might add that this bureaucracy was formed in military classrooms, as René Dreifuss noted: "The industrial and technological entrepreneurs linked to the multinational structure transmitted and received training in public administration and business objectives in the Superior War School," sharing an ideology of national security and entrepreneurship in which "discipline and hierarchy are seen as essential components of an industrial system."[38]

This point is not secondary. Bernardo reminds us that the four emerging powers (BRICS) share the institutional element of a "bureaucratic capitalism" in which the state plays a prescribed role. Through the use of the state bank BNDES, Brazil has for some time been able to apply a coherent industrial policy, placing it among the top ten industrial powers since the 1970s. This form of capitalism inserted private entrepreneurs (techno-bureaucrats) in the state structure, as it did during the military dictatorship and now does through the PT government. It is a kind of statism supported by multinational companies.[39]

The governments of Lula and Rousseff have had the advantage of enjoying high levels of internal cohesion, largely due to the success of social policies to reduce poverty and neutralize social conflict. That social cohesion "is an indispensable factor for effective imperialist expansion," says Bernardo.[40] It is especially effective in a period when the old power centers are in decline and new centers are beginning to sprout, centers that must necessarily constitute their own periphery.

A good example of this cohesion is the perception in Brazilian society regarding military and foreign policy. One of the goals set by the National Defense Strategy was precisely that the population engage in debates about Brazil's position regionally and globally, and the role of the armed forces. A comprehensive IPEA study on Brazilians' social perception in relation to national defense illustrates the internal cohesion achieved. Sixty-seven percent of Brazilians believe that it is very likely or fairly likely that the country will be at the receiving end of foreign military aggression that attempts to appropriate Amazonian resources, while 63 percent believe the country could be attacked for its pre-salt oil reserves.[41] More interesting still, 35 percent of Brazilians (almost half if one excludes nonresponders) stated that the main threat comes from the United States and that Brazil's key allies are in the region.[42]

When people are asked about confidence in the armed forces, 82 percent answered that they have a lot or quite a lot, while only

244 • *The New Brazil*

17 percent say they have little or no confidence.[43] These levels of support are well above military approval ratings in other regional countries, and reveal a significant degree of national cohesion. Something similar happens with the question of military equipment expenditure: 70 percent say they think it should be increased substantially or a lot, compared to only 4 percent saying it should be reduced.[44] It seems clear that society has a strong empathy with the objectives set by the National Defense Strategy, and that the state and society broadly share a single vision of the world and Brazil's place within it.

An open scenario

In previous chapters, we saw how a trend that emerged during the military regime flourished in all its intensity in the twenty-first century under the Lula government. That trend, slowly maturing, is the will towards turning Brazil into a global power, as one of four emerging nations changing the global balance of power. Aside from the United States and Brazil, there are no intermediate powers in Latin America capable of playing an important role in reshaping the regional map, as Argentina and Mexico once were.

Strategists from the Superior War School (ESG) were the first to highlight the regional vocation of Brazil, noting that South America is the most important region for the United States to maintain global dominance. World War II showed the geopolitical importance of the region in US strategy, because it safeguarded sources of raw materials—minerals essential to its defense industry—and also secured its rear flank in the South Atlantic.[45]

Moniz Bandeira considers Brazil the only possible rival to US hegemonic influence in the region. In his view, one shared by the ESG, Plan Colombia is designed to control the petroleum in that country rather than fight guerrillas and drug trafficking, which is why between 10 and 15 percent of the Colombian troops and their US military advisers are deployed along the country's five oil pipelines and other facilities—to protect energy infrastructure and foreign oil companies. The Brazilian military's main concern is that "the Colombian army has become the largest and best equipped—relatively speaking—in South America," threatening the sovereignty of the Amazon.[46] One of the reasons that led President George W. Bush "to restore the Fourth Fleet to the South Atlantic"[47] according to Moniz Bandeira (and here he coincides with Brazilian political, military, and business elites) is the discovery of large oil fields in Brazil's offshore platform.

He insists that the creation of UNASUR and the South American Defense Council dismantles the inter-American system created by Washington with the Organization of American States (OAS), the Rio Treaty (Inter-American Treaty of Reciprocal Assistance), and the Inter-American Defense Board. He concludes that in light of South America being the largest global exporter of food, one of the largest oil producers, and considering its vast mineral reserves and water, "one cannot rule out the hypothesis of war with a technologically superior power," or conflicts involving Venezuela and Bolivia, and therefore Brazil's national security.[48]

Guilherme Sandoval Góes, coordinator of the Division of Geopolitical Affairs and International Relations of the ESG, said that Brazil took a significant step in 1986 in creating the South Atlantic Zone of Peace and Cooperation (ZPCSA) to counteract the United States' continental strategy. The ZPCSA, in his opinion, "has an important role in neutralizing a possible US initiative to create the South Atlantic Treaty Organization (SATO), which would consolidate US hegemony in this important geostrategic region."[49]

According to Sandoval Góes, South American regional strategy should focus on five areas: strengthening integration, constructing a South American identity in terms of defense, integrating defense industries, promoting sustainable economic growth, and making South America a power hub in the world system. To prevent the geopolitical subordination of the region, he advocates "benign Brazilian leadership in South America," which could convert the region into "a vital space for the international strengthening of Brazil." He further urges multipolar international cooperation on several fronts with the European Union and the Asian block.[50] If these steps do not materialize, South America could become simply an object of Washington's economic exploitation without political autonomy.

There is an interesting coincidence between the vision of the ESG and the Institute for Strategic Thinking (IPEA), two of the main centers of strategic thinking. In general, their analysis coincides with the worldview adopted by a broad spectrum of analysts including advocates of the world-systems theory. The economist José Luis Fiori, working for the IPEA, emphasizes how the defeat in Vietnam in 1973 led the United States to consolidate a military empire—a process that accelerated after the collapse of the Soviet Union in 1991, leading to a new political geometry with US economic dominance, but also the emergence of new regional powers, including China.[51]

The peculiarity of South America is that, throughout the twentieth century, it did not consolidate an integrated and competitive system of national and state economies, as Asia did after decolonization. For this reason, says Fiori, "there was never a hegemonic dispute in South America between its states and their national economies, and none of the states fought for continental hegemony with the great powers."[52] In two centuries of independence, the new nations moved seamlessly from British to US hegemony, and then to the period of the Washington Consensus. However, at the end of the first decade of the twenty-first century it is possible to see two major geopolitical and economic transformations—the leadership of Brazil in South America and the growing importance of China in the regional economy.

Brazil began to attend to its South American agenda during the 1980s and took center stage in the late 1990s, when the Initiative for the Integration of Regional Infrastructure in South America (IIRSA) was, as we've seen, launched during a summit of presidents convened by Cardoso in 2000. Under Lula's government, it became the "main point of reference."[53] Despite these efforts, consciousness of the region's importance has yet to translate into concrete policies. Ricardo Sennes, coordinator of the University of São Paulo International Analysis Group, argues that there is an implicit "preference for a pattern of regional relationships based on Brazilian political and economic capabilities and not on regional integration."[54] In this sense, Brazilian regional policy is more like that of the US (a series of bilateral agreements based on the interests of the hegemon) than the European model which is constructing integration based on a high level of institutionalization.

What is certain is that Brazil signed a strategic military agreement with France in September 2008, including conventional and nuclear submarines that, once operational, will make Brazil the biggest naval power in the South Atlantic—a development that will change its relationship with the United States. The 2008 crisis, says Fiori, "increased regional economic asymmetries and led to new differences and conflicts between regional governments and the Brazilian government."[55] Brazil's new military supremacy creates an unprecedented situation in the region.

Regionalization—meaning the intensification of regional ties—has outpaced institutional integration.[56] It would appear that business elites and the state bureaucracy are quite behind the Foreign Ministry and the military in understanding the importance of America of the South (referring to the spatial concept coined by military strategists) as a launchpad for Brazil's ambitions as a global power.

The economic data speaks for itself. Between 2001 and 2009, Brazil's exports to Mercosur went from 2.4 percent to 10.3 percent of total exports, a figure surpassed only by China. It is even more interesting to note that the bulk of Brazil's industrial exports are destined for South America. In 2008, 60 percent of its electronics exports went to South America, as did 40 percent of automotive industry exports, 35 percent of textiles, 32 percent of machinery and equipment, and 31 percent of electrical equipment. Similarly, 28 percent of chemical and petrochemical exports, 18 percent of pulp and paper, and 16 percent of steel went to other South American countries.[57] Overall, Brazilian industrial exports to the region account for between a quarter and a third of its total exports.

The second strategic shift in the region, the impressive entrance of China, also generates new problems and imbalances. In this case, it is primarily an economic challenge: between 2003 and 2008, China went from representing 5.4 percent to 12.7 percent of the regional exports, but its gross value grew 700 percent. That led to a decline in Brazilian participation in some markets, such as Argentina.[58] As for Chinese investment, Latin America has become its second destination behind Asia. The Brazilian government is concerned by this trend, since massive Chinese imports of minerals and soybeans, and their investments in land purchases and hydrocarbons, could "weaken the density of the national productive structure as well as decrease strategic control over energy sources (petroleum) and natural resources (land and mines), while increasing external structural vulnerability."[59]

The IPEA concludes that competitive pressure from the Chinese manufacturing industry is shrinking industrial exports from Brazil, generating a sharp trade deficit in high-technology products and reducing the share of technology-intensive exports to third markets like Latin America, Europe, and the United States.[60]

Furthermore, the effects of the 2008 crisis tend to slow the integration project, intensifying asymmetries and competition between countries. The four main issues here are not new, but they are aggravated: economies directed toward the export market, poorly integrated and rarely complementary; national and social asymmetries and inequalities within each country and across the region; the lack of an efficient continental infrastructure; and the lack of permanent regional objectives capable of unifying a strategic vision.[61] These are objective and structural difficulties that can only be overcome with a powerful political will.

The South American region can continue being a periphery exporting commodities, a condition imposed since the era of colonialism, or it can wager on endogenous development, which can ensure an autonomous trajectory. But making that decision requires, as Fiori notes, that "the region solves its security dilemma endogenously," to stop relying on the umbrella of the United States, and instead, for all South American countries to become strategic allies.[62]

At this point, Brazil has two alternatives—to become a privileged periphery or a leader of regional countries constructing their own autonomy. Compared to the other emerging markets (India, Russia, and China), Brazil has the huge advantage in that it can expand peacefully in a region free of conflicts. It also has the world's sixth largest reserves of uranium and can soon begin exporting enriched uranium. It is among the five largest oil reserves in the world, it has the largest biofuel industry, three of the ten largest banks in the world are Brazilian, and it has some of the largest global multinationals. An expansive trajectory was launched by Lula in 2003, but its leaders must make some key decisions:

> First, its global project needs to be defined, including its specific relation to European and US values, diagnostics, and positions regarding major international themes and issues. And secondly, Brazil will have to decide whether or not to retain its position as strategic military ally to the US, Britain, and France, with the right to access top-shelf technology—as Turkey and Israel have—but keeping the US military and its key European allies within its area of influence, protection, and strategic decision making. In other words, Brazil must decide its place in the world.[63]

Brazil can maintain an instrumental relationship with the region, as defined by the Superior War School military strategists and construction companies, which essentially agree on a kind of expansionism that subordinates the region to their interests, or they can opt for a more egalitarian type of integration, in which the São Paulo bourgeoisie and the state bureaucracy will need to make concessions. The mass opposition of the Bolivian people to the construction of a highway funded by the BNDES and executed by the OAS construction company is the most tangible sign of the kind of popular rejection to "endogenous" imperialism that follows in the footsteps of previous empires.

There are other possibilities. The construction of a new regional architecture based on the three pillars of the Bank of the South, the South Fund, and the strengthening of national currencies through the creation of a South American monetary system may be a necessary step to disconnect the region from the dollar.[64]

Nevertheless, Brazil is delaying the implementation of these measures due to narrow national interests. Regional integration with a decoupling from the dollar will not be the work of transnational companies but of nation-states. It is still unclear whether the new ruling elite, with its PT cadres and trade unionist influence in pension funds, will have the political courage and clarity necessary to lead this process in a time when the world is entering a period of systemic chaos.

For the people and small countries of the region, new opportunities and greater challenges are unfolding. It will be necessary to set limits on the imperialist expansionism of the Brazilian bourgeoisie and its state—as indigenous Bolivians have done—to impose conditions, to negotiate to prevent a repeat of colonial history, so that the majority do not return to being peripheries of a new center, now a regional center, specializing in capital accumulation by appropriating the commons. It is possible because the majority of South Americans, including the majority of the Brazilian people, are suffering under the same drive towards modernization. In this sense, Brazilians resisting the construction of Belo Monte, the San Francisco River transposition, or megaprojects such as Jirau and Santo Antônio can and should form a bloc of resistance to protect the environment and the sovereignty of indigenous peoples, alongside those who defend the TIPNIS in Bolivia, those who oppose dams in Peru, and those who resist agribusiness in Paraguay.

10
Antisystemic Movements in Brazil

"Currently in Brazil there is no popular reaction, no direct confrontation; the class struggle is taking a very molecular form, diffuse and unable to take a political form: it has become a 'private' struggle. It is an expression of class struggle, but not a political struggle. There are hidden confrontations, a daily conflict, every day, but—especially among the poor—no confrontation with those above."
—*Francisco de Oliveira*

On 12 November, a job foreman on the Belo Monte dam ordered four workers to porter huge logs that could clearly only be moved with machines. They refused, because under their contract they were not required to carry out such tasks. That same day they were fired. Unrest began to stir immediately around the worksite and workers "threatened to burn down their accommodation huts."[1] The next day the company asked workers to choose delegates for sit-down talks, and the four fired workers were reinstated to calm things down. Four days later, 138 workers were fired and brutally expelled from the construction site: forty members of the elite Belém police squad threw the workers onto buses and sent them back to Maranhão. The company bosses accused the "delegates" of being responsible for the expulsions as a means of delegitimizing them before their fellow workers.

A week later, on November 25, a strike began on site, which was suspended a few days later under union pressure. The journalist Ruy Sposato, of the Xingu Vive para Siempre Movement based in Altamira, the city nearest the site, followed the debates and resistance to Belo Monte dam. Sposato tells how the workers decided to suspend the strike upon the advice of the Construction Workers Union of Pará:

> The union took the initiative in the negotiations because the workers had no desire to create a commission or a strike leadership given the dismissals that had occurred. This need for anonymity created fresh problems for organizing. On the advice of the union, onsite assemblies were held to decide what demands would be brought before the General Superintendence of Labor [...] After an afternoon of talks, the union managed to convince workers that it would be better to suspend the strike without negotiating, because the company said it would immediately solve the problems of water and food, and the rest of the demands would be discussed only after the strike was lifted.[2]

The union legally represents the Belo Monte workers, but some of the workers do not recognize it because there is not a single construction worker in its local leadership. At the outbreak of the first strike, according to Sposato, "the union did not send a representative." Worse still, the delegates for the negotiations were probably chosen by the union (since there was no evidence that they had held real assemblies), and they were accompanied by Avelino Ganzer, Joint Social Secretary of the Presidency of the Republic, linked to the CUT (Unified Workers' Central).

Working conditions on site are pitiful. The workers rise at four in the morning, drink coffee in company canteens, and at five, climb aboard the buses to get to the work site. They work until 5:30PM, eat and return to their quarters between 6:30 and 7PM.

Their salary is US $500 a month, and overtime is not paid double. The food is rank and the water provided is unfit for drinking. About 250 workers have been hospitalized due to poisoning. The workers are isolated from the city, and the nearest Internet access in Altamira, fifty kilometers away, is precarious.

The press remained completely silent. To highlight their plight, the workers hijacked a company truck. At this point, Sposato contacted Monte Belo workers to report on the labor dispute.[3] On the fourth day of the strike, the four workers "delegated" by the union went to the regional labor delegation offices, where union leaders had already agreed on a solution to the labor dispute with the company and the government representative.

The union belongs to the Força Sindical (Union Power) group, which at that time had a close relationship with Labor Minister Carlos Lupi and who, a few days after the negotiations with the Belo Monte workers, was forced to resign over allegations of corruption in his ministry. When the strike began in November 2011, construction at Belo Monte had just begun and there were less than 4,000 workers on site although there are now an estimated 20,000 workers in total. The interesting thing about the events in Belo Monte is that they reveal a pattern of behavior by workers who, like former plantation slaves, were ready to use arson in response to slave-like conditions, and who opt for anonymity instead of representation, rejecting the official union. Here Sposato describes the alliances formed on either side of the conflict:

> The spontaneous actions of workers ended because of pressure from the union apparatus, the government representative, and the construction company, all insisting that the strike be suspended. So the workers suspended the strike, with the threat that it could be re-implemented at any time. From this moment, the workers, demanding improvements, were pitted against the union, the government, and the company, who had formed a block to end the strike.[4]

What happened in Belo Monte is very similar to what had already happened in the course of the Jirau and Santo Antônio disputes, and also on other Growth Acceleration Program (PAC) and World Cup 2014 construction sites. Throughout 2011, there were major labor disputes at all these sites, with nearly 80,000 workers going out on strike on the PAC sites alone. The triple alliance between unions, government, and business seen in Jirau was also employed in Belo Monte. However, it is not that the union had been co-opted, or that their leaders betrayed the workers. The shareholding structure of the Norte Energia company, responsible for the construction of the Belo Monte dam, reveals complex union interests.

Table 10: Composition of shareholders of Norte Energia (2011)

	percent
Eletrobras	15.00%
Chesf	15.00%
Eletronorte	19.98%
Petros	10.00%
Funcef	5.00%
Caixa Fip Cevix	5.00%
Neoenergia SA	10.00%
Amazonia Cemig	9.77%
Others	10.25%

Source: Norte Energia S.A.

The first three companies are controlled by the federal government. Petros and Funcef are the employees pension funds of Petrobras and Caixa Economica Federal, both state enterprises. Neoenergia SA is a company in which Previ, the pension fund for workers of state-owned Banco do Brasil, has a 49 percent stake. In short, the Brazilian government controls directly or indirectly about 70 percent of the shares of the company constructing Belo Monte. In several ways, unions have a decisive weight, either through pension funds that control about 25% of the shares, or by their significant presence in the highest echelons of the federal government, where decisions are made on megaprojects. Almost half the positions of trust in the Lula and Dilma administrations have been linked to the labor movement, primarily bankers, teachers, and oil workers, with a large majority originating from the CUT.[5] Furthermore, the union presence in the three largest pension funds (Previ, Petros, and Funcef) is crucial.

The BNDES finances 80 percent of the Belo Monte project, whose budget is, according to the Xingu Vivo para Siempre movement, some $17 billion, to be transferred to private banks at a below-market interest rate—which is to say, it will be subsidized by the State, and repayable over thirty years.[6] Thus, union/government management plays a critical role in guiding the loans, creating conglomerates such as Norte Energia, and overseeing business decisions. The union/government/corporation "bloc" pointed out by Sposato encapsulates the new configuration of Brazilian power. And this new form of power has no qualms about calling in the military police to restore order on the state's megaprojects.

The union's new position can be understood by identifying their interests. With the country's rise to the status of a global power, the remaking of the ruling class has formed a new elite, by merging union cadres (linked to pension funds and state administration) with the old elites. The big unions, those clustered at the more specialized, better-paid end of the labor spectrum, are part of a power bloc and not the sort of labor aristocracy the socialist movement considered such sectors in previous historical periods.

The concept of labor aristocracy appears in Engels's 1892 preface to *The Condition of the Working Class in England*, and refers to the gentrification of a sector of the working class as a result of the colonial phenomenon.[7] Later, Lenin developed and updated the concept: "Imperialism has the tendency to create privileged sections also among the workers, and to detach them from the broad masses of the proletariat."[8] Secondly, he considers that a part of the workers agreed to be led by "men bought by, or at least paid by, the bourgeoisie."[9] Both cases are temporary situations with material benefits for certain sectors of the working class. They are not, therefore, a new structural reality, but a sector of the workers benefiting from the extraordinary profits of monopoly capital, because of their place in production or their organizational capacity, or both.

A qualitative leap takes place with the creation of pension funds. In the early-twentieth century, a bureaucratic layer appeared within the labor movement, as described by Lenin, with their own interests. The concept prompted heady debate in the Second International, leading to splits. What João Bernardo defines as "the transformation of unions into capitalist investors," begins in the second half of the twentieth century. Now unions are increasing their revenues by making investments with the funds coming from members' contributions. While this may seem appalling to those interested in emancipation and revolution, the development of pension funds is just another engine for capital accumulation and, furthermore, financial speculation. Unions around the world play dominant roles in these pensions funds, and Brazil is no different.

At this point, union leaders who control the funds and occupy strategic positions in the state apparatus—and through them control many Brazilian multinationals—are part of the ruling class. This is a qualitative change that cannot be overlooked and manifests itself when serious labor conflicts arise, such as those at Jirau and Belo Monte. It is neither chance, nor error, nor a case of co-optation that those same union leaders are working with the state and the corporations to prevent or to destroy strikes.

Thus, May 1st celebrations are generally funded by state and private companies. The two Mayday celebrations in São Paulo in 2011—one held by the CUT and the other by five other unions—were held at a cost of $2.8 million. Petrobras contributed $350,000; Caixa Economica Federal, Banco do Brasil, and Eletrobras contributed between $90,000 and $120,000 each. Private companies also lent a hand: Brahma, Casas Bahia, Carrefour, Pao de Acucar, BMG, and the big banks Bradesco and Itau each contributed between $50,000 and $120,000. The two celebrations featured extravagant shows and raffles for twenty cars.[10]

The point I want to emphasize is that we are facing a new reality, a rupture from the old bureaucratic tendencies of union leaders, to a new scenario for which we have not yet developed the necessary concepts. Sociologist Francisco de Oliveira goes even further, noting that it is "an epistemological revolution for which we do not possess an adequate theoretical tool."[11]

Stagnation and decline of struggle

All social movements pass through long periods of low activity, of defensive struggles and stagnation, with core leaders unable or unwilling to rebuild the capacity to struggle. Under the two Lula governments, this condition has intensified in both the labor and social movements.

If we take the union movement, we see that in 1989 there were nearly 4,000 strikes in Brazil,[12] a high point in a decade of massive labor struggle. In 1992, the number of strikes had fallen to 554, which would remain the average in subsequent years. During the 2000s, that number fell even lower: 420 in 2001, 304 in 2002, 299 in 2005, and 411 in 2008.[13] Note that in the eight years of Lula administrations there were fewer strikes than in 1989 alone.

There have been other notable changes. Força Association, like the CUT, chose to support the Lula and Dilma Rousseff administrations. None of the demonstrations during those years, with the exception of the May 1st celebrations, attracted more than 25,000 workers, and most of the demands were focused on defending economic growth as a means of increasing employment rates and salaries.[14] Since 2003, there have been successive ruptures in the CUT, giving rise to a couple of new unions—Conlutas (National Coordination of Struggles) and Intersindical. In 2011, both labor factions—the government-linked official faction and the opposition or "class" union—held meetings to affirm their positions. Interestingly, the MST, which usually mobilizes with the opposition sectors and the class-union faction, attended the two most important meetings of the official faction (the National Assembly of Social Movements, first held May 31, 2010 in São Paulo, and the Conclat, held on June 1 by CUT, Força Sindical, UGT, CTB, and Nova Central).[15]

Another national union conference, also called Conclat, was convened in Santos by the class-union sector with the support of Conlutas, Intersindical, MTST (Movement of Homeless Workers), MAS (Advanced Movement Union), MTL (Earth, Labor, and Freedom Movement) and the Pastoral Obrera of São Paulo. It was attended by 3,115 delegates, 800 observers and more than a hundred guests from twenty-five countries.[16] The conference failed because the hegemonic parties failed to agree with the PSTU and PSOL on the name of the new union. The PSTU was intransigent about keeping the Conlutas name, leading 35 percent of the delegates and five of the seven organizations to withdraw from the event. Divisions within the class faction and the government's success in keeping the MST as an ally throughout the election campaign of 2010 weakened the opposition social movement and showed the continuing hegemonic clout of Lula and the PT within the organized union bases.

As the OSAL-Brasil team pointed out, "the cycle of antisystemic struggles led by unions since 1978 has lost momentum," partly caused by structural changes in the world of labor, but mostly due to the "hypertrophy of the role of professionalized leaders and an increasing institutionalization of conflicts."[17] For new unions, the greatest challenge is to be and to act differently than the official trade unions. The main problem faced is not so much what political/union line they take, but which sector of the workers they intend to target. If radical and anticapitalist unions prioritize workers with secure and well-paid jobs, especially in government or large companies with consolidated pensions, they would have to manage huge and bureaucratic institutions whose members have no solidarity with other workers. These workers have no intention of changing a world that does not treat them that badly: their aspiration is to be able to consume more.

Nevertheless, a significant portion of Brazilian workers still labor in appalling conditions. We have mentioned the workplace conflicts taking place on huge megaprojects, dams, refineries, and public infrastructure works overseen by the PAC. Similar atrocious working conditions are found in the meatpacking, cattle, and poultry industries. These sectors employ some 800,000 workers, and between 20 and 25 percent of them suffer work-related health problems. Workers are forced to perform at unacceptable levels, especially in the poultry industry, where employees perform seventy to 120 movements per minute when the health advisory recommends not exceeding thirty to thirty-five.[18] The multinational Brasil Foods, supported by generous loans from the BNDES and accounting for 9 percent of global exports of animal protein, confirms that at one of its plants almost 70 percent of workers suffer work-related ailments, 30 percent sleep poorly, and between 12 and 14 percent have considered suicide because of the pressure of work.[19]

Companies claim that they have to accelerate the work pace in order to compete internationally. In interviews about working conditions in meatpacking plants, workers, trade unionists, and specialists have reported an epidemic of accidents and injuries due to the repetitiveness of the work, awkward postures, exposure to cold and moisture, and other problems.

Even before the wave of company mergers and internationalization promoted by the Lula government, long-term meat processing industry workers were prone to ailments like pneumonia and rheumatism. "Today a young man aged 25 to 30 with five or six years work experience is showing signs of acute pain and permanent damage," said a trade unionist.[20] Unlike the isolation of workers who build hydroelectric dams in inhospitable jungle conditions, meat processing workers are based near large cities and form unions, so their problems receive some media attention. Nevertheless, they still have difficulties asserting their rights, to some extent because large Brazilian companies and state unions have investments in these workplaces.

The workers building stadiums and other infrastructural works related to the 2014 World Cup are also among the most negatively affected by the acceleration of economic growth. Although 50 percent of the resources for these projects come from the BNDES, which uses money from the FAT (Fund for Workers), labor laws are routinely violated. Up to November 2011, the Joint National People's World Cup Committees documented ten strikes in twelve stadium projects, almost always demanding higher wages; better safety, health, and food; and denouncing excessive working rhythms. At the Grêmio Stadium site in Porto Alegre, construction workers burned down their living quarters after a deadly work-related accident. This is a pattern of action similar to what we have seen on the construction sites of hydro-electric dams.[21]

Before the strike, workers on the new Cuiabá stadium in Mato Grosso earned just 587 reals (about $325) monthly; at the Belo Horizonte Stadium, the salary was 605 reals; and in Pernambuco even less, just 589 reals a month. The 3,000 workers building the stadium in Fortaleza, Ceara, reported working up to fifteen hours a day (from 7AM to 10PM, seven days a week) because of delays in the Odebrecht project.[22] Military police have intervened several times to prevent workers' assemblies and arrest those who stand out as troublemakers. These are the workers most affected by Brazil's rise to the status of a global power, and it is here that a more militant unionism could take root.

The "have-nots": reconfiguration and change

Those from below, the lowest of the low, workers without a roof over their heads, without land, without a job, without rights, the poorest in Brazil, are the ones who most need to organize themselves for change. This social sector has established one of the most important antisystemic movements in Latin America, the Movement of Landless Rural Workers (MST). Not only is it the most important movement in Brazil, but its powerful political culture has become an essential reference for other movements in Brazil and beyond. The forms of action and organization of the homeless and unemployed movements has also been inspired by the MST.

The retreat of social struggle in Brazil affects all social movements. However, the struggle's general ebb affects the rural peasant movements and the labor movement differently. In the country-side, there is a clear decline in the number of land occupations, camps, and the number of people involved, as well as growing conflicts over previously occupied land, suggesting a direct offensive by the agribusiness industry on squatters. The MST and other similar movements are not as affected by the increased levels of bureaucratization occurring in the labor movement, and do not participate in the bloc that is in power. However, the MST, alongside *favela* inhabitants and poor urban neighborhoods, are the sectors most attacked and criminalized by elites. This is why we cannot really call the situation a "crisis," a concept that we should only apply when the foundations of a movement fade: it is more of a reconfiguration or reorientation.

From a quantitative point of view, the most complete data comes from the Pastoral Land Commission (Comisión Pastoral de la Tierra, CPT), which annually publishes a comprehensive report on land conflicts, including occupations, camps, and murders. Data from the last decade leaves no doubt: The conflicts between landowners and occupiers remain consistent, but the number of new occupations and existing camps has fallen.

Table 11: Land Conflicts 2001–2011

	2001	2002	2003	2004	2005	2006	2007	2008	2009	2010	2011*
Conflicts	366	495	659	752	777	761	615	459	528	349	275
Occupations	194	184	391	496	437	384	364	252	290	180	144
Camps	65	64	285	150	90	67	48	40	36	35	20

Source: Comisión Pastoral de la Tierra
* from January to September

If we include all rural conflicts, including the struggle for land, water and labor, the level of conflict is higher or equal to the average of the decade but the number of families involved is reduced—in land conflicts from 2008 onwards and in conflicts overall from 2010. Indeed, the number of people involved in land occupations reached its peak in 2003 with 1,190,578, and similar levels were maintained until 2005 when the number began declining. In 2009, there were 628,000 people involved in occupations and rural conflicts, in 2010 the figure was 559,000, and in the first nine months of 2011 it fell to 342,000.[23] Throughout the decade the number of land disputes fell by half, and occupations are a third less than in 2004 and 2005, with the actual number of camps falling precipitously.

There are several reasons for the decline. The first is that the large infrastructure works and mega-projects attract poor workers who previously were living in camps or were part of the occupations.[24] The second reason is the slow pace of land reform, which has seen a dramatic decrease in the amount of land recovered during the Lula government, a reality that discourages farmers from occupying and resisting for years on end, while holding out in canvas huts. In Rio Grande do Sul, for example, land decrees for 130,000 hectares were given between 1995 and 2002, compared to only 36,000 hectares between 2003 and 2010.[25] The third reason is related to social policies. MST coordinator Joao Pedro Stedile has said that the *Bolsa Familia* (Family Basket) social program has improved the situation of many families and contributed to keeping them out of the land struggle.[26]

The fourth, and probably key, reason for the decline has to do with structural changes in the countryside. Between 2003 and 2009 inequality declined by 8 percent in rural areas, compared to a figure of 6.5 percent in cities. The average rural income grew by 42 percent and poverty fell from 35 to 20 percent of the rural population.[27] Income transfers from social policies, employment growth, and an increase in the minimum wage explain these changes, which have led to the significant upward mobility of rural families. With these changes, the pressure from below diminished and other demands took center stage, such as the demand for education, health, road improvement, and credit in the form of loans and subsidies for production.

Moreover, the extraordinary advance of agribusiness, fervently supported by the administrations of Lula and Dilma, has led to crisis in the struggle for land reform. The geographer Mançano Bernardo Fernandez argues that the hegemony of agribusiness is causing a crisis among farmers to the degree that 90 percent of all family farmers face serious economic difficulties.[28] In his opinion, the struggle for land is impossible when farmers suffer a marked deterioration in their economic situation and thus seek work in other sectors of the economy. "The camp model, considering the hardship involved for the families, must be reconsidered," says Fernández.[29]

This is a key point, because if the occupations are the main form of struggle, the camps are the first step, and a real education in land struggle, according to movement analysis. In September 2011, there were twenty camps with 2,000 families around Brazil, compared to almost 300 in 2003.[30] It seems the camp model as a first step into the land struggle is not working, so it is true that the tactic should be reconsidered and, with it, the whole process of movement formation. A pattern of social action born more than three decades ago near the end of the dictatorship, with the first occupations in Rio Grande do Sul, was effective for over twenty years: to organize the landless into a movement, to occupy unproductive land en masse, to work the land, and to resist eviction. When police evicted the occupation, the ex-squatters would form a camp on the side of the road nearby and remain in protest. The real organization of the movement took place in the permanent camps, demonstrating how those from below could organize every level of the movement.[31]

The second variant of this problem is, as Porto Gonçalves notes, the need to reconfigure the land struggle into a struggle for territory, the "common home of different peoples and cultures in the world."[32] The current period is characterized by a significant increase in violence employed by landowners as the movement declines and agribusiness makes inroads. A careful analysis of rural violence in 2010 leads to the conclusion that 96 percent of it has involved landowners, business owners, and illegal property owners, all "historical segments of the dominant power in the country"—as well as a new addition: mining companies. The victims of violence are the people who survive by traditional uses of the land, lakes, rivers, swamps, and forests, which is to say Indians, fishermen, hunter gatherers, and river-bank dwellers, including landless settlers who benefited from agrarian reform. A central fact is that, among the 604 rural conflicts of 2010, 57 percent of the victims are "traditional populations" such as those outlined above, and 43 percent are "sectors that traditionally have been central to the struggle for land reform, such as the landless movement and the settlers."[33]

We are witnessing a shift caused by the intensification of capitalism, turning "traditional peoples" into subjects of resistance. This requires rethinking the centrality of the conflict between the monocultural *latifundista* landowners and small farmers with or without land. It is imperative, therefore, to reconsider the centrality of land reform, understood traditionally as land distribution. In this new political context, more important than a piece of land are "the material conditions of reproduction as signs that affirm differences,"or in other words, a space in which other cultures can reproduce their way of life, maintaining and affirming their differences.[34] It means recognizing populations from different ecosystems with other ways of living: from African descendants who lay claim to their *quilombos* (free republics of slave escapees) to rubber tappers, peasant farmers, *sertão* (big desert) communities, coconut and Brazil nut harvesters, and other people of diverse life cultures. Considering such sectors of society as subjects is to go beyond a certain "economist" mode of thinking, which understands people and life as simply "relations of production."

The agrarian reform settlements are suffering a brutal offensive by agribusiness, affecting their production and making it increasingly difficult to survive in the settlements, to the point that many people must seek work elsewhere as "cheap labor in the service of capital."[35] The strength of the commodities production sector is such that it not only causes the expulsion of family farms and traditional communities, but also forces agrarian reform settlers to work as laborers in large-scale soybean and sugarcane monoculture businesses, or on Brazil's grand megaprojects.

In the last months of 2011, a debate began over the future of the landless movement, in the wake of a public letter from MST, MTD, Consulta Popular, and Via Campesina militants.[36]

I will not go into the details of the letter or the various responses, because that is up to each and every social movement and militant to analyze. The letter expressed unease with the direction of social struggles in Brazil and their attitude toward the Lula and Dilma administrations. However, I do not think the bureaucratization and institutionalization of the movements are the underlying reasons for the problems. No doubt these tendencies have gained ground in all our regional movements as they transform into organizations.[37] But I also have no doubt that the vast majority of the poor, the sector that represents the social basis of antisystemic movements, are choosing to improve their lives within market relations and with the support of the state. In other words, whereas earlier those from below were organizing to struggle they are now in the labor market and taking advantage of social welfare. However, despite the poor's current accommodation of the state and market, radicals need not accept this situation without proposing alternatives and continuing to offer resistance.

Francisco de Oliveira, founder of PT, and subsequently the PSOL, and vocal critic of the Lula administration, told an anecdote that explains this reality. In a meeting to support the candidacy of Plinio de Arruda Sampaio, PSOL, in the 2010 elections, an informal survey was conducted among social sectors. The findings showed that the popular sectors did not want to expropriate money from the rich because in their opinion, "we are all in this together," and they support Lula "because they don't want to fight." He concluded his story with a summary of the current dilemmas: "This is the mindset of Lula's government social bases. And this is what the social movements are up against."[38]

Despite these enormous challenges, I still see a will within the MST to persist in struggle and open up new fronts of action. In 2011, at the annual *April Vermelho* (Red April) mobilization, MST militants undertook seventy occupations in ten different states, the third biggest offensive this decade.[39] This indicates the continued capacity for mobilization in the land struggle despite all the difficulties outlined, ensuring that the movement has not abandoned its goals.

Among the million settler families, most of them linked to the occupation movement, the MST organized work projects to strengthen the family agriculture base, and therefore stave off their inclusion into the commodity-production chain of agribusiness. The MST promoted agroecology, against the use of agrichemicals.[40] This is a very ambitious campaign that encourages a different farming culture than the hegemonic, via the political formation of the settlers. The MST must move from a movement for land reform towards a movement of settlers for agrarian reform. Another line of action prioritized by the MST is organizing among the urban poor. Such work began in 1997 with the creation of the Homeless Workers Movement (MTST). However, it has met with enormous and unforeseen difficulties in the form of fierce territorial battles between drug traffickers and leftist political movements not related to MST. In the mid-2000s, the movement decided to focus on building urban communes, the first and most successful being the Hélder Câmara commune in the municipality of Jandira, in the metropolitan region of São Paulo.

The existing class struggle seems fragmented among three conflicts: resistance to megaprojects, the struggle against the expansion of agribusiness in rural areas, and the fight against the frenzied speculation in urban areas caused by the 2014 World Cup and 2016 Olympic Games. No social actor has emerged who matches the capacities of the landless movement, which was able to synthesize the peasant struggle during the era of the military dictatorship with the centuries-old struggle of the rural poor for land. Nevertheless, even in this difficult moment, various forms of resistance continue, even if they are far from reconfiguring a new cycle of struggle like the one that emerged in the late 1970s in Brazilian factories and fields against a military-regime-driven modernization process that excluded whole sectors of society.

Cycles of struggle are not invented nor imposed artificially. They arise spontaneously when the conditions are ripe, unplanned and without a ready-made program. To paraphrase a well-known Chinese proverb—one cannot just throw down seeds and expect the plant to grow. We can only plow the land, hoe the weeds, and add a little water in the hope—never the certainty—that the seed takes. I think that this is the kind of activity that a lot of activists in Brazil and Latin America, and increasingly all around the world, have been occupying themselves with of late.

11
The June 2013 Uprisings: Below and Behind the Mobilizations

The huge mobilizations in June 2013 in 353 cities and towns in Brazil surprised the political system as much as analysts and the media. Nobody expected that there would be so many demonstrations in so many cities for so long. As happens in these cases, analysts were quick to comment. They initially focused on the immediate problems highlighted by the actions—urban transport, rising fare prices, and the poor quality of service for commuters—but slowly began to address the day-to-day dissatisfaction felt by a large part of the population. While there was widespread acknowledgment that basic family income had risen during the last decade of economic growth, commentators began to focus on economic inclusion through consumption as the root of the dissatisfaction, alongside the persistence of social inequality.

In this analysis, I would like to address the new forms of protest, organization, and mobilization from a social movement perspective. These new forms emerged within small activist groups composed mainly of young people that began organizing in 2003, the year Luiz Inácio Lula da Silva took office. Unlike political parties, trade unions, and other traditional organizations formed in the early eighties, the new groups were key to the June mobilizations because of their ability to organize and involve the broadest sectors of society in the struggle, and to employ forms of action and organization that set them apart from their predecessors.

In most cases, commentators have overgeneralized, often giving an almost magical role to "social networks" in mobilizing the millions of people in the street. "With nimble fingers on their cell phones and connected by social networks, youth have taken to the streets all around the world to protest," said former President Luiz Inácio Lula da Silva.[1] "Beyond social media, the people are unorganized," said leading intellectual Luiz Werneck Vianna.[2] Others analysts linked the "Revolution 2.0" to a new middle class and argued that the June struggles in Brazil are continuous with the Arab Spring and the Spanish *indignados* (the outraged).[3]

In this chapter, I assert—in tune with James C. Scott—that we can find the key to what is happening in the public arena in the daily practice of the popular sectors, particularly in what Scott calls "hidden spaces" where the subordinated develop discourses that are antagonistic to power: "The acts of daring and haughtiness that so struck the authorities were perhaps improvised on the public stage, but they had been long and amply prepared in the hidden transcript of folk culture and practice."[4] It is necessary to focus on the continent behind and below the visible coast of the political, says Scott, to understand a new political culture. We can better understand the new forms of protest and organization in Brazil if we look closely at the practices that the small activist groups have forged over the last decade.

To avoid generalizations, I will focus specifically on one of the principle actors in the June protests and one that embodies these new forms of organization and action. The Movimento Passe Livre (Free Fare Movement, MPL) helped to detonate the massive explosion of demonstrations in June. The MPL were responsible for calling the initial demonstrations that were brutally repressed by the police and that, in turn, led to general public outrage. Other key social organizations involved were the Comitês Populares da Copa (Popular Committees for the World Cup), the

Centro de Midia Independente (Indymedia Brazil, CMI), and the Movimento dos Trabalhadores Sem Teto (Homeless Workers Movement, MTST). The hip-hop scene in São Paulo and in peripheral urban settlements also played an important role.

Salvador, Florianópolis, Porto Alegre

Mass protests of tens of thousands of students against the increase of the bus fare from 1.30 to 1.50 reals shook the city of Salvador in the state of Bahia from August 13 to mid-September 2003. More than 40,000 people blocked roads, shut down key intersections, and held their ground against police repression. This wave of protests became known as the *Revolta do Buzu* (bus revolt) and many consider it the birth of the *passe livre* (free fare) movement, which demanded free bus fare for students.

It was a movement of poor and lower-middle-class students who typically spent about 30 percent of their income on transport. The official student associations, which were remote from students' daily lives, played no role in the mobilizations. Instead it was a rapidly radicalizing movement made up of people who had not previously participated in demonstrations. These were young people without political experience but accustomed to challenging authority (sneaking onto buses, hanging around on street corners, listening to *pagode,* and dancing capoeira). They turned their backs on the "leadership" of the student organizations and political parties and were at the forefront of the street blockades erected to resist the police.[5]

The student multitudes rejected the official organizations that claimed to represent them and made decisions in large assemblies, where they distributed common tasks. They held assemblies at the street blockades that spread throughout the city and made decisions by consensus. The assemblies functioned in a strictly horizontal manner, and they rejected a proposal to set up committees, to "prevent the formation of a new student bureaucracy in the streets."[6] The general feeling among the protesters was that institutionalization would lead them to lose what they had won in the streets.

Nevertheless, members of official student organizations pro-claimed themselves representatives of the movement and negoti-ated an agreement with the city of Salvador that helped demobilize the protests without achieving any objectives.[7] Numerous analysts agree that while militants from left-wing parties were responsible for convening the first demonstration in Salvador, they were left aside once the movement expanded exponentially.[8]

In parallel, the Campanha pelo Passe Livre Estudiantil (Stu-dent Free Fare Campaign) was active in Florianópolis from 2000 onwards, although there were also small groups with similar demands in São Paulo and other cities. The Juventude Revolução (Revolutionary Youth) organization, which had links to the Workers Party, began local agitating for free fares among secondary students and organized small demonstrations, leading to a mobilization of 15,000–20,000 students in 2004, in a city of 400,000 inhabitants.[9]

The Workers Party leadership expelled the activist collective responsible for initiating the free fares movement from the Juven-tude Revolução after it asserted its independence from the party by arguing that youth "should not be watched over by an adult organization."[10] Argentine filmmaker Carlos Pronzato's docu-mentary about the Salvador uprising, *Revolta do Buzu*, circulated among activists and inspired emerging groups in Florianópolis and other cities. In May 2004, the Florianópolis municipality once again increased transport fees, which had already grown by 250 percent over the previous ten years. Following ten days of massive demonstrations, and blockades of the bridges linking the island with the mainland of the city during rush hour, protest-ers successfully stopped the fare increase. A campaign of direct action accompanied the mass protests, in which students refused to pay the bus fare, jumping turnstiles or opening the rear doors of buses. Like the demonstrators in Salvador, the students held mass assemblies in public spaces.[11]

We get a sense of the new forms of protest and organization from participants' accounts of the events:

> [Present at the protests were] hundreds of secondary school students, community movements from the

north and south of the island, college students, mothers, fathers, teachers, actors, public functionaries, trade unionists, and other workers. Artists from the hip hop movement, as well as capoeira groups livened up the marches. After a few days, large assemblies occupying the Avenida Paulo Fontes (accessing the Central Terminal, the largest in the city), renamed Uprising Street, had become a fixture. Community leaders, representatives from organized groups, and people without organizational or institutional affiliation participated and spoke at the assemblies. An older lady would speak with indignation about a particular problem, to be followed by a young man putting forward a proposal for action. The foundations for the movement were built right there and then in these large assemblies.[12]

As in Salvador, official student institutions and political parties did not play a prominent role in Florianópolis. The CMI, the Brazilian Indymedia, was vital in covering the demonstrations and providing an outlet for protesters' demands and discourse. When groups in several cities decided to set up a national organization, the CMI was crucial in the coordination of the groups, leading to the first Free Fare Movement gathering during the 2005 World Social Forum in Porto Alegre, without the support of any political party.[13]

On the morning of January 29, defying the suffocating heat beneath the white marquee tents of the *Intergalactika Caracol* youth camp within the World Social Forum, dozens of young people began to form into a circle convened by the Florianópolis MPL and the CMI. In all, about 250 activists from sixteen different delegations from twenty states participated. The meeting started in the morning, continued throughout the afternoon, and concluded with the passage of important resolutions calling for the formation of a national movement. The young activists, ranging from fifteen to twenty-five years of age, took turns talking, as almost everyone paid close attention and took notes. A few wore *Passe Livre* t-shirts and some wore the traditional red shirts of the *Sem Terra*.

Reflecting on that first meeting, participants emphasized the importance of the gathering, particularly its autonomous character: "We were aware that it didn't occur because some large organization called for it, but rather as an expression of a specific need of the movement—the need for a national body to coordinate the various struggles that had been taking place without any organization or defined group behind them."[14] Activists realized from the beginning that the movement had the potential to go beyond student demands. Transportation is central to the reproduction of labor power and capital accumulation, and represents the first stage of the sale of labor power. The MPL activists recognized that their demands would impact "the owners of the means of production and the circulation of commodities."[15]

With the formation of the federal Free Fare Movement, its National Plenary approved a document proclaiming itself "autonomous, independent and nonpartisan but not anti-partisan," defining its strategic goal as "the transformation of the current conception of urban public transport, rejecting the commercial conception of transport and beginning the struggle for free and decent public transport for all of society, beyond the control of the private sector."[16] The movement's practice of direct action, horizontalism, and anticapitalism is outlined in later documents.

According to Marcelo Pomar, the student movement opted for a consensus process, rejecting bureaucratic entities and parties, with resolutions "eventually agreed upon in the National Plenary." Despite the enormous challenges inherent in consensus-based decision-making processes, the activists felt that it was the most appropriate mode of organization "given that these were the first steps in the construction of a movement."[17]

A new political culture

In this dynamic manner, the MPL was formed and it had a presence in most major Brazilian cities for the next couple of years. However, like most social movements in Brazil, the organization entered into a period of retreat midway through the decade, before returning in strength by the end of the decade.

But to really understand a movement, one needs to look beyond the demonstrations and public statements, and go deeper into its inner world. How do activists relate to one another? How do they carry out meetings and gatherings? Basically, we need to explore the culture of the movement to understand its way of seeing the world. With this in mind, I will follow the evolution of the Free Fare Movement through its major events and campaigns and explore what was happening within the movement; in other words, I will focus on the face-to-face relationships in the movement's daily life.

Following its founding, the Free Fare Movement organized several days of actions and held the Second National Meeting in July 2005 in Campinas. During this three-day meeting, two small radical left parties, Revolucionário Operário (Revolutionary Worker) and Construção Socialism (Constructing Towards Socialism) made attempts to reverse the decisions made in Porto Alegre about horizontalism and autonomy. Many of those present saw this as an attempt to co-opt the incipient movement and, in response, reaffirmed the commitment to horizontality and autonomy: "a federation of groups constitutes the movement." Although it has a national-level working group, it has no coordinating body, which activists believed would introduce a hierarchical structure into the movement.[18]

On October 26, the Free Fare Movement convened a day of action commemorating the adoption of free fare for students in Florianópolis, a date that became known as the Free Fare National Day of Struggle. They organized events in thirteen cities, including three demonstrations in São Paulo, and launched a national newspaper distributed in ten cities. The demonstrations ranged from 100–500 people and in some cities demonstrators burned turnstiles.[19] The following year, the Second National Meeting was held on July 28–30 at the MST Florestan Fernandes National School in São Paulo. It was an important gathering that helped to consolidate the movement and marked a big step forward in strategy to demand free fare for the entire population, not just students.

Participating in the gathering, where they devised a federal structure based on the principles of horizontality, autonomy, independence, and decision making by consensus, were 160 activists from thirteen collectives. They set up working groups focused on media, organization, and legal support as well as a study group on transportation issues. Among the attendees was the engineer Lúcio Gregori, who, from 1990 to 1992 in São Paulo, had served as the Transportation Secretary in the municipal administration of the then-militant Workers Party leader Luiza Erundina. Gregori held the view that transport should be a public service and therefore free. He argued that once a fare is charged, a mechanism is established to divide those who can use it and those who cannot, and therefore, the imposition of a fare represents the privatization of something that is common to all—public transport. He pointed out that just as health and education are free public services, so too the costs of transportation should be borne by those who benefit from the service: "the ruling class that needs public transport for employees to get to the workplace."[20]

The movement went through some major changes around this time. Although the MPL had managed to set up an independent federal structure and set the tone of debate on transport issues in society, there was an ebb in the struggle, grassroots groups were generally weak, and some activists felt defeated because they had not won their main demand. The movement's active core initiated a change in the strategy: instead of demanding free fares for students, they would demand free fares for all.

The MPL group in Brasilia (population 2.5 million) had between forty and eighty members. After 2006, and a seven year period without fare increases, that number fell to between eight and twenty activists. They engaged in three types of activities: "direct actions; raising awareness of public transport and urban mobility issues, with a focus on class, race and gender; and lobbying the government for free fares."[21] Highly dedicated young students made up these small activists groups and they took their activities very seriously. They held a month-long activist training camp in 2001, which was suggestive of the intensity of their efforts.[22]

During the formation of the Free Fare Movement in 2005, the activists drew up a list of the cities' secondary schools and held dozens of carefully prepared workshops.[23] The day-to-day work of each group involved weekly or biweekly plenary meetings, various specialized work groups, and small, stable study groups, with almost daily contact among the core activists. Some of the principle actions of the Free Fare Movement were street performances, using music, dance, and theater, that involved long hours of preparation.

Autonomous activism requires a greater level of dedication than most members of political parties recognize. Furthermore, everything must be done without any institutional support, so activists rely on collective effort and creativity. Strong bonds of trust and solidarity emerge in these collective groups, to the extent that some activist groups could be considered living communities. Activists often share a house or live within the same neighborhood and frequent the same social spaces, and this level of co-existence is a powerful cohesive force that blurs the line between friendship and militancy, creating a climate of fraternity that is reaffirmed at regional or federal gatherings. Needless to say, this militant lifestyle goes together with an ethic that does not separate words and deeds, the personal and the collective, or decision makers and activists. It is a way of doing things that is counter to the hegemonic political culture, including the left parties.

During the period of retreat in 2006, "the movement entered into a complex and often tense process of reflection, trying to understand where it had 'failed' in the fight against fares."[24] For example, people within the São Paulo Free Fare Movement felt that failing to curb increases in 2006 and the lack of ideas on how to continue the struggle had a significant internal impact: "Activists felt cheated, exhausted, and several left; the movement entered a long period of restructuring."[25] This period extended into 2010, although it varied from region to region.

The adoption of the zero-fare strategy was just the first policy shift. The movement also attempted to broaden its popular base and affirmed its commitment to anticapitalism. When it gave up the "Free Fare" slogan, it embraced a demand that would appeal to the entire population, not just students. By drawing on technical advice from militants such as the engineer Lúcio Gregori and forming study groups, the Free Fare Movement deepened its knowledge of urban transport and developed a spacial and racial understanding of the political consequences of urban segregation. The movement began to situate itself in a long history of powerful struggles and revolts against fare increases from 1974 to 1981 in Rio de Janeiro, São Paulo, the Baixada Flauminense, and the satellite cities of Brasilia and Salvador.[26] All of this allowed the Free Fare Movement to become a point of reference in debates on transport and the "right to the city," which is a premise of the zero-fare demand.

The MPL's second shift in strategy to broaden its social base had even deeper implications as it related to the class character of the movement and how the oppressed *feel* oppression. In Brasilia, "from 2007 to 2008, the MPL increased work in secondary schools and neighborhoods on the peripheries," explains the activist Paíque Duques Lima.[27] In São Paulo, the MPL "saw the need to diversify their campaign fronts, beginning work in some communities, especially in the south zone," which is the poorest part of the city.[28] However, the population that they encountered when they began working in the urban peripheries was already organized by community associations, political parties, and NGOs, who were resisting evictions caused by real estate speculation in anticipation of the 2014 World Cup. These areas were also dealing with local drug issues as well. As Paíque Duques from Brasilia noted, "the MPL followed in the steps of the Comitês Populares de la Copa (Popular Committees of the World Cup)," which at this point "had begun to gain political leverage within entire neighborhood struggles."[29]

Their work in the poor communities on the periphery changed the profile of the movement. If organizing in the São Paulo peripheries lent greater political legitimacy to the Free Fare Movement, in Brasilia it changed the movement's racial and class composition. If the initial founders were predominantly young, white people from the middle and lower-middle classes, after 2008, there was an influx of "youths from cities around Brasilia" (Guara, Taguatinga, São Sebastião, Ceilandia, and Samambaia) as well as poor families and black people.[30] These were people who had been unable to find "their" place in formal institutions, whether it was a leftist party, a union, or a student's group.

From this perspective, the movement positions its identity against a set of oppressions: class, gender, race, and—not explicitly—age. In effect, the movement stands against all forms of oppression, and through its practice seeks to avoid the traditional division of labor by gender and skin color. The Free Fare Movement's composition reflects its commitment to the poor, people of color, women, and those without access to transport and thus, access to the city. People of color (black, brown, and mestizo) began joining the movement, recognizing that the Free Fare Movement embodied a struggle against discrimination and also, according to Paíque Duques Lima, that core black activists in the MPL participated in the antiracist movement.

When Brazilian urban social movements began their resurgence in 2010, the MPL had already established itself as a national organization in the major cities, with fluid links to other social movements and a voice in the public debate on transport and urban reform. It had thousands of trained, experienced activists who, in five years of activism, had organized hundreds of street actions (from flyering to demonstrations of 10,000 people), occupations of public buildings, occupations of bus terminals, and road blockades, as well as organizing their own communications media that reached hundreds of thousands of Brazilians. Although still a relatively small movement, it was by no means marginal, as evidenced by the participation of well-known personalities such as the former mayor of São Paulo, Luiza Erundina, during the Zero Fare campaign launch in 2011. So for instance, in Brasilia there were 200–300 people heavily involved, and the constant coming and going of people helped the movement's political culture spread to other sectors of society.

As protest activities transcended the boundaries of the movement, they were taken up by other similar groups and movements.

Paíque Duques reflects that "the formation of MPL forged a culture of political action that developed beyond its specific set of issues," because its organizational experience influenced activists working on issues beyond public transport.[31] This new culture of struggle and organization took place far from institutionalized groups or parties, in relatively autonomous social spaces; spaces where hidden discourses flourish and dissident cultures are forged, as James C. Scott notes. By analyzing the relationship between social space and hidden discourse, Scott emphasizes the breakdown of the border between theory and practice, which is evident in groups such as the Free Fare Movement: "Similar to popular culture, hidden discourse does not exist as pure thought; it exists only insofar as it is practiced, articulated, expressed and disseminated within marginal social spaces."[32]

However, the Free Fare Movement is more than just an expression of an alternative youth culture or the cultures found in poor neighborhoods. It is "an organization with principles and strategic perspectives," as was made clear during the second gathering held in July 2005 in Campinas.[33] According to Duques, it is a "grouping of anticapitalists with efficient mechanisms of resistance to domination and bureaucratic or market co-optation."[34] Various cultures come together in the melting pot of the organization, from hip hop and popular culture to Brazil's leading organization of resistance, the *Movimento dos Trabalhadores Sem Terra* (Rural Landless Movement). The Zapatistas and other antiglobalization movements also inspire the MPL. It appears that no one culture is hegemonic within the MPL.

The movement's politics emerge from within, and they are the fruit of the long debates and hands-on experience at the forefront of the revolts in Salvador and Florianópolis. Leo Vinicius, an activist and writer in the Florianópolis Free Fare Movement, explains how leadership works in the movement during times of upheaval:

> When I talk of *leadership,* I don't mean command and obedience or manipulating the masses. I'm talking about a group that thinks, plans, discusses, and studies

the social issues surrounding the popular revolt and the day-to-day questions of the uprising in order to meet the needs of the movement.… The best and most relevant leadership in these cases is the one that understands how to foster autonomous practices created and produced by the social mobilization.[35]

They are grassroots groups made up of activist-intellectuals who are able to organize and work with popular sectors and also identify projects and strategies that promote social change from below. Their characteristics allow us to say that a new political culture emerged in Brazil in the first decade of the century: a new organizational and activist culture embedded in small and medium-sized groups that became publicly visible during the mass protests in June 2013.

The Pan American Games as rehearsal

"People have the illusion that they will profit from the World Cup events, but the truth is that they will be brutally suppressed," said Roberto Morales, deputy adviser to Marcelo Freixo of the Socialism and Liberty Party (PSOL), a year and a half before the Confederations Cup.[36] Morales participates in the Comitê Popular da Copa (World Cup Popular Committee) that emerged during the Pan American Games in Rio de Janeiro in 2007, when locals resisted the forced relocations that made way for games' facilities.

The experience of the Pan American Games was instrumental in convincing the activists of the coming disaster. In the ensuing years, the city has hosted or will host four mega-sporting events that will lead to long-term changes in the urban fabric, affecting mainly poor residents: the 2011 World Military Games, the 2013 Confederations Cup, the 2014 World Cup, and the 2016 Olympic Games.

For activists with the World Cup Popular Committee, the Pan American Games were a watershed that revealed the Brazilian government's inability to manage public funds in a democratic, transparent manner or to create space for effective dialogue with civil society on the legacy of the Games.[37] For the social movement, the games provided an opportunity to create a broad and stable organization that could bring people together, overcoming localism and fragmentation.

At this time, urban movements in Rio were riven by division, as were student and land reform movements.[38] According to the investigation of Marques, De Moura, and Lopes, demonstrations and street actions against the Pan American Games began in 2006, and focused on the forced evictions caused by the construction of sports infrastructure. Between April 2006 and October 2007, there were as many as forty-five demonstrations protesting the Games in Rio held in July.[39]

During the first stage, from April 2006 to April 2007, neighborhood groups resisting eviction organized the demonstrations. They had the support of professional associations (geographers, in particular), municipal council people, the MST, the association of Rio *favelas*, and the Order of Lawyers of Brazil. They organized street actions, meetings, and seminars to highlight how these publicly funded mega-events benefited the private sector and hurt the poor. Three months before the Games, 5,000 activists participated in "The City—A Right For Everyone" conference in São Paulo, an event that was cosponsored by the MST, the Intersindical and Conlutas trade unions, as well as the PSOL and other left parties.[40]

On May 1, 2007, more than forty organizations convened a rally in a *favela* threatened with eviction, a coalition led by local social and political organizations and joined by social groups from across the city. The coordinating committee organized numerous demonstrations throughout the year and decided to hold an event on the opening day of the Games, July 13. More than a hundred activists from a coordination of sixty groups organized the protest on the opening day of the Games. Defying the climate of fear of protest in the city, 1,500 protesters attended. Inside the Maracaná Stadium, Lula was booed by protesters to such an extent that he was unable to finish his address.[41]

The coordinating committee of social movements continued organizing resistance to *favela* home demolitions caused by the Pan American Games and many consider it a key element in creating the network of social movements that came together in the lead-up to the June uprising.[42]

The two main organizing groups—the Popular Committee on the World Cup and Olympics, and the National Popular Committees for the World Cup—built on the experience of the Pan American Games and formed groups in each of the twelve cities chosen to host the 2014 World Cup matches. In its report, *Mega-Events and Human Rights Violations in Brazil,* the World Cup Popular Committee claims that a total of 170,000 people will be affected by the construction works, and outlines the numerous problems accompanying the mega-events, from the violation of housing rights to labor issues, as well as the lack of environmental impact studies.

In twenty-one *villas* (townships) and *favelas* in seven cities hosting the World Cup, says the report, the state is implementing "strategies of war and persecution, including marking out houses with paint without explanation, the invasion of homes without court orders, and misappropriation and destruction of property."[43] All those affected live in low-income areas with varying degrees of precariousness and working in the informal economy. "The lack of information and prior notification creates a climate of instability and fear about the future," says the report, which paralyzes affected families and puts them at the mercy of the authorities or speculators.[44]

The Popular Committees, like the Free Fare Movement, devoted a lot of energy to research, followed by widespread dissemination of their findings. Their report concludes that only a handful of construction companies—those benefiting from the privatization of the stadiums—carry out the huge public-work programs for the mega-events. In addition to benefiting from the construction contracts, the small group of companies also take long-term control of the privatized facilities constructed with public funds. The sheer scale of the infrastructure construction (highways, airports, stadiums, and transport) leads the authors of the report to come to the same conclusion as the Free Fare Movement: citizens' right to the city is being violated.

Researching and publishing such reports is one dimension of the Popular Committees activity; the other is organizing mobilizations and working with affected communities. In March 2010, the political climate changed when the Urban Social Forum took place in Rio, consolidating the coalition of movements against mega-events. In 2011, the Popular Committees organized thirteen public activities in Rio alone, involving mobilizations, public forums, seminars, demonstrations of support for affected communities, and a protest march outside of the 2014 World Cup qualifiers.[45]

One can see the change in the political climate in the electoral landscape in Rio de Janeiro. PSOL activist Marcelo Freixo was elected to the state congress in 2006 with 13,500 votes. He became president of the Human Rights Commission of the Rio parliament and chaired committees investigating militias and arms trafficking in the city. On the basis of his campaigning against corruption and mafias, his grassroots support grew and Freixo won reelection in 2010 with 177,000 votes. In the 2012 municipal elections, he ran for mayor without any major financial backing and very little television time, relying instead on grassroots support, young people's social networks, popular artists like Caetano Veloso and Chico Buarque, and personalities like Frei Betto. He chose Marcelo Yuka as candidate for vice-mayor, a former rap musician who was shot in a robbery, which rendered him a paraplegic. Despite heavy rains, 15,000 attended his campaign finale, despite heavy rains. Caetano Veloso said he had not participated in a political event since Lula's campaign for president in 1989. "I'm here as a resident and voter of Rio de Janeiro to simply say what a joy and honor it is to vote for a candidate like Marcelo Freixo, who represents dignity in Brazilian politics." Freixo didn't win, but obtained more than 900,000 votes, 28 percent of the electorate.[46]

Construction work on stadiums for the 2014 World Cup—some unveiled during the 2013 Confederations Cup—remains the most controversial public issue, even among athletes. Much of the criticism focuses on the refurbishment of the legendary Maracaná Stadium, which is a symbol of the country's great soccer prowess. Renovations took three years, longer than its initial construction, and cost more than $600 million, double the cost of South Africa's Soccer City Stadium where the 2010 World Cup final was held. A business consortium in which Odebrecht, Brazil's biggest construction company, holds 90 percent of the shares, has leased the Maracaná Stadium for thirty-five years. This consortium is also a major donor to political parties, particularly the governing Worker's Party.[47]

However, even more than the cost of the construction, the soccer-mad public is angry about feeling excluded from the national sport. More than 203,000 spectators—8.5 percent of the population of Rio de Janeiro—attended the 1950 World Cup final in the newly opened Maracaná Stadium. Working-class people made up 80 percent of the total attendance in the "general" and "popular" standing-room-only sections. After several remodels, the stadium's current capacity is 75,000, less than 1 percent of the population of the city. The gentrification of the sport is visible in the reconstruction of Maracaná to suit the requirements of FIFA (Fédération Internationale de Football Association, soccer's international governing body). The once rowdy, packed and disorderly bleachers have been replaced with sterile rows of seats where crowd participation is limited to choreographed "waves" and the orderly fluttering of mini-flags. The refurbishment aims to create a "multi-purpose arena" to host concerts and shows with segregated corporate boxes equipped with private bars, television screens, and air conditioning, which elites access directly by car via a private ramp, thereby avoiding any contact with the "multitude."[48]

The tickets are far more expensive than previous World Cups: Categories 1, 2, and 3 in terms of the best seating views are priced at $203, $192, and $112, compared to $126, $75, and $57 in the 2006 World Cup in Germany and $160, $120, and $80 in South Africa in 2010. Only category 4 tickets are cheaper than in Germany ($25 versus $45) but more expensive than in the last World Cup.[49] In addition, facilities built for the 2007 Pan American Games such as the velodrome and Aquatic Park were demolished because they failed to conform with the World Cycling and Aquatic Federation's requirements, at the cost of $50 million for public expenditure.

In 2011, Atletas pela Cidadania (Athletes for Citizens) formed as a platform for promoting a public debate around the sports and social impact of the mega-events. Sixty top athletes supported the effort, including popular soccer players like Kaka, Dunga, Dani Alves, and Cafu. During the 2012 municipal election campaign, Atletas pela Cidandania petitioned mayoral candidates in eleven cities to make a commitment to supporting public use of the event facilities. Shortly before the large demonstrations that marked the Confederations Cup in April, fifty-seven top athletes from varied sports signed a petition against the demolition of the Maracaná complex, which includes swimming pools, running tracks, a municipal school, and an Indian Museum, to make way for parking lots and shopping centers. The petition read: "Sporting [in Brazil] is now in a sad state. There is long-term planning and evaluation for construction and infrastructure investments, but none for the development of sport."[50]

Reflecting the opinion of many Brazilians regarding the myriad construction works for the World Cup, the Popular Committees noted: "The historical stadiums are being destroyed to be rebuilt as consumption and tourism centers like shopping malls. Tickets to national and state championships are too expensive and out of reach for the 'traditional' fan."[51]

Debating the character of the June mobilizations

Considering the trajectory of the new urban movements, the massive demonstrations in June 2013 came as no surprise. The scale and duration of the protests, as well as the radicalism of many of the protesters, is striking, but not the general outrage against the increase in transport costs and deep anger at the Confederations Cup setup.

Taking into account this brief overview of the Free Fare Movement and the Popular Committees, I want to challenge some common falsehoods about the June demonstrations. My hope is to contribute to a debate about today's popular struggles. I have attempted to approach the events from the perspective of the people themselves, rather than that of the government or political parties. While the perspective of the government and parties is always relevant, when millions take to the streets it seems ethically inappropriate to frame their decisions as response to external stimuli. That would be a rather colonial way of thinking. As Ranahit Guha, founder of the school of postcolonial studies stated, "the farmer knew what he was doing when he revolted."[52]

It was not a spontaneous act, but the massive expansion of existing movements. Every fare increase since 2003 has been met with demonstrations, rallies, street blockades, the destruction of turnstiles, the disruption of bus service, and the occupations of transport terminals. There were even significant uprisings against fare increases in Salvador in 2003 and Florianópolis in 2004 and 2005. The Free Fare Movement has been organizing street protests for over eight years, legitimizing struggle and establishing a tradition of mobilization against the fare increases that make Brazil's transport costs the highest in the world.[53] This has established an equation in the mind of the public in large cities: *fare increase = protest.*

While the media has mostly focused on transport issues as the catalyst for the June protests, one aspect has received scant coverage. The Popular Committees have succeeded in changing the public perception of the impact of the infrastructural works for mega-events; there is widespread understanding that cities are being redesigned for the speculative market and for the benefit of a few. In addition to raising consciousness, the Committees have mobilized a sizable sector of the affected population and expanded their base of operations, similar to the MPL. "The Popular Committees started to have an impact in neighborhoods resisting evictions," points out MPL activist Duques Lima.[54] Six months before the June demonstrations, activists from the Popular Committees were actively organizing with the inhabitants of the Vila Autódromo and Morro da Providencia neighborhoods in Rio de Janeiro, where they resisted the demolition of buildings and stood firm against eviction orders.[55]

Between March 2011 and May 2013, the Committees held seventy-eight events in Rio de Janeiro alone, including fifteen street demonstrations. They organized a campaign to preserve the Maracaná Stadium with the slogan "O Maraca é nosso!" ("The Maraca is Ours!"). Popular artists like Chico Buarque, who sported the slogan on his shirt at media events, supported the effort. Four demonstrations were held in front of the Maracaná, including two marches to the stadium and a protest on the day that it reopened.[56]

In truth, the most astonishing feature of the June demonstrations was the sheer number of people doing more or less exactly what the activists had been doing for years. Firstly, there was a popular overflow from below and, secondly, mass feelings of solidarity and outrage against police repression. These things were not entirely spontaneous. Following Gramsci, Guha argues that there is no place for pure spontaneity in history, and framing popular revolts as acts of mere spontaneity is elitist to the extreme. It implies that mobilization from below is "completely dependent on the intervention of charismatic leaders, advanced political organizations, or the upper classes."[57] Likewise, those who argue that social networks played a prominent role in mobilizing the masses provide another example of this kind of elitist analysis, which is detached from reality.

This is an anticapitalist struggle. FIFA is one of the largest multinationals in the world, controlled by a cabal of corrupt businessmen. Its power is such that it can dictate policy to countries, demanding the introduction of special legislation, privileges, and tax exemptions in the sale of FIFA products. It even has the power to force governments to stop local companies from selling unauthorized products. Brazil adopted the controversial World Cup General Law on June 5, 2012 after years of debate. Nevertheless, the Federal Public Prosecutor requested that the Supreme Court intervene, charging that several of its articles are unconstitutional.[58] The protest marches at the Confederations Cup matches in June are a direct and explicit challenge to the World Cup General Law that the government and FIFA negotiated.

The anticapitalist character of the June protests and the movements propelling them is evident in their resistance to capitalist accumulation around mega-events and mega-projects, which we could describe as "urban extractivism." The Zero Fare campaign is a response to urban extractivism, promoting access to social rights such as health, education, and culture, and "the right to be able to move around the city itself, and, from that, to meet up, to reflect, and to produce the tools to transform it."[59]

Another member of the Free Fare Movement, Marcelo Pomar, argues for the de-commodification of public transport—transforming it into a basic public service—the costs of which should be borne by those who benefit from the flow of goods and people. "Public transportation costs are a sophisticated mechanism of social control," argues Pomar, that allow the dominant class to enclose the popular sectors in urban slums.[60]

The effort to break this control mechanism is inherently anti-capitalist. The MPL argues that the Zero Fare Campaign is a struggle for all and changes everything; it is a means to subvert the transport system and, thus, the whole structure of the city. Spatial, social, racial, and gender segregation restrict urban mobility to the point that, to give one example, people living in Brasilia's satellite towns and working in the city's planned city center feel like prisoners in the suburbs. As night falls, "a kind of curfew takes hold in the city, affecting those who depend on public transport."[61]

The huge construction works for the World Cup and the Olympics are creating a similar dynamic of exclusion in other cities. For instance, Rio's poor are being shifted to the northern and western peripheries while the city center is being converted into a space for tourism and business. The construction of the Puerto Maravilla dock to accommodate cruise ships is an example; it will allow tourists to visit the Morro da Providencia by cable car in order to avoid the surrounding *favela*. Construction during sporting mega-events provides authorities with an opportunity to implement plans for new city centers and to demarcate "sacrifice zones" in centrally located, poor neighborhoods wherein they plan to move the inhabitants to the peripheries, another sacrifice to the new plans.

The fight against property speculation is an anticapitalist struggle. The best way to understand rebellions of the poor and marginalized is to recognize that they are conscious of who they are, where they fit in the system, and what they themselves can do to change it.

This is an urban movement demanding the right to the city. Rural movements have been the backbone of popular movements in Brazil since the colonial period, but now centers of resistance are concentrating in the cities. The struggle for urban reform carried out by the main social movements (Free Fare, MTST, the World Cup Committees, CMI, etc.) has many similarities with the rural struggle for land reform. The *latifundista* (large farms) system and agribusiness are to the countryside what spatial segregation and real estate speculation are to the city.

Two aspects should be highlighted. Firstly, these are new kinds of movements, formed when the Workers Party (PT) came to power, and therefore they confront a new configuration of state power. This new form of state power is an alliance between PT leadership and the Brazilian bourgeoisie, who enjoy not only excellent relations but also the same national project and global perspective. Secondly, a group of high-ranking trade unionists have entered the financial sector through management of pension funds and control of the BNDES, the largest development bank in the world.[62]

Governments have changed how they deal with protest and social movements. Recent struggles in Brazil, from resistance to the Belo Monte hydroelectric dam to the campaign for free transport and against mega-events, now confront a different form of governance. With the apparent decline in the level of poverty in Brazil today, a less obvious form of inequality remains that cannot be measured quantitatively. Spatial, racial, class, gender, and generational segregations are not seen as part of overall, systemic patterns of oppression. Sometimes massive rebellions are necessary to break the everyday routines that hide oppression.

Brazil's new configuration of power uses disproportional force against the social movements. On June 24, the Special Police Operations Battalion (BOPE) entered the Complexo da Maré *favelas*— the most heavily populated *favela* in the city—with guns blazing. Nine people were killed, including one policeman. Trade unions called a demonstration two weeks later and yet failed to include the Maré slaughter or police brutality in their long list of demands. As journalist Eliane Brum points out: "Brazil will not change while the middle class feels more for the wounded of São Paulo than the dead of da Maré" and notes that police use rubber bullets to injure in the city center but live ammunition to kill in the *favelas*.[63]

A new political culture. When a new political culture emerges it needs to differentiate itself from the hegemonic culture that went before it. In this case, it seems clear that the modes of struggle and organization created toward the end of the dictatorship, when the CUT trade union and the Workers Party were formed, no longer correspond to the needs of current antisystemic struggles. We recall that the riots of 2003 and 2004, and the founding principles of the MPL in 2005, flatly rejected the traditional bureaucratic culture and instead emphasized horizontalism, which is to say, collective leadership, consensus to avoid the consolidation of majorities, and autonomy from the state and political parties.

Thus far, the social organizations shaped by this political culture have kept their distance from the mainstream labor movement but collaborate with the more militant trade union factions, as well as progressive organizations. Many of the new urban groups are inspired by Brazil's main radical organization, the Rural Landless Movement (MST, known as Sem Terra), respecting their deep experience and adapting some of Sem Terra's forms of struggle to the urban environment. The main difference between these two political cultures is found in their form of organizing: the Sem Terra's top-down structure in contrast with the urban movement's horizontalism.

Nevertheless, the MST and the new urban movements could coalesce in coming years if they can work together on concrete projects, as has already happened in some cases. This would be a huge step forward for political and social struggles in Brazil and would offer a positive example for other social movements around the continent. An alliance between Brazil's two main emancipatory movements—rural and urban—would most likely lead to a qualitative leap in Latin America's antisystemic struggles.

Notes

Introduction

1 Giovanni Arrighi and Beverly Silver, *Caos y orden en el sistema-mundo moderno* (Madrid: Akal, 2001).

2 Giovanni Arrighi, *Adam Smith en Pekín* (Madrid: Akal, 2007).

3 Ibid., 375–381.

4 Territorio Indígena y Parque Nacional Isiboro Sécure.

5 "Brasil quer acelerar usinas em vizinhos para garantir energia," *Folha de São Paulo*, February 14, 2012.

6 "Múltis brasileiras trazem US$21 bilhões das filiais," *Valor*, February 6, 2012.

Chapter 1

1 "Embajador brasileño muestra su tristeza por la quema de la bandera de su país," *La Nación*, Asunción, 16 May, 2008, accessed 10/20/2011, www.lanacion.com.py/articulo.php?archivo=1&edicion=1&sec=1&art=186859.

2 "Protesta en contra de Hidroeléctrica de Inambari terminó sin resultados," *Los Andes*, Juliaca, December 14, 2009, accessed 10/20/2011, www.losandes.com.pe/Regional/20091214/30921.html. *Ronderos* or *rondas campesinas* are community organizations through which the indigenous and farmers defend themselves against rustlers, criminals, or whatever outside danger threatens the community.

3 "La región Puno protesta contra hidroeléctrica del Inambari," *Los Andes*, Juliaca, March 5, 2010, accessed 10/20/2011, http://www. losandes.com.pe/Politica/20100305/33711.html.

4 Ministerio de Energía y Minas de Perú, "Acuerdo para el suministro de electricidad al Perú y exportación de excedentes al Brasil," Lima, June 16, 2010.

5 "Mayor parte de energía irá a territorio brasileño," *La Primera*, Lima, May 29, 2010; and "El espejismo de la integración energética," César Campodónico, *La República*, Lima, June 19, 2010.

6 "Disminuye la popularidad de Evo Morales," *Infobae*, September 29, 2011, accessed 10/21/2011, http://america.infobae.com/ notas/34601-Disminuye-la-popularidad-de-Evo-Morales.

7 Ruy Mauro Marini, "La acumulación capitalista mundial y el subimperialismo," *Cuadernos Políticos* 12, México, ERA, April–June, 1977.

8 Mathias Seibel Luce, *O subimperialismo brasileiro revisitado: a política de integraçâo regional do governo Lula (2003–2007)* (Porto Alegre: Universidad Federal de Rio Grande do Sul, 2007); Fabio Bueno and Raphael Seabra, "El capitalismo brasileño en el siglo XXI: un ensayo de interpretación," May 25, 2010, accessed 10/21/2011, http://www. rosa-blindada.info/?p=351; Pedro Henrique Pedreira Campos, *O imperialismo brasileiro nos sécalos XX e XXI: uma discusâo teórica*, presented at the XXI Annual Conference of the International Association for Critical Realism, Niterói, Universidad Federal Fluminense, July 23–25, 2009; and Virginia Fontes, *O Brasil e o capital-imperialismo* (Rio de Janeiro, EPSJV, UFRJ, 2010). Other articles in which the concept appears include Carlos Tautz, "Imperialismo brasileiro," May 11, 2005 in www.asc-hsa.org/files/Imperialismo_Brasileiro.pdf; and Andrés Mora Ramírez, "¿Subimperio o potencia alternativa del sur?" September 14, 2009, accessed 10/21/2011, http://alainet.org/ active/33011.

9 Ruy Mauro Marini, "La acumulación capitalista mundial y el subimperialismo," 67.

10 Ruy Mauro Marini, *Subdesarrollo y revolución* (Mexico: Siglo XXI, 1974), 26.

11 Ibid., 191.

12 Ibid., 192.

13 Ibid., 60.

14 Ibid., 37.

15 Ibid., 54.

16 Ibid., 193–194.

17 Ruy Mauro Marini, "La acumulación capitalista mundial y el subimperialismo."

18 Ruy Mauro Marini, *Subdesarrollo y revolución*, 76.

19 Ibid., 17.

20 Golbery do Couto e Silva, *Geopolítica del Brasil* (México: El Cid Editor, 1978), 8–9.

21 Ibid., 56–57.

22 Ibid., 60.

23 Ruy Mauro Marini, *Subdesarrollo y revolución*, 74.

24 Paulo Schilling, *¿Irá Brasil a la guerra?* (Montevideo: Fundación de Cultura Universitaria, 1973), 74.

25 Ibid., 4.

26 Ibid., 80.

27 James Dunkerley, *Rebelión en las venas. La lucha política en Bolivia 1952–1982* (La Paz: Quipus, 1987), 170.

28 Ibid., 171.

29 Marcelo Quiroga Santa Cruz, *Oleocracia o patria*, México, Siglo XXI, 1982.

30 Paulo Schilling, *¿Irá Brasil a la guerra?*, 86.

31 James Dunkerley, *Rebelión en las venas*, 177.

32 Marco Aurelio García, "O lugar do Brasil no mundo," in Emir Saderand Marco Aurelio García, *Brasil entre o pasado e o futuro* (São Paulo: Boitempo, 2010), 163.

33 Juan Antonio Pozzo Moreno, "Breve reseña histórica de las relaciones paraguayo brasileñas," *ABC*, Asunción, June 28, 2008.

34 Paulo Schilling, "Itaipu: energía y geopolítica," 1978, accessed 10/20/2011, http://www.manuelugarte.org/modulos/biblioteca/s/shilling_expansionismo_brasilenio/expansionismo_brasilenio_parte3.htm.

35 Ibid.

36 Juracy Magalhaes, *Minhas Memórias Provisorias* (Rio de Janeiro: Ed. Civilização Brasileira, 1982), 201–203, cited by Pozzo Moreno.

37 Paulo Schilling, "Itaipu: energía y geopolítica."

38 Ibid.

39 Golbery do Couto e Silva, cited by Paulo Schilling, *¿Irá Brasil a la guerra?*, 16.

40 Ruy Mauro Marini "Dialética da dependência," in Roberta Traspadini and João Pedro Stédile, *Ruy Mauro Marini: Vida e obra* (São Paulo: Expressão Popular, 2005), 138.

41 Ibid.

42 Ruy Mauro Marini, "La acumulación capitalista mundial y el subimperialismo," 1.

43 Ibid., 3.

44 Ibid., 8.

45 Ibid.

46 Ibid., 10.

47 Ibid., 17.

48 Ruy Mauro Marini, *Subdesarrollo y revolución*, 57–58.

49 Ibid., 61.

50 Ibid., 71.

51 Ibid., 78.

Chapter 2

1 Departamento Intersindical de Assesoria Parlamentar, *Boletim do DIAP*, No. 242, Brasilia, October, 2010.

2 "Construtoras ajudam a eleger 54 percent dos novos congresistas," *Folha de São Paulo*, November 7, 2010.

3 Ibid.

4 Instituto Ethos and Transparency Internacional, *A Responsabilidade Social das Empresas no Processo Eleitoral, Edição 2010*, São Paulo, 2010, 30.

5 Ibid., 32.

6 From *Boletim do DIAP*.

7 In CMI Brasil, June 11, 2005, www.midiaindependente.org/pt/blue/2005/06/319720.shtml.

8 *Mensalão* (*mensal* - monthly) in reference to the monthly payments received by dozens of MPs based on a scheme put together by leaders of the PT and the federal government.

9 The FAT is a fund administered by the Ministry of Labor to fund unemployment insurance and social development programs based on employer and workers contributions.

10 Francisco de Oliveira, *Crítica à razão dualista o Ornitorrinco* (São Paulo: Boitempo, 2003), 146.

11 Armando Boito Jr., "A hegemonia neoliberal no governo Lula," *Crítica Marxista* 17, Rio de Janeiro, Editora Revan, 2003.

12 Ibid.

13 The ABC is the industrial region of São Paulo metropolitan area, whose name derives from the initials of the cities that make up the core of the region—Santo André, São Bernardo do Campo and São Caetano do Sul.

14 Armando Boito Jr., "A hegemonia neoliberal no governo Lula," 17.

15 Fabiana Scoleso, "Sindicatos dos metalúrgicos do ABC: as novas relações entre capital e trabalho na década de 1990," presentation at *III Simposio de Lutas Sociais na América Latina*, GEPAL, Paraná, Universidad Estadual de Londrina, September 24–26, 2008.

16 Marcelo Badaró Mattos, "A CUT hoje e os dilemas da adesão à ordem," *Outubro* 9, São Paulo, Instituto de Estudios Socialistas, 2003.

17 *Pelego*, referring to the skin taken from a sheep in the language of the Rio de la Plata. In Brazil, the term "pelego" was first popularized during the government of Getúlio Vargas in the 1930s. Imitating the Labor Charter of Benito Mussolini, Vargas decreed the Unionization Act in 1931, subjecting union constitutions to the Ministry of Labor. A union leader close to the government and with ties to the state was called a "pelego." Under the military dictatorship that began in 1964, a military-backed unionist was also a "pelego."

18 Armando Boito Jr., "A hegemonia neoliberal no governo Lula," 9.

19 Ibid., 12.

20 Marcelo Badaró Mattos, "A CUT hoje: os dilemas de adesão à ordem."

21 Ibid.

22 Ibid.

23 Ibid.

24 Rudá Ricci, "A CUT vai caminhando para ser a antiga CGT do século XXI," Instituto Humanitas Unisinos, September 2, 2008, accessed 12/15/13, http://www.ihu.unisinos.br/entrevistas/16373-a-cut-vai-caminhando-para-ser-a-antiga-cgt-do-seculo-xxi-entrevista-especial-com-ruda-ricci.

25 Armando Boito, Andréia Galvão, and Paula Marcelino, "Brasil: o movimiento sindical e popular na década de 2000," *OSAL*, Buenos Aires, *Clacso* 26, October, 2009, 39.

26 The first position in Armando Boito et al. The second in Andréia Galvão, "O movimento sindical frente ao governo Lula," *Outubro* 14, São Paulo, Instituto de Estudios Socialistas, 2006.

27 Armando Boito, Andréia Galvão, and Paula Marcelino, "Brasil: o movimiento sindical e popular na década de 2000," 37.

28 Celina Souza, "Sistema brasileño de gobierno local," in Catia Lubambo, Denilson Bandeira, and André Melo (eds.) *Diseño institucional y participación política: experiencias en el Brasil contemporáneo* (Buenos Aires: FLACSO, 2006), 146.

29 Andréia Galvão, "O movimento sindical frente ao governo Lula," 144. Unlike Fuerza Sindical, the CUT gets no dividends, but negotiates loans with lower interest rates that can attract more affiliates.

30 Ibid.

31 Armando Boito; Andréia Galvão, and Paula Marcelino, "Brasil: o movimiento sindical e popular na década de 2000," 48.

32 Maria Celina D'Araujo Soares, *A elite dirigente do governo Lula* (Rio de Janeiro: Fundação Getúlio Vargas, 2009), 9.

33 Ibid., 15.

34 Ibid., 32–37.

35 Ibid., 42.

36 Ibid., 78.

37 Ibid., 117–125.

38 Machado dos Santos, Vivian "Por dentro do FAT," *BNDES magazine* 26, Rio de Janeiro, December, 2006, 3–14.

39 Francisco de Oliveira, *Crítica à razão dualista. O ornitorrinco*, 146.

40 "Evolução do desembolso do BNDES," BNDES, accessed 12/25/13, http://www.bndes.gov.br/siteBNDES/bndes/bndes_pt/Institucional /Relacao_Com_Investidores/Desempenho/#desembolso2010.

41 "As finanças do BNDES: Evolução recente en tendencias," *Revista do BNDES* 31, Rio de Janeiro, June, 2009, 4.

42 Ibid., 37.

43 "Datos de Pensions & Investments," www.pionline.com.

44 Maria Chaves Jardim, "Entre a solidariedad e o risco: Sindicatos e fundos de pensão em tempos de governo Lula," Doctoral Thesis, Universidad Federal de São Carlos, Programa de Pos-Graduación in Ciencias Sociales, 2007, 60.

45 Ibid., 73.

46 "Fundos de pensão tem desafío de mudar cultura do brasileiro de nao poupar," *Folha de São Paulo*, November 17, 2010.

47 Carlos de Paula, "O Cenário da Previdência Complementar Hoje en na Próxima Década," 31st Congreso Brasileiro dos Fundos de Pensão, Previc (Superintendencia Nacional de Previdencia Complementar, Olinda, November 18, 2010.

48 Ibid.

49 La Fundación Getúlio Vargas (FGV) classifies the population by family income: Class A and B more than 4,891 reals a month in 2010, Class C between 1,064 and 4,591 reals, Class D between 768 and 1,064, and Class E less than 768 reals per family. The minimum wage in 2010 was 510 reals or $300 a month ($1 is approximately 1.70 reals).

50 *PREVI magazine* 53, Rio de Janeiro, PREVI, August 2010.

51 Ibid.

52 *PREVI magazine* 51, Rio de Janeiro, PREVI, June 2010.

53 D'Araujo, Maria Celina, *A elite dirigente do governo Lula*, 74–76.

54 Ibid., 76.

55 "PT e PMDB querem manter domino em fundo de pensão," *Jornal DCI*, accessed 5/29/13, http://www.prevhab.com.br/stPublicacoes. aspx?secao=0&item=587.

56 Ibid.

57 *Veja* magazine, March 4, 2009.

58 "Estudo mostra que governo é sócio de 119 empresas," *Agencia Estado*, December 2, 2010, accessed 10/20/11, http://economia. estadao.com.br/noticias/economia+geral,estudo-mostra-que-governo -e-socio-de-119-empresas,45860,0.htm (accessed 20/10/2011).

59 "Fundo de pensão Previ acumulou, em 10 anos, rentabilidade de 553,35 percent," *Valor*, May 19, 2010.

60 *Diario do Grande ABC*, November 30, 2010.

61 "Fundo de pensão da Petrobras vira sócio da controladora de Itaú," *Folha de São Paulo*, November 26, 2010.

62 "O PT e os fundos de pensão," *Piauí* magazine 35, August, 2009.

63 Maria Chaves Jardim, "Entre a solidariedad e o risco: Sindicatos e fundos de pensão em tempos de governo Lula," 172–173.

64 Ibid., 171–172.

65 Ibid., 173.

66 Ibid., 189.

67 Ibid., 192.

68 Ibid., 237.

69 "Dirigentes eleitos de fundos de pensão apoiam Lula," *Associação Nacional dos Participantes de Fundos de Pensão*, http://www.anapar. com.br/boletins/boletim_66.htm.

70 Maria Chaves Jardim, "Entre a solidariedad e o risco: Sindicatos e fundos de pensão em tempos de governo Lula," 248–249.

71 Ibid., 252–254. All data on the funds of the elite come from the same work, 254–260.

72 "O PT e os fundos de pensão," *Piauí magazine* 35, August 2009.

73 Ibid., 266.

74 Sindicato dos Bancarios: http://www.spbancarios.com.br/profission-alcursos.asp?c=9.

75 Maria Chaves Jardim, "Entre a solidariedad e o risco: Sindicatos e fundos de pensão em tempos de governo Lula," 265.

76 "Programa do Governo do PT 2002," cited in Maria Chaves Jardim, 75.

77 *Valor Económico*, May 29, 2003, cited in Maria Chaves Jardim, 163.

78 "Seminario Internacional sobre Fundos de Pensão," accessed 03/14/11, http://www.anapar.com.br/boletins.php?id=113.

79 Adacir Reis, intervention in the I Seminario Internacional sobre Fundos de Pensão, accessed 03/14/11, http://www.ancep.org.br/imprensa/materias/semin_inter.htm#6.

80 Oded Grajew, intervention in the I Seminario Internacional sobre Fundos de Pensão, accessed 03/14/11, http://www.ancep.org.br/imprensa/materias/semin_inter.htm#6.

81 Interview with Oded Grajew, *GV Executivo*, São Paulo, Fundación Getúlio Vargas, São Paulo, 4/1, February/April, 2005, accessed 06/09/12, http://rae.fgv.br/gv-executivo/vol4-num1-2005/oded-grajew.

82 Ibid.

83 Maria Chaves Jardim, "Domesticação e/ou Moralização do Capitalismo no Governo Lula: Inclusão Social Via Mercado e Via Fundos de Pensão," *Dados* 1, Rio de Janeiro, 2009, 123.

84 Ibid., 150.

85 Ibid., 152.

86 Francisco de Oliveira, *Crítica a razão dualista. O ornitorrinco*, 147–148.

87 Ibid., 148.

88 Ibid., 147.

89 Francisco de Oliveira, "O momento Lenin," *Novos Estudos* 75, São Paulo, Cebrap, July 2006, 23–47.

90 Ibid., 40–41

91 Maria Chaves Jardim, "Entre a solidariedad e o risco: Sindicatos e fundos de pensão em tempos de governo Lula," 223.

92 Ibid., 214–215.

93 Ibid., 217.

94 Severino Cabral, *Brasil megaestado*, Rio de Janeiro, Contraponto, 2004, 30.

95 Ibid., 129.

96 Ibid., 49.

Chapter 3:

1 Gabinete de Segurança Institucional, "Anais do VII Encontro

Nacional de Estudos Estratégicos," Brasilia, 2008, 372.

2 Núcleo de Assuntos Estratégicos, "Projeto Brasil 3 Tempos," *Cadernos NAE*, No. 1, Presidencia de la República, July, 2004, Brasilia.

3 Ibid., 87.

4 Alberto Moniz Bandeira, *Presencia de Estados Unidos en Brasil* (Buenos Aires: Corregidor, 2010).

5 Ibid., 431 and ff.

6 Núcleo de Assuntos Estratégicos, *Cadernos NAE* 1, 88.

7 Alberto Moniz Bandeira, *Presencia de Estados Unidos en Brasil*, 453.

8 Ibid., 501.

9 More details about the participation of the United States in the 1964 coup in Moniz Bandeira, 501–533.

10 Núcleo de Assuntos Estratégicos, *Cadernos NAE* 1, 92.

11 Ibid., 93.

12 Ibid., 94.

13 Created as Oficina de Pesquisa (Investigation) its name was changed to IPEA in 1967.

14 Núcleo de Assuntos Estratégicos, *Cadernos NAE* 1.

15 Ibid., 97.

16 Ibid., 103.

17 Ibid., 104.

18 Ibid., 112.

19 "Cenário Diadorim. Esboço de um Cenário Desejável para o Brasil. Projeto Brasil 2020," *Parcerias Estratégicas* 6, Brasilia, Secretaria de Assuntos Estratégicos, March 1999, 35.

20 Núcleo de Assuntos Estratégicos, *Cadernos NAE* 1, 5.

21 Núcleo de Assuntos Estratégicos, "Agenda para o futuro do Brasil," *Caderno NAE* 8, Brasilia, May 2007, 5.

22 Leyes 11.204 of December 5, 2005 and 11.754 of July 23, 2008, respectively.

23 Núcleo de Assuntos Estratégicos, *Cadernos NAE*, 1, 42, and 51.

24 Núcleo de Assuntos Estratégicos, *Cadernos NAE*, 8, 55.

25 Ibid.

26 Ibid., 16.

27 *Los Cuadernos del NAE* were, through 2010, dedicated to biotechnology, climate change, political reform, prospective scenarios, the future of Brazil, digital inclusion, the fuel matrix, macroeconomic modeling, and nanotechnology. In terms of lecture series, the most common were social development, foreign policy, culture, education, institutional security, mines and energy, science and technology, health, agricultural development, sports, ports, planning, social security, racial equality, and social communication.

28 Secretaria de Assuntos Estratégicos, *Brasil 2022*, Brasilia, 2010, 5.

29 Ibid., 15.

30 Ibid., 18–19.

31 Ibid., 16.

32 Ibid., 26.

33 Ibid., 40.

34 Ibid., 53.

35 Ibid., 58.

36 Secretaria de Assuntos Estratégicos, *Brasil 2022*, "Relações Exteriores. Importância estratégica," accessed 01/10/12, http://www.sae.gov.br/brasil2022/?p=52.

37 Tratado Constitutivo de la Unión de Naciones Suramericanas," http://www.comunidadandina.org/unasur/tratado_constitutivo.htm.

38 Translator's note: *Itamaraty* refers to the Brazilian Ministry of External Relationships.

39 "Unasur enfoca sus políticas de Defensa en propuesta de fabricación de aviones," *EFE*, Lima, November 11, 2011, accessed 01/11/12, http://www.abc.es/agencias/noticia.asp?noticia=997234.

40 "Declaración conjunta de Puricelli y Amorim," Ministerio de Defensa de la República Argentina, September 5, 2011, accessed 01/11/12, http://www.mindef.gov.ar/prensa/comunicados.php?notId=1969.

41 "Brasil e Argentina discutem produção de blindados leves," *Valor*, September 6, 2011.

42 *El Mundo*, Madrid, May 17, 2010.

43 *Caros Amigos* 51, São Paulo, June 2001.

44 Samuel Pinheiro Guimarães, *Desafios brasileiros na era dos gigantes* (Rio de Janeiro: Contraponto, 2006), 259.

45 Ibid., 263.

46 Ibid., emphasis in the original.

47 Samuel Pinheiro Guimarães, *Quinhentos anos de periferia* (Rio de Janeiro: Contraponto, 1999), 90.

48 Samuel Pinheiro Guimarães, *Desafios brasileiros na era dos gigantes*, 265–266.

49 Ibid., 268.

50 Ibid., 270.

51 Ibid., 276.

52 Ibid., 425–426.

53 Ibid., 306.

54 Ibid., 320.

55 Samuel Pinheiro Guimarães, "Mudanza de clima e energía nuclear," *Valor*, June 11, 2010, accessed 06/20/10, http://www.sae.gov.br/site/?p=3663.

56 Ibid.

57 Samuel Pinheiro Guimarães, "A América do Sul em 2022," *Carta Maior*, July 26, 2010, accessed 06/10/11, http://www.cartamaior.com.br/templates/materiaMostrar.cfm?materia_id=16822.

58 Ibid.

59 Roberto Mangabeira Unger, "Pôr fim ao governo Lula," *Folha de São Paulo*, November 15, 2005, 2.

60 Richard Rorty, "Unger, Castoriadis and the Romance of a National Future," in Robin W. Lovin and Michael J. Perry (eds.), *Critique and Construction: A Symposium on Roberto Unger's Politics* (New York: Cambridge University Press, 1987), 30.

61 As well as Rorty's text, one can consult Perry Anderson, "Roberto Unger y las políticas de transferencia de poder," in *Campos de batalla* (Bogotá: Tercer Mundo Editores, 1995), 209–236; Geoffrey Hawthorn, "Practical Reason and Social Democracy: Reflections on Unger's Passion and Politics," in Robin W. Lovin and Michael J.

Perry (eds.), *Critique and Construction*, 90–114.

62 Boitempo Editorial (São Paulo) has published seven of Mangabeira Unger's books to date: www.boitempo.com.

63 Geoffrey Hawthorn, "Practical Reason and Social Democracy," 90.

64 Perry Anderson, "Roberto Unger y las políticas de transferencia de poder," 228.

65 All these initiatives form part of Mangabeira Unger's letter to President Lula, in which he resigns as a minister. See "Carta programática ao Presidente (digitada)," June 29, 2009, http://www.law.harvard. edu/faculty/unger/portuguese/propostas.php.

66 Ibid., 1.

67 Ibid., 2.

68 Ibid., 7.

69 Roberto Mangabeira Unger, "Uma visão de longo prazo para o Brasil," discourse during the VII Encuentro Nacional de Estudios Estratégicos, in Gabinete de Seguridad Institucional, "Anais VII Encontro Nacional de Estudos Estratégicos," Brasilia, Presidencia de la República, November 6–8, 2007, Vol. 2, 2008, 467.

70 Ibid., 472.

71 Ibid., 473.

72 Ibid., 477.

73 Ibid., 487.

74 *Istoé magazine*, "O general de Mercadante," January 20, 2003, accessed 03/27/11, http://www.terra.com.br/istoegente/181/reportagens /oswaldo_muniz.htm.

75 Presented in 2001 as a conclusion in "Política, Estrategia y Alta Administración," *Revista Eletrónica Brasiliano & Asociados* 28, São Paulo, Brasiliano & Asociados, March 2007, accessed 03/31/11, http://www.brasiliano.com.br/revistas_anteriores.php?PHPSESSID =68e832a68fa6162c568e1b8a4b09d4de.

76 "Brasilia propone una OTAN sudamericana," *Agencia Periodística del Mercosur*, November 16, 2006, accessed 03/31/11, http://lists.econ.utah. edu/pipermail/reconquista-popular/2006-November/044587.html.

77 Ibid.

78 "Diferencial do Brasil está no agronegócio," *Carta Maior*, July 3,

2006, accessed 03/31/11, http://www.cartamaior.com.br/templates/materiaMostrar.cfm?materia_id=11588.

79 Ibid.

80 Acronym for European Aeronautic Defence and Space Company (EADS), a European corporation created in 2000 by the merger of Aeroespacial MATRA in France, CASA of Spain, and Germany's Daimler Chrysler. Fabricates Airbus commercial aircraft, military aircraft, missiles, and rockets.

81 "A volta da Engesa: O Brasil que produz armas de guerra," *Revista Istoé*, August 19, 2007, accessed 03/21/11, http://www.istoe.com.br/reportagens/16703_A+VOLTA+DA+ENGESA.

82 "EADS Defence & Security e Organização Odebrecht unem forças no Brasil para estabelecer uma parceria de longo prazo," accessed 03/21/11, http://www.odebrecht.com.br/sala-imprensa/press-releases?id=14268.

83 "Odebrecht cria empresa de gestão na área de Defesa," September 17, 2010, accessed 03/31/11, http://economia.ig.com.br/empresas/industria/odebrecht+cria+empresa+de+gestao+na+area+de+defesa/n1237778550208.html.

84 "Odebrecht adquire controle da fabricante de mísseis Mectron," *Folha de São Paulo*, March 25, 2011, accessed 04/02/11, http://www1.folha.uol.com.br/mercado/893738-odebrecht-adquire-controle-da-fabricante-de-misseis-mectron.shtml.

85 "Odebrecht cria empresa de gestão na área de Defesa."

86 *Foreign Policy*, October 7, 2009, accessed 01/10/12, http://rothkopf.foreignpolicy.com/posts/2009/10/07/the_world_s_best_foreign_minister.

Chapter 4

1 *Diario da Manhá*, Goiania, 10 February, 2003, accessed 04/03/11, http://www.achanoticias.com.br/noticia.kmf?noticia=2809013.

2 Mario Augusto Jakobskind, "Aprendiendo de Vietnam," in *Brecha*, Montevideo, February 18, 2005; and *Observatorio da Imprensa*, January 25, 2005, accessed 04/03/11, http://www.observatoriodaimprensa.com.br/artigos.asp?cod=313JDB003.

3 Câmara dos Deputados, Departamento de Taquigrafia, "Depoimento do Comandante Militar da Amazônia General Cláudio Barbosa de Figueiredo," Comissâo de Relaçôes Exteriores e Defesa Nacional,

Brasilia, October 2, 2003, 32.

4 Paulo Roberto Corrêa Assis, "Estrategia da resistencia na defesa da Amazonia," Núcleo de Estudos Estratégicos Mathias de Alburquerque (NEEMA), Amazonia II, Rio de Janeiro, Tauari, 2003.

5 João Roberto Martins Filho, "As Forças Armadas Brasileiras no pós Guerra Fria." Fortaleza, *Revista Tensões Mundiais* 3, 2006, 78–89.

6 Luiz Alberto Moniz Bandeira, *As relações perigosas: Brasil-Estados Unidos (De Collor a Lula, 1990–2004)* (Rio de Janeiro: Civilização Brasileira, 2010), 271.

7 Ibid., 272–274.

8 João Roberto Martins Filho, "As Forças Armadas brasileiras e o Plano Colómbia," in Celso Castro (ed.) *Amazônia e Defesa Nacional* (Rio de Janeiro: Fundação Getúlio Vargas, 2006), 13–30.

9 Juan Gabriel Tokatlian, "La proyección militar de Estados Unidos en la región," *Le Monde Diplomatique*, Buenos Aires, December, 2004.

10 Ibid., 276.

11 "Os militares, o governo neoliberal e o pé americano na Amazonia," *Reportagem*, October 18, 2000, accessed 04/30/11, http://www. oficinainforma.com.br/includes/imprimir_pv.php?id=493.

12 Humberto Trezzi, "EUA já têm 20 guarnições na América do Sul," *Zero Hora*, Porto Alegre, March 25, 2001, accessed 01/02/11, www. oocities.org/toamazon/toaguarnicao.html.

13 Raúl Zibechi, "El nuevo militarismo en América del Sur," Programa de las Américas, May, 2005, in http://alainet.org/active/8346.

14 Ministerio de Defesa, "Estratégia Nacional de Defesa," Brasilia, 2008, 1.

15 Ibid., 2.

16 Ibid., 5.

17 Ibid., 6.

18 Samuel Pinheiro Guimarães, *Desafios brasileiros na era dos gigantes* (Rio de Janeiro: Contraponto, 2006), 353.

19 Ministerio de Defesa, "Estratégia Nacional de Defesa," 7.

20 Ibid., 16.

21 This is an armed confrontation in which there is a great disparity between the forces, and thus they are forced to go beyond the traditional military strategy.

22 Ministerio de Defesa, "Estratégia Nacional de Defesa," 18.

23 Ibid., 22.

24 "Nova cartada do Exército brasileiro," *Zero Hora*, Porto Alegre, April 18, 2010, accessed 01/02/11, http://planobrasil.com/2010/04/18/nova-cartada-do-exercito-brasileiro/.

25 "Brasil planeja frota nuclear," *O Estado de São Paulo*, November 21, 2010, accessed 01/02/11, http://www.estadao.com.br/noticias/impresso,brasil-planeja-frota-nuclear,643152,0.htm.

26 "Produção de helicópteros coloca Brasil entre gigantes mundiais," in *Defesanet*, April 13, 2011, accessed 04/19/11, http://www.defesanet.com.br/aviacao/noticia/596/Producao-de-helicopteros-coloca-Brasil-entre-gigantes-mundiais.

27 This is a long-range helicopter, powerful and fast, capable of carrying twenty-nine soldiers with all their equipment, and two pilots.

28 "Brasil ganha espaço nos planos da Eurocopter," *Valor*, April 12, 2011, accessed 01/02/11, http://www.investe.sp.gov.br/noticias/lenoticia.php?id=14881.

29 Ibid.

30 "Senado aprova reestruturação das Forças Armadas," *O Estado de São Paulo*, August 4, 2010, accessed 01/02/11, http://www.estadao.com.br/noticias/nacional,senado-aprova-reestruturacao-das-forcas-armadas,590449,0.htm.

31 That is the argument of the Brazilian Navy, accessed 02/28/11, https://www.mar.mil.br/menu_v/amazonia_azul/amazonia_azul.htm.

32 *Marinha em Revista*, Brazil Navy, December 2010, 6–10.

33 "Militares expandem simulação de ataque ao pré-sal," in *O Globo*, July 13, 2010, accessed 04/28/11, http://oglobo.globo.com/pais/mat/2010/07/13/militares-expandem-simulacao-de-ataque-ao-pre-sal-917139348.asp.

34 http://www.defesabr.com/blog/index.php/14/07/2010/militares-expandem-simulacao-de-ataque-ao-pre-sal/ (accessed 04/28/11).

35 "Strategic Concept. For the Defense and Security of The Members of the North Atlantic Treaty. Organisation," accessed 04/28/11, www.nato.int/lisbon2010/strategic-concept-2010-eng.pdf.

36 Pepe Escobar, "Bienvenidos a OTANstán," in *Rebelión*, November

21, 2010 accessed 01/02/11, http://www.rebelion.org/noticia. php?id=117083.

37 "Importante Jobim lança o Mare Brasilis," *Defesanet*, accessed 11/30/10, http://www.defesanet.com.br/dn/17SET10.htm.

38 Ibid.

39 "Ministro da Defesa ataca estratégia militar de EUA e Otan para o Atlântico Sul," *Folha de São Paulo*, November 4, 2010, accessed 04/28/11, http://www1.folha.uol.com.br/mundo/825261-ministro -da-defesa-ataca-estrategia-militar-de-eua-e-otan-para-o-atlantico-sul. shtml.

40 Ibid.

41 "Brasil planeja frota nuclear," *O Estado de São Paulo*.

42 Ministerio de Defesa, "Estrategia Nacional de Defesa," 28.

43 Ibid., 27.

44 "Lula amplía 45 percent gasto com defesa em 5 anos," *O Estado de São Paulo*, 25 April, 2010, accessed 01/02/11, http://www.estadao. com.br/noticias/impresso,lula-amplia-45-gasto-com-defesa-em-5- anos,542748,0.htm.

45 "Brasil debe fazer investimento militar para ter voz," *Folha de São Paulo*, April 8, 2011.

46 Rodrigo Fracalossi de Moraes, "Ascensão e queda das exportações brasileiras de equipamentos militares," *Boletim de Economia e Política Internacional* 3, Brasilia, IPEA, July, 2010, 60.

47 Ibid., 64.

48 Renato Dagnino, *A Indústria de Defesa no Governo Lula*.

49 Ibid., 80–81.

50 Ibid., 18, 51–52.

51 "O fim de uma batalha aérea," *Veja*, September 9, 2009, accessed 04/19/11, http://veja.abril.com.br/090909/fim-batalha-aerea-p-100.shtml.

52 Portal *IG*, September 17, 2010, accessed 04/22/11, http://economia .ig.com.br/empresas/industria/odebrecht+cria+empresa+de +gestao+na+area+de+defesa/n1237778550208.html.

53 "Odebrecht adquire controle da fabricante de mísseis Mectron," *Folha de São Paulo*, March 26, 2011.

54 Portal *IG*, September 17, 2010.

55 *Embraer S. A.,* December 10, 2010, accessed 04/22/11, http://www. embraer.com/pt-BR/ImprensaEventos/Press-releases/noticias/Pagi- nas/EMBRAER-CRIA-UNIDADE-EMPRESARIAL-DEDICADA -AO-MERCADO-DE.aspx.

56 *Embraer S. A.,* March 15, 2011, accessed 04/22/11, http://www. embraer.com/pt-BR/ImprensaEventos/Press-releases/noticias /Paginas/ORBISAT.aspx.

57 "Embraer compra 50 percent da Atech, empresa de tecnologia de defesa," *Folha de São Paulo*, April 12, 2011.

58 "O cargueiro militar tático," accessed 04/23/11, http://www.defesabr. com/Fab/fab_embraer_kc-390.htm; and *Exame magazine*, April 22, 2010. The KC-390 travels at 800 km per hour (the Hercules at 610), it costs $50 million (instead of $80 millon), and weighs 23.6 tons, instead of the 20 tons of the Hercules.

59 "Volta às armas. Reaparelhamento das Forças Armadas," *Istoé*, April 21, 2011; and *Defesanet* 14 April 2011, accessed 04/23/11, in http:// www.defesanet.com.br/laad2011/noticia/611/EMBRAER-Defe- sa-e-Seguranca-e-FAdeA-Assinam-Contrato -de-Parceria-para-o-Programa-KC-390.

60 "Exército Brasileiro e Iveco assinam contrato de produção da viatura blindade de transporte de pessoal," *Iveco*, accessed 04/22/11, http:// web.iveco.com/brasil/sala-de-imprensa/Release/Pages/01_Exercito BrasileiroeIveco.aspx.

61 "Em recuperação, Avibras poderá ser vendida ou ter a União como sócia," *Valor*, April 19, 2011, accessed 01/02/11, http://www.defe- sanet.com.br/defesa/noticia/657/Em-recuperacao—Avibras-podera- ser-vendida-ou-ter-a-Uniao-como-socia.

62 Ibid.

63 "A promisora KMW," *Defesanet*, 18 April, 2011 accessed 04/24/11, http://www.defesanet.com.br/laad2011/noticia/631/A-Promisora -KMW-.

64 Ibid.

65 *Valor*, April 18, 2011.

66 "Industria de Defesa: Novos tempos," *Revista da Indústria*, No. 163, in *Defesanet*, September 2, 2010, accessed 04/24/11, http://www. defesanet.com.br/com_def/RI_163.htm.

67 Ministerio de Defesa, "Estrategia Nacional de Defesa," 49.

68 "Avanza el proyecto nuclear de Brasil," *La Nación*, Buenos Aires, September 9, 2009, accessed 04/24/11, http://www.lanacion.com. ar/1172321-avanza-el-proyecto-nuclear-de-brasil.

69 Pedro Silva Barros and Antonio Philipe de Moura Pereira, "O Programa Nuclear Brasileiro," *Boletim de Economia e Política Internacional* 1, Brasilia, IPEA, July 2010, 71.

70 Odair Dias Gonçalves, "O Programa Nuclear Brasileiro: Passado, Presente e Futuro," *Anais VII Encontro Nacional de Estudos Estratégicos*, Brasilia, Gabinete de Segurança Institucional, Vol. 3, 2008, 85.

71 Luiz Alberto Moniz Bandeira, *Presencia de Estados Unidos en Brasil.*

72 Ibid., 408–409.

73 Ibid., 412.

74 "O Brasil quer a bomba atómica," interview with José Goldemberg, *Epoca*, June 25, 2010, accessed 04/26/11, http://revistaepoca.globo. com/Revista/Epoca/0,,EMI150601-15518,00.html.

75 Luiz Alberto Moniz Bandeira, *As relações perigosas,* 144.

76 Odair Dias Gonçalves, "O Programa Nuclear Brasileiro," 88.

77 Luiz Alberto Moniz Bandeira, *As relações perigosas,* 144.

78 Odair Dias Gonçalves, "O Programa Nuclear Brasileiro," 89.

79 Speech by Fernando Enrique Cardoso upon signing the TNP, June 20, 1997, cited by Moniz Bandeira, *As relações perigosas,* 148.

80 Odair Dias Gonçalves, "O Programa Nuclear Brasileiro," 89.

81 Ibid., 90.

82 Ibid., 93.

83 "Brasil quer autosuficiência na produção de urânio até 2014," November 26, 2009, *Defensanet*, accessed 04/27/11, http://pbrasil.wordpress. com/2009/11/26/brasil-quer-autosuficiencia-na-producao-de-uranio -ate-2014/.

84 Ibid.

85 "Reator de submarino nuclear fica pronto em 2014 e será modelo para usinas," *Agencia Brasil*, May 23, 2010, *Portalnaval*, accessed 04/27/11, http://www.portalnaval.com.br/noticia/30289/reator-de-submarino-nuclear-fica-pronto-em-2014-e-sera-modelo-para-usinas.

86 "Brasil negocia venda de urânio enriquecido," *O Estado de São Paulo*, February 7, 2011, accessed 01/02/11, http://economia.estadao.com.br/noticias/economia percent20brasil,brasil-negocia-venda-de-uranio-enriquecido,53914,0.htm.

87 "José Alencar defende que Brasil tenha bomba atômica," *O Estado de São Paulo*, September 24, 2009, accessed 04/26/11, http://www.estadao.com.br/noticias/nacional,jose-alencar-defende-que-brasil-tenha-bomba-atomica,440556,0.htm.

88 Hans Rühle, "Is Brazil Developing the Bomb?," *Der Spiegel*, July 5, 2010, accessed 04/26/11, http://www.spiegel.de/international/world/0,1518,693336,00.html.

89 Ibid.

90 "Brasil pode estar construindo bomba atômica, conjectura pesquisador alemão," interview with Hans Rühle, *Deutsche Welle*, Brasilia, May 11, 2011, accessed 04/27/11, http://www.dw-world.de/dw/article/0,,5564374,00.html.

Chapter 5

1 "Empréstimos do BNDES crescem 23 percent em 2010 e chegam a R$ 168 bi," *Folha de São Paulo*, January 24, 2011.

2 Ibid.

3 Francisco de Oliveira en "A reorganização do capitalismo brasileiro," *IHU Online*, November 11, 2009, accessed 02/12/11, http://www.ihu.unisinos.br/noticias/27407-conjuntura-da-semana-especial-a-reorganizacao-do-capitalismo-brasileiro.

4 Marcio Pochman, "Estado brasileiro e ativo e criativo," interview with Patricia Fachin, *Revista IHU* 322, São Leopoldo, Universidade do Vale do Rio dos Sinos, March 22, 2010, 16.

5 Ibid.

6 *Exame*, May 12, 2009.

7 "Relatorio Anual 2009," *Previ*, 16, accessed 12/19/10, www.previ.com.br.

8 "Em 18 meses BNDES gasta R$ 5 bi para criar gigantes," *Folha de São Paulo*, October 4, 2009.

9 "JBS e Bertín anunciam formaçâo de gigante de carne bovina," *Valor*, September 16, 2009.

10 See the company's webpage: www.jbs.com.br.

11 "Política industrial quer incentivar formação de multinacionais brasileiras," *Folha de São Paulo*, June26, 2007.

12 "Grupo Votorantim compra a Aracruz com ajuda do BNDES," *Folha de São Paulo*, January 21, 2009.

13 Ibid.

14 Agência Nacional de Telecomunicações, January 16, 2012, accessed 02/02/12, http://www.anatel.gov.br/Portal/exibirPortalInternet.do.

15 "Supertele ganha corpo com financiamento do BNDES," *Valor*, February 8, 2008.

16 "Nova tele terá forte presenta do governo," *Folha de São Paulo*, July 20, 2008; and "Relatorio 2008," *Previ*, www.previ.com.br.

17 Braskem, www.braskem.com.br; and "A reorganização do capitalismo brasileiro," *Revista IHU*, No. 322, São Leopoldo, Universidade do Vale do Rio dos Sinos, March 22, 2010.

18 Ibid; and Braskem, accessed 02/27/12, http://www.braskem-ri.com. br/show.aspx?idCanal=OxIsNDdQ/sz37EhqiG8SFA==.

19 "As relações obscuras entre o polo petroquímico gaúcho, a Braskem e o governo federal. Entrevista especial com Carlos Eitor Rodrigues Machado," *IHU Online*, May 11, 2009, accessed 05/15/11, http://www.ihu. unisinos.br/entrevistas/22099-as-relacoes-obscuras-entre-o-polo -petroquimico-gaucho-a-braskem-e-o-governo-federal-entrevista -especial-com-carlos-eitor-rodrigues-machado.

20 Efraín León Hernández, "Energía Amazónica. La frontera energética amazónica en el tablero geopolítico latinoamericano," Doctoral thesis, Posgrado de Estudios Latinoamericanos, Universidad Nacional Autónoma de México, 2007, 123.

21 Ibid., 124.

22 "Petrobras batiza Tupi de Lula," *Folha de São Paulo*, December 29, 2010.

23 "Entenda o que é a camada pré-sal," *Folha de São Paulo*, August 31, 2008; and "A exploração do pré-sal e o futuro brasileiro," *Jornal da Universidade* 113, Porto Alegre, Universidade Federal de Rio Grande do Sul, November 2008.

24 Ibid.; and "Petrobras batiza Tupi de Lula."

25 Pedro Silva Barroso and Luiz Fernando Sanná Pinto, "O Brasil do pré-sal e a Organização dos Países Exportadores de Petróleo (OPEP),"

Boletim de Economia e Política Internacional 4, Brasilia, IPEA, October/December 2010, 11.

26 "Petrobras já planeja novo gasoduto e dez plataformas no pré-sal," *Valor*, December 27, 2010, accessed 02/11/12, http://www.valor.com.br/arquivo/695277/petrobras-ja-planeja-novo-gasoduto-e-dez-plataformas-no-pre-sal.

27 Carlos Walter Porto Gonçalves and Luis Enrique Ribeiro, "A luta pela reapropriaçâo social dos recursos naturais na América Latina: o caso da Petrobras no Ecuador," *Rede Brasileira de Justiça Ambiental*, 2006, accessed 02/10/11, http://www.justicaambiental.org.br/_justicaam biental/pagina.php?id=1773.

28 "La estrategia de Petrobras para convertirse en la mayor empresa de A. Latina," July 25, 2010, accessed 02/18/11, http://www.americaeconomia.com/negocios-industrias/la-estrategia-de-petrobras-para -convertirse-en-la-mayor-empresa-de-america-latin.

29 "Petrobras é a quarta maior empresa de energía do mundo," *Folha de São Paulo*, January 27, 2009.

30 "Oferta da Petrobras soma R$120,360 bilhões, a maior da história," *O Globo*, September 23, 2010, accessed 02/18/11, http://oglobo. globo.com/economia/oferta-da-petrobras-soma-120360-bilhoes-maior-da-historia-2947969.

31 *O Globo*, September 24, 2009, accessed 02/02/11, http://oglobo. globo.com/economia/com-capitalizacao-petrobras-vira-segunda -maior-petrolifera-do-mundo-2947426.

32 "Entenda a capitalização da Petrobras," *Folha de São Paulo*, September 1, 2010; and "Governo eleva a fatia na Petrobras para 48 percent," *Reuters*, São Paulo, September 24, 2010.

33 *Valor*, December 27, 2010.

34 "Petrobras terá operação submersa no pré-sal," *Valor*, December 28, 2010, accessed 02/19/11, http://valor-online.jusbrasil.com.br/politica /6431412/petrobras-tera-operacao-submersa-no-pre-sal.

35 Ibid.

36 Giorgio Romano Schutte and Pedro Silva Barros, "A geopolítica do etanol," *Boletim de Economia e Política Internacional* 1, Brasilia, IPEA, January 2010, 34.

37 Ibid., 35.

38 União da Indústria de Cana-de-Açúcar (UNICA), http://www.unica.com.br/dadosCotacao/estatistica.

39 Giorgio Romano Schutte and Pedro Silva Barros, "A geopolítica do etanol," 35.

40 Ibid., 35.

41 "Biocombustibles," *Cadernos NAE* 2, Brasilia, Núcleo de Asuntos Estratégicos de la Presidencia de la República, October, 2004, 131.

42 Revista Época, June 13, 2008, accessed 02/15/11, http://revistaepoca.globo.com/Revista/Epoca/0,,EMI5865-15273.html.

43 Ibid.

44 http://www.unica.com.br/dadosCotacao/estatistica, accessed 01/15/11.

45 *O Estado de São Paulo*, suplemento agrícola, February 2007.

46 Silvia Ribeiro, "Biocombustibles y transgénicos, *La Jornada*, November 26, 2006.

47 "Biocombustibles," *Cadernos NAE* 2.

48 Keiti da Roicha Gomes, "Presença estrangeira na produção de commodities: o caso da indústria de etanol no Brasil," *Boletim de Economia e Política Internacional* 4, Brasilia, IPEA, October/December, 2010, 27.

49 Ibid.

50 Ibid., 19.

51 Ibid., 20.

52 Ibid., 21.

53 "Grandes grupos ocupam o espaço de familias tradicionais nas usinas," *O Estado de São Paulo*, November 1, 2009, accessed 02/19/11, http://www.estadao.com.br/noticias/impresso,grandes-grupos-ocupam-o-espaco-de-familias-tradicionais-nas-usinas,459503,0.htm.

54 Keiti da Roicha Gomes, "Presença estrangeira na produção de commodities: o caso da indústria de etanol no Brasil," 24–25.

55 "Petrobras planeja conter 'estrangeiros' no álcool," *Folha de São Paulo*, December 11, 2010.

56 Ibid.

57 For more details see the official PAC page: http://www.brasil.gov.br/pac/.

58 Ibid.

59 Agencia Nacional de Energía Eléctrica (ANEEL), *Atlas de energia elétrica do Brasil*, Brasilia, 2008, 57.

60 Empresa de Pesquisa Energética, *Balanço Energético Nacional 2010*, Rio de Janeiro, 2010, 17 and 169.

61 Ibid., 17.

62 PAC 2, Relatorio, 76, accessed 01/19/11, http://www.brasil.gov.br/pac/pac-2.

63 "Entenda a polémica envolvendo a usina de Belo Monte," *O Globo*, April 19, 2010, accessed 03/25/11, http://oglobo.globo.com/politica/entenda-polemica-envolvendo-usina-de-belo-monte-3020673.

64 Altamira is a municipality of 160,000 square kilometers, the size of Uruguay, and it has 110,000 inhabitants. It is 800 km from Belém, the capital of the state of Pará.

65 "Belo Monte: una monstruosidade apocalíptica"; interview with Erwin Kräutler in *Revista IHU* 337, São Leopoldo, August 2, 2010. All the data about the Belo Monte rebellion comes from this source.

66 Ibid.

67 *IHU Online*, February 11, 2011, accessed 02/12/11, http://www.ihu.unisinos.br/index.php.

68 *Jornal do Brasil*, February 7, 2011; and "Nota pública do painel de especialistas sobre a UHE Belo Monte," February 4, 2011, *Rio Vivos*, accessed 02/11/11, http://www.riosvivos.org.br/canal.php?c=526&mat=17044.

69 "Usina hidrelétrica de Belo Monte testa projeto energético de Lula," *Folha de São Paulo*, April 18, 2010.

70 "Belo Monte o leilâo que nao Houve," *Folha de São Paulo*, April 23, 2010; "Um parecer oficial contra Belo Monte," *O Globo*, April 23, 2010; and "Aneel confirma dois consorcios na disputa por Belo Monte," *Valor*, April 16, 2010.

71 "Fundos de pensáo estatais terâo 10 percent da usina de Belo Monte," *O Estado de São Paulo*, May 15, 2010, accessed 03/02/11, http://www.estadao.com.br/noticias/impresso,fundos-de-pensao-estatais-terao-10-da-usina-de-belo-monte,552018,0.htm.

72 "Odebrecht, Camargo e Andrade vâo construir usina de Belo Monte," *O Estado de São Paulo*, August 15, 2010, accessed 02/15/11, http://

www.estadao.com.br/noticias/impresso,odebrecht-camargo-e
-andrade-vao-construir-usina-de-belo-monte,595196,0.htm
(accessed 15/02/2011).

73 "Amazônia é prioridade de expansão de fontes energéticas, diz Eletrobrás," *Folha de São Paulo*, February 10, 2011.

74 "Manifesto de empresários defende BNDES, mas especialistas
criticam política de fomento," *O Globo*, August 6, 2010, accessed
02/15/11, http://oglobo.globo.com/economia/manifesto-de
-empresarios-defende-bndes-mas-especialistas-criticam-politica
-de-fomento-2969438.

75 Ibid.

76 "Doce grupos ficam com 57% de repasses do BNDES," *Folha de São
Paulo*, August 8, 2010.

77 Joaquín Eloi Cirne de Toledo, *O Globo*, August 6, 2010.

78 *Folha de São Paulo*, February 2, 2010.

79 Sérgio Lazzarini, *Capitalismo de laços* (Rio de Janeiro: Elsevier, 2011).

80 *O Globo*, December 5, 2010.

81 Sérgio Lazzarini, *Capitalismo de laços*, 10.

82 Ibid., 11.

83 Ibid., 32.

84 Ibid., 33.

85 Ibid., 38.

86 Mansueto Almeida, "A concentração do investimento e da produção
em poucos setores," interview, *Revista IHU* 338, São Leopoldo, Universidade do Vale do Rio dos Sinos, August 9, 2010, 5–8.

87 "Fundo de pensão da Petrobras vira sócio da controladora do Itaú,"
Folha de São Paulo, November 26, 2010.

88 Among the collectives that form the "Plataforma BNDES" are:
ATTAC Brasil, Central Única de los Trabajadores, Comisión Pastoral
de la Tierra, Consejo Indigenista Misionero, Movimiento de Afect-
ados por Represas (MAB), Movimiento de Trabajadores Rurales Sin
Tierra, and Movimiento Nacional de Derechos Humanos.

89 See http://www.plataformabndes.org.br/index.php/quem-somos
(accessed 02/19/10).

90 The complete document here: http://www.plataformabndes.org.br/
index.php/pt/analises-do-desenvolvimento/45-principal/499-car-
ta-dos-atingidos-pelo-bndes- (accessed 02/19/10).

91 Ibid., 191.

Chapter 6

1 "Zé Mineiro, o patriarca da JBS, mantém os pés no châo," Aída do
Amaral Rocha, in *Valor*, November 8, 2009, http://www.sysrastro.
com.br/sysrastro/det_noticia.phpnot_codigo=6329&PHPSES-
SID=7c4e84b678c10368f2607b9d94e3ce31.

2 "JBS: The Story Behind The World's Biggest Meat Producer," Karen
Blanfeld, in *Forbes*, April, 2011, accessed 05/15/11, http://blogs.
forbes.com/kerenblankfeld/2011/04/21/jbs-the-story-behind-the-
worlds-biggest-meat-producer/.

3 Ibid.

4 "BNDES terá 35% da JBS após trocar debêntures," *Valor*, May 19,
2011, accessed 01/02/12, http://www.fazenda.gov.br/resenhaeletron-
ica/MostraMateria.asp?cod=722581.

5 Afonso Fleury, Maria Tereza Leme Fleury, and Germano Glufke, "El
camino se hace al andar: La trayectoria de las multinacionales brasileñas," in *Business Review*, first quarter, Universia, Madrid, 2010.

6 See official site: www.camargocorrea.com.br.

7 www.andradegutierrez.com.br.

8 Pedro Henrique Pedreira Campos, "As orígens da internacionalização
das empresas de engenharia brasilerias," in *Empresas transnacionais brasileiras na América Latina: um debate necesario* (São Paulo:
Expressão Popular, 2009), 105.

9 Ibid., 106.

10 Ibid., 108.

11 "Multinacionais brasileiras. A rota dos investimentos brasileiros no
exterior," *KPMG*, 2008, www.kpmg.com.br.

12 Pedro Henrique Pedreira Campos, "As orígens da internacionalização
das empresas de engenharia brasilerias," 109.

13 Ibid., 112.

14 Ibid., 112–113.

15 Ibid., 12.

16 Roberto Iglesias, "Os interesses empresariais brasileiros na América do Sul: investimentos diretos no exterior," Brasilia, CNI, 2007, 35.

17 Javier Santiso, "La emergencia de las multilatinas," *Revista de la CEPAL* 95, Santiago, August 2008.

18 Ibid., 20.

19 Ana Claudia Alem and Carlos Eduardo Cavalcanti, "O BNDES e o apoio à internacionalização das empresas brasileiras: algunas reflexões," in *Revista do BNDES* 24, Brasilia, December, 2005.

20 Ibid., 17.

21 "Pivó de crise, Odebrecht saúda cúpula e pede 'integraçâo'," *Folha de São Paulo*, December 15, 2008.

22 *Boletim SOBEET* 77, Sociedad Brasileña de Estudos de Empresas Transnacionales y de la Globalización Económica, São Paulo, January 26, 2011.

23 Gustavo Bittencourt and Rosario Domingo, "Inversión extranjera directa en América Latina: tendencias y determinantes," Montevideo, *Cuaderno de trabajo* 6, Facultad de Ciencias Sociales, 1996, 60.

24 Ziga Vodusek, *Inversión extranjera directa en América Latina. El papel de los inversores europeos* (Washington: Banco Interamericano de Desarrollo, 2002), 21.

25 CEPAL, *La inversión extranjera directa en América Latina y el Caribe* (New York: United Nations, 2010), 45.

26 *Boletim SOBEET* 79, São Paulo, April 26, 2011; and UNCTAD, *Investment Trend Monitor* 8, United Nations, New York, January 24, 2012.

27 UNCTAD, *Investment Trend Monitor* 8, 6.

28 Márcia Tavares, "Investimento brasileiro no exterior," 12; and CEPAL, *La inversión extranjera directa en América Latina y el Caribe*, New York, United Nations, 2009, 69.

29 Ibid., 13.

30 Ibid., 19.

31 "Multiancionais brasileiras," *KPMG*.

32 Banco Central do Brasil, "Capitais Brasileiros no Exterior," accessed 05/29/11, http://www.bcb.gov.br/?cbe.

33 Fernando Ribeiro and Raquel Casado Lima, "Investimentos brasileiros na América do Sul: desempenho, estratégias e políticas," Rio de Janeiro, Funcex, July 2008, 36.

34 Luis Fernando Novoa, "O Brasil es seu 'desdobramento': o papel do BNDES na expansâo das empresas transnacioanis brasilerias na América do Sul," in Instituto Rosa Luxemburg Stiftung, *Empresas transnacionais brasileiras na América do Sul*, 189.

35 Luciano Coutinho interview by Agencia Brasil, April 29, 2008, cited by Luis Fernando Novoa, 193.

36 Ana Claudia Alem and Carlos Eduardo Cavalcanti, *Revista do BNDES*, 56.

37 Ibid.

38 Ibid., 197.

39 BNDES, "Política de desenvolvimento produtivo. Innovar e investir para sustentar o crescimento," BNDES, May 2008, 17.

40 Ibid.

41 Ibid.

42 Ibid., 24.

43 Ibid., 28.

44 Ana Saggioro García, "Empresas transnacionais: dupla frente de luta," Instituto Rosa Luxemburg Sitftung, *Empresas transnacionais brasileiras*, 14.

45 Ibid., 13.

46 *O Estado de São Paulo*, May 11, 2011, accessed 05/29/11, http://economia.estadao.com.br/noticias/Economia+Brasil,dilma-instala-hoje-camara-de-politica-de-gestao,not_66426.htm.

47 Antonio Palocci had to resign his post on June 7, 2011, due to accusations of embezzlement. He was replaced by Senator Gleisi Hoffmann, a PT member.

48 "Dilma corteja empresário Jorge Gerdau para seu governo," *Folha de São Paulo*, November 30, 2010.

49 *Agencia Brasil*, May 16, 2011, accessed 05/29/11, http://agenciabrasil.ebc.com.br/noticia/2011-05-16/dilma-camara-de-politicas-de-gestao-vai-aumentar-competitividade-e-reduzir-burocracia.

50 Raúl Zibechi, "La rebelión obrera de Jirau," *La Jornada*, April 8,

2011; and "Rebelión en la Amazonia brasileña," *Programa de las Americas*, April 12, 2011.

51 *O Estado de São Paulo*, November 14, 2010.

52 http://www.imd.org/about/pressroom/pressreleases/Brazilian-Company-Votorantim-Honoured-as-Top-Family-Business-in-the-World.cfm (accessed 06/12/2011).

53 This can be found at *Historianet*, "Nacioanalismo e imperialismo," accessed 06/12/11, http://www.historianet.com.br/conteudo/default. aspx?codigo=717. Also in Mino Carta, "Ermirio e as seis irmãs," in *Retratos do Brasil* (São Paulo: Editora Política, 1985), 83–84.

54 Data at http://www.odebrecht.com.br.

55 "Marcelo Odebrecht," *Istoé*, December 10, 2008, accessed 02/07/12, http://www.istoedinheiro.com.br/noticias/2547_MARCELO+ODE-BRECHT.

56 Ibid.

57 ADESG, *Revista da Associação dos Diplomados da Escola Superior de Guerra*, Special Edition, 2011, 20.

Chapter 7

1 Instituto Humanitas Unisinos, "A rebeliâo de Jirau," *Conjuntura da Semana*, São Leopoldo, March 28, 2011, accessed 07/24/11, http://www.ihu.unisinos.br/index.php?option=com_noticias&Itemid=18&task=detalhe&id=41771.

2 Efraín León Hernández, *Energía amazónica. La frontera energética amazónica en el tablero geopolítico latinoamericano*, Posgrado de Estudios Latinoamericano, México, UNAM, 2007, 137.

3 Ibid., 138.

4 *Folha de São Paulo*, February 19, 2009.

5 *O Globo*, March 13, 2009.

6 Entrevista a Maria Ozánia da Silva, *IHU Online*, March 14, 2011, accessed 07/24/11, http://www.ihu.unisinos.br/index.php?option=com_noticias&Itemid=18&task=detalhe&id=40843%20.

7 Leonardo Sakamoto, "A luta por respeito e dignidade," http://www.ihu.unisinos.br/index.php?option=com_noticias&Itemid=18&task=detalhe&id=41526.

8   *Folha de São Paulo*, March 20, 2011.

9   Leonardo Sakamoto, "A luta por respeito e dignidade."

10 Instituto Humanitas Unisinos, "A rebelião de Jirau."

11 The alliance is made up of: Movimiento Xingu Vivo para Siempre, Alianza Tapajós Vivo, Movimiento Rio Madera Vivo, and Movimiento Teles Pires Vivo.

12 "O conflito en Jirau e apenas o incio do filme," *IHU Online*, São Leopoldo, March 24, 2011, accessed 07/30/11, http://www.ihu.unisinos.br/index.php?option=com_noticias&Itemid=18&task=detalhe&id=41666.

13 "Mortes em obras do PAC estao acima dos padroes," *O Globo*, March 26, 2011, accessed 07/30/11, http://oglobo.globo.com/economia/mat/2011/03/26/mortes-em-obras-do-pac-estao-acima-dos-padroes-924098487.asp.

14 Nota de MAB, March 18, 2011, accessed 07/24/11, http://www.ihu.unisinos.br/index.php?option=com_noticias&Itemid=18&task=detalhe&id=41490.

15 *O Estado de São Paulo*, March 19, 2011.

16 *O Estado de São Paulo*, March 18, 2011.

17 "Dilma quer saída para greves em obras do PAC," *Jornal Valor*, March 24, 2011.

18 Instituto Humanitas Unisinos, "A rebelião de Jirau."

19 Ibid.

20 See Chapter 2.

21 *Lucha Indígena* 59, Lima, July 2011, 2.

22 "Perú cancela hidrelétrica da OAS e da Eletrobrás," *Valor*, June 15, 2011.

23 *El Comercio*, Lima, April 5, 2011, accessed 08/01/11, http://elcomercio.pe/politica/738151/noticia-asesores-brasilenos-ayudan-ollanta-humala-su-imagen_1.

24 See Chapter 1.

25 "Amazonia: a última fronteira de expansão do capitalismo," in Conjuntura da Semana, *IHU Online*, June 6, 2011, accessed 12/21/11, http://www.ihu.unisinos.br/cepat/cepat-conjuntura/500017-conjuntura-da-semana-amazonia-a-ultima-fronteira-de-expansao-do-capitalismo-brasileiro.

26 Efraín León Hernández, *Energía amazónica,* 136.

27 Mario Osava, "Nuevas potencias emergen sobre aguas ajenas," *IPS,* April 2011, accessed 07/25/11, http://ipsnoticias.net/nota.asp?idnews=97958.

28 "Governo prevé até 2020 mais 24 hidrelétricas," *O Globo,* June 4, 2011, accessed 01/02/11, http://g1.globo.com/economia/noticia/2011/06/governo-preve-ate-2020-mais-24-hidreletricas.html.

29 Efraín León Hernández, *Energía amazónica,* 123.

30 "Brasil estuda construir hidrelétricas em 7 países da América Latina," *Folha de São Paulo,* August 11, 2011.

31 Ibid.

32 Interview with Lucía Ortiz and Bruna Engel, *Revista IHU* 342, São Leopoldo, 40–43.

33 "Usina-plataforma, o novo conceito em hidrelétricas," *Corriente Contínua* 224, Brasilia, Eletronorte, January 2009.

34 Ibid., 15.

35 Ibid., 14.

36 "Tapajós tendrá 5 usinas inspiradas nas plataformas de petróleo," *IHU Online,* July 5, 2009, accessed 01/02/12, http://www.ihu.unisinos.br/noticias/noticias-arquivadas/23686-tapajos-tera-5-usinas-inspiradas-nas-plataformas-de-petroleo.

37 Interview with Lucía Ortiz and Bruna Engel, *Revista IHU* 342, 41.

38 Interview with Leandro Scalabrin in *Revista IHU* 341, 16.

39 Patricia Molina, "El Proyecto de Aprovechamiento Hidroeléctrico y de Navegabilidad del río Madera en el marco de la IIRSA y del contexto de la globalización!," in Fobomade, *El Norte Amazónico de Bolivia y el Complejo del Río Madera* (La Paz: 2007), 32.

40 Jorge Molina Carpio, "Análisis de los estudios de impacto ambiental del Complejo Hidroeléctrico del Río Madera, Hidrología y sedimentos," in Fobomade, 49

41 Iván Castellón Quiroga, "Aerca de las represas en la cuenca del río Madera," in Fobomade, 118.

42 "Mega represas: ¿exportar o depdredar?," accessed 08/04/11, http://www.ecosistemas.cl/web/noticias/documentos/1363-megarepresas-iexportar-y-depredar-.html.

43 "Los retos de Brasil como economía emergente," *IBCE*, accessed 08/04/11, http://www.ibce.org.bo/principales_noticias_bolivia/29072011/noticias_ibce_bolivia.asp?id=21951.

44 "Mega represas: ¿exportar o depredar?"

45 Patricia Molina, "Bolivia-Brasil: Relaciones energéticas, integración y medio ambiente," in Fobomade, 29.

46 Ibid.

47 Ibid., 30.

48 Guilherme Carvalho, *La integración sudamericana y Brasil* (Rio de Janeiro, Action Aid, 2006), 64.

49 "América do Sul debe ousar mais, diz FHC," *Folha de São Paulo*, September 1, 2000.

50 "FHC pede reciprocidade em abertura," *Folha de São Paulo*, September 2, 2000.

51 Between 1961 and 2002 the IDB approved loans of $18 billion: 51 percent to energy projects; 46 percent to land transport, and 3 percent to telecommunications, marine, river, and air transport. Brazil received 33 percent of the funds.

52 Andrés Barreda, "Análisis geopolítico del contexto regional," in Patricia Molina (Ed) *Geopolítica de los recursos naturales y acuerdos comerciales en Sudamérica* (La Paz: Fobomade, 2005), 16.

53 Carlos Walter Porto Gonçalves, "Ou inventamos ou erramos. Encruzilhadas de Integração Regional Sul-americana," IPEA, 2011 (unpublished), 12.

54 Ibid., 12–13.

55 In Elisangela Soldatelli, *IIRSA. E esta a integração que nós queremos?*, Porto Alegre, Amigos da Terra, December 2003, 4.

56 Guilherme Carvalho, *La integración sudamericana y Brasil*, 36.

57 Mónica Vargas, "Integración de la Infraestructura Regional Sudamericana: Proyectos en Bolivia," in Patricia Molina, 72.

58 The CAF is a multinational finance institution created in 1970 and the FONPLATA was created in 1971 to finance integration projects. See: www.caf.com and www.fonplata.org.

59 Elisangela Soldatelli, *IIRSA. E esta a integração que nós queremos?*, 16.

60 "Resumen de la cartera IIRSA. Actualizado a enero de 2011," www.

iirsa.org.

61 Andrés Barreda, "Geopolítica, recursos estratégicos y multinacionales," December 20, 2005, accessed 08/10/11, http://alainet.org/active/10174&lang=pt<font%20color=.

62 Ibid.

63 Ibid.

64 Silvia Molina, "El rol de Bolivia en la integración sudamericana," in Patricia Molina, 61.

65 Ibid., 64.

66 Alvaro García Linera (coord.), *Sociología de los movimientos sociales en Bolivia* (La Paz: Diakonía/Oxfam, 2004), 218.

67 Félix Patzi Paco, *Insurgencia y sumisión. Movimientos indígeno-campesinos (1983–1998)* (La Paz: Comuna, 1999), 162.

68 Anuario Sena, "Costos sociales y ambientales de la carretera Villa Tunari-San Ignacio de Moxos," Fobomade, May 13, 2011, accessed 08/16/11, http://www.fobomade.org.bo/art-116.

69 Subcentral TIPNIS, "Memoria. Foro Departamental: Territorio Indígena y Parque Nacional Isiboro Sécure," (Cochabamba: Cenda/Fobomade, 2010), 17–18.

70 Ibid., 30.

71 Rosa Rojas, "Quieran o no habrá carretera," *Ojarasca* 172, La Jornada, August 2011.

72 Anuario Sena, "Costos sociales y ambientales de la carretera Villa Tunari-San Ignacio de Moxos."

73 Ibid.

74 Ibid.

75 Ibid.

76 Marcel Achkar and Ana Domínguez, "IIRSA: Otro paso hacia la des-soberanía de los pueblos sudamericanos," Programa Uruguay Sustentable-Redes Amigos de la Tierra, Montevideo, 2005. 18.

77 Ana Esther Ceceña, Paula Aguilar, and Carlos Matto, "Territorialidad de la dominación," Buenos Aires, Observatorio Latinoamericano de Geopolítica, 2007, 12.

78 José Luis Fiori, "Brasil e América do Sul: o desafío da inserção internacional soberana," Brasilia, Cepal/Ipea, 2011, 18.

79 Carlos Walter Porto Gonçalves, "Ou inventamos ou erramos. Encruzilhadas de Integração Regional Sul-americana," 20.

80 Ibid., 23.

Chapter 8

1 "Sapatos da China, fazendas e hotéis" in Valor, November 6, 2009 and "Ernesto Corrêa: Conheça o empresário mais miterioso do Brasil" in *IG Economía*, 27 April, 2011, accessed 09/05/11, http://economia.ig.com.br/empresas/conheca+o+empresario+mais+misterioso+do+brasil/n1300100882833.html.

2 "Empresario deja frigorífico por cemento," *El País*, Montevideo, January 20, 2011, accessed 09/05/11, http://www.elpais.com.uy/110120/pecono-542094/economia/Empresario-deja-frigorifico-por-cemento/.

3 *Veja*, August 13, 2008, http://veja.abril.com.br/130808/holofote.shtml (accessed 09/12/11).

4 The life history of Corrêa is based on the articles in Note 1.

5 Marcelo Cervo Chelotti, "Novos territórios da reforma agária na Campanha Gaúcha," *Campo-Território*, Revista do Laboratório de Geografia Agrária, Universidad Federal de Uberlândia 10, August 2010, 214.

6 "O fim do Estado de direito II," May 7, 2002, reproduced on the Diego Casagrande website: (www.diegocasagrande.com.br), accessed 09/12/11, http://www.varican.xpg.com.br/varican/Bpolitico/Fimdoestadir.htm.

7 Mitsue Morissawa, *A historia da luta pela terra e o MST* (São Paulo: Expressão Popular, 2001), 123 ff.

8 Marcelo Cervo Chelotti, "Novos territórios da reforma agária na Campanha Gaúcha," 202.

9 Marcelo Cervo Chelotti, "Agroecología em assentamentos rurais: estrategia de reprodução camponesa na Campanha Gaúcha," *Agrária*, Revista do Laboratório de Geografia Agrária, Universidad de São Paulo, Departamento de Geografía 7, July–December 2007, 95.

10 Flamarion Dutra Alves et al, "Territorialização camponesa, identidade e reproduçôes sociais: os assentamentos rurais na metade sul do Rio Grande do Sul," *Campo-Territorio* 4, Uberlândia, Universidade Federal de Uberlândia, August 2007, 90.

11 Flamarion Dutra Alves, "As faces do desenvolvimento rural no Sul Gaúcho: produçâo agroecológica familiar e monoculturas empresariais," *Agrária* 7, São Paulo, Laboratório de Geografia Agrária, Universidad de São Paulo, July–December 2007, 43.

12 Marcelo Cervo Chelotti, "Novos territórios da reforma agária na Campanha Gaúcha," 212.

13 Ibid., 216.

14 "Fuerte empresario brasileño capitalizó al frigorífico PUL," *El País*, Montevideo, April 13, 2003, accessed 09/14/11, http://www.elpais.com.uy/03/04/12/pecono_37061.asp.

15 Diego Piñeiro, "Dinámicas en el mercado de tierras en América Latina. El caso de Uruguay," Santiago, FAO, September, 2010, mimeo.

16 "Carne uruguaya: a melhor do mundo," *El País*, September 26, 2007, accessed 09/14/11, http://www.elpais.com.uy/Suple/Agropecuario/07/09/26/agrope_304912.asp.

17 "La creciente extranjerización de la economía uruguaya," *Brecha*, separata, November 28, 2008; and "Uruguai teme a invasâo de brasileiros," *Valor*, July 25, 2011.

18 "Lugo se quejó de Brasil en la OEA," *La Nación*, Asunción, October 29, 2008.

19 "Tensión por los brasiguayos," *Página 12*, Buenos Aires, October 25, 2008.

20 "Un general brasileño dice que invadirá Itaipu si Lula lo ordena," Última Hora, Asunción, October 18, 2008.

21 Ibid.

22 "Tensión por los brasiguayos," *Página 12*.

23 "No Paraguai, o rei da soja é brasileiro," in *IG*, March 23, 2011, accessed 09/14/11, http://economia.ig.com.br/no+paraguai+o+rei+da+soja+e+brasileiro/n1238185176716.html.

24 "Dominios de brasiguayos," *Página 12*, Buenos Aires, November 22, 2008.

25 Marcos Glauser, *Extranjerización del territorio paraguayo*, Asunción, BASE-IS, 2009.

26 "Cerca del Brasil, lejos de Dios," *E´A* 14, Asunción, January–February, 2010, 9–16.

27 Ibid., 15.

28 Marcos Glauser, *Extranjerización del territorio paraguayo*, 30.

29 Ibid., 31.

30 Ibid., 32.

31 "Cerca del Brasil, lejos de Dios," *E´A*, 13.

32 "Soja em franca expansâo no Paraguai," *Valor*, September 16, 2011, accessed 01/02/12, http://www.valor.com.br/empresas/1008846/soja-em-franca-expansao-no-paraguai.

33 Marcos Glauser, *Extranjerización del territorio paraguayo*, 162.

34 Ricardo Canese, *La recuperación de la soberanía hidroeléctrica del Paraguay* (Asunción: Editorial El Ombligo del Mundo, 2007), 80 ff.

35 Pablo Herrero Galisto, "Deudas binacionales: el mismo camino de dominación y saqueo," Asunción, Jubileo Sur/Américas, July 2008.

36 "Notas Reversales entraron en vigencia a partir del 14 de mayo," May 16, 2011, accessed 09/17/11, http://www.itaipu.gov.br/es/sala-de-prensa/noticia/notas-reversales-entraron-en-vigencia-partir-del-14-de-mayo.

37 "Bolivia después de la tormenta," Raúl Zibechi in *Programa de las Américas*, February 3, 2011.

38 Andrés Soliz Rada, "Evo, ¿fin de ciclo?," *Bolpress*, January 15, 2011, accessed 09/19/11, http://www.bolpress.com/art.php?Cod=2011011506.

39 Alejandro Almaraz, "Siete preguntas sobre hidrocarburos, carreteras y otros," *Página Siete*, La Paz, January 11, 2011.

40 Ibid.

41 "Império brasileiro emerge na Bolìvia," *Folha de São Paulo*, May 22, 2005, A18.

42 "40% de la soya estaría en manos brasileñas," *La Razón*, Santa Cruz, November 15, 2010, accessed 09/18/11, http://www.la-razon.com/version.php?ArticleId=121085&EditionId=2346.

43 "Gobierno revela reservas probadas de condensado," *Observatorio Boliviano de Industrias Extractivas*, September 11, 2011, accessed 09/19/11, http://plataformaenergetica.org/obie/content/13685.

44 Pablo Villegas, "La industrialización del gas y la refundación de YPFB en 5 meses," in *Petropress* 24, Cochabamba, Cedib, February, 2011, 35.

45 *Gaceta Oficial de Bolivia*, La Paz, May 1, 2006.

46 Andrés Soliz Rada, "¿Hubo nacionalización?," *Bolpress*, January 10, 2011, accessed 09/18/11, http://www.bolpress.com/art.php?cod=2011011005.

47 Ibid.

48 Jorge Márquez Ostria, "La industrialización de los hidrocarburos. ¿Realidad o ficción?," *Petropress* 21, Cochabamba, Cedib, August 2010, 31.

49 Pablo Villegas, "La industrialización del gas," 38.

50 *HidrocarburosBolivia*, September 20, 2011, http://www.hidrocarburosbolivia.com/nuestro-contenido/noticias/45950-petrobras-adjudico-a-technip-y-haldor-topsoe-la-ingenieria-basica-para-la-fabrica-de-fertilizantes-que-industrializara-gas-natural-bolivian.

51 Pablo Villegas, "La industrialización del gas," 51.

52 *Petropress* 25, Cochabamba, Cedib, May, 2011, 3.

53 Franz Chavez, "Brasil mantiene poderío en producción de gas boliviano," *IPS*, January 13, 2011 accessed 09/19/11, http://ipsnoticias.net/nota.asp?idnews=96978.

54 Ibid.

55 Patricia Molina, "Petrobras en Bolivia: petróleo, gas y medio ambiente," in Jean Pierre Leroy and Juliana Malerba (Eds.), *Petrobras, ¿integración o explotación?* (Rio de Janeiro: FASE, 2005).

56 Efraín León Hernández, *Energía amazónica*, 156–157.

57 Eduardo Tamayo, "Las deudas se pagan, las estafas no," *ALAI*, November 20, 2008, accessed 09/25/11, www.alainet.org/active/27559.

58 Natalia Landivar, "Os padrões de comportamento das 'transbrasileiras' no Equador: extra-territorializando a responsabilidade do Estado Brasileiro," in Instituto Rosa Luxemburg Stiftung, *Empresas transnacionais brasileiras na América Latina*, 119.

59 Christian Zurita, "Norberto Odebrecht: monumento a la vergüenza," in Fernando Villavicencio, et al, *El discreto encanto de la revolucón ciudadana* (Quito: 2010), 239.

60 Ibid., 244.

61 Ibid., 231.

62 Natalia Landivar, "Os padróes de comportamento," 122.

63 Christian Zurita, "Norberto Odebrecht," 229.

64 Ibid., 230.

65 "Empreiteiras recebem R$ 8,5 por cada real doado a campanha de políticos," *O Globo*, May 7, 2011, accessed 01/02/12, http://oglobo. globo.com/economia/empreiteiras-recebem-85-por-cada-real-doa-do-campanha-de-politicos-2773154.

66 Napoleón Saltos, Fernando Villavicencio, and Comisión Especial Caso Petrobras, *Ecuador: peaje global. ¿De la hegemonía de USA a la hegemonía de Brasil?* (Quito: PH Ediciones, 2007), 43. About the history of Petrobras in Ecuador see: Natalia Landivar and Enéas da Rosa, "Obligaciones extraterritoriales del Estado Brasileño: una breve mirada a las actividades de Petrobras en Ecuador," in Jean Pierre Leroy and Julianna Malerba, *Petrobras: ¿integración o explotación?*, 49–54; and Alexandra Almeida, "A Petrobras no Equador," in Instituto Rosa Luxemburg Stiftung, *Empresas transnacionais brasileiras na América Latina*, 28–42.

67 *El Universal*, Quito, July 15, 2011.

68 Diario *Hoy*, Quito, September 25, 2011, accessed 09/25/11, http:// www.hoy.com.ec/noticias-ecuador/la-produccion-de-petroler-as-privadas-disminuyo-502077.html.

69 Proyecto Yasuní-ITT in http://yasuni-itt.gob.ec/¿que-es-la-iniciativa-yasuni-itt/, (accessed 01/02/12).

70 Robert Evan Ellis, "El impacto de China en Ecuador y América Latina," Bogotá, Universidad Jorge Tadeo Lozano, 2008.

71 Agencia ANDES, "Cooperación Ecuador-China se fortalece en sectores estratégicos," September 14, 2011, accessed 01/02/12, http:// andes.info.ec/tema-del-dia/cooperacion-ecuador-china-se-for-talece-en-sectores-estrategicos-91584.html.

72 Occidental Petroleum Corporation (OXY) operated in Block 15 in the east of Ecuador, extracting more than 100,000 barrels of oil per day, a third of all oil extracted by private companies from Ecuador. The indigenous and social movements considered OXY's departure from the country one of their greatest triumphs.

73 Napoleón Saltos et al, *Ecuador: Peaje global*, 10.

74 Alejandro Moreano, "Ecuador en la encrucijada," *OSAL* 19, Buenos Aires, January–April 2006, 65–74.

75 Claudio Scaletta, "La retirada de la burguesía nacional," *Página 12*, November 14, 2005.

76 Carlos Bianco, Pablo Moldovan, and Fernando Porta, *La internacionalización de las empresas brasileñas en Argentina* (Santiago: Cepal, 2008), 33.

77 Ibid., 34.

78 Ibid., 44.

79 *Energía del Sur*, February 10, 2011, accessed 09/30/11, http://energiadelsur.blogspot.com/2011/02/cristobal-lopez-dueno-del-grupo-casino.html.

80 Petrobras Argentina in www.petrobras.com.ar.

81 Carlos Bianco, Pablo Moldovan and Fernando Porta, "La internacionalización."

82 *Cronista Comercial*, Buenos Aires, February 1, 2011.

83 "Mayor inversión de Brasil en Argentina," *Clarín*, Buenos Aires, September 28, 2011.

84 "Anunciaron una millonaria inversión brasileña en una planta siderúrgica," *La Nación*, Buenos Aires, September 11, 2008.

85 *Agencia Brasil*, June 6, 2011.

86 IPEA, "Regiâo Norte do Brasil e Sul da Venezuela: Esforço binacional para a Integração das cadeias produtivas," May 11, 2011, Brasilia, 6.

87 "A integração de infraestrutura Brasil-Venezuela: A IIRSA o eixo Amazônia-Orinoco," Relatório de Pesquisa, IPEA, Brasilia, May 11, 2011.

88 Ibid.

89 Ibid.

90 Decreto No.6.592, Predencia da República, accessed 09/30/11, http://www.planalto.gov.br/ccivil_03/_Ato2007-2010/2008/Decreto/D6592.htm. Emphasis added.

91 Golbery do Couto e Silva, *Geoplítica del Brasil* (México: El Cid, 1978).

92 Paulo Schilling and Luzia Rodrigues, "Além das fronterias," *Teoria e Debate*, São Paulo, Fundaçâo Perseu Abramo, April, 1989.

93 See http://www.espectador.com/1v4_contenido. php?id=181101&sts=1 (accessed 10/01/11).

94 "Governo brasileiro emite alerta ao continente," *Defesanet*, October 8, 2008.

95 "Declaración Conjunta de los Presidentes de la República de Bolivia, Carlos D. Mesa Gisbert, y de la República Federativa del Brasil, Luiz Inácio Lula da Silva," Nota 350, July 8, 2004, Brazil Embassy in Bolivia, accessed 10/01/11, http://www.brasil.org.bo/n287es.htm.

96 Mario Osava, "Dilema del gas y de la integración," *IPS*, May 27, 2005, accessed 12/30/11, http://ipsnoticias.net/print.asp?idnews=33999.

97 Kintto Lucas, "Disputa geopolítica Brasil-Estados Unidos," *Brecha*, Montevideo, August 19, 2005.

98 *Prensa Latina*, Quito, August 16, 2005.

99 Eleonora Gosman, "El espionaje de Brasil se expande en Latinoamérica," *Clarín*, Buenos Aires, May 7, 2005.

100 "En Brasil, la ocupación de tierras de los colonos genera preocupación," *ABC Color*, Asunción, July 2, 2011, accessed 01/02/12, http://www.abc.com.py/nota/en-brasil-la-ocupacion-de-tierras-de-los-colonos-genera-preocupacion/.

Chapter 9

1 Among others, David Harvey, *El nuevo imperialismo* (Madrid: Akal, 2004); Giovanni Arrighi, *El largo siglo XX* (Madrid: Akal, 1999); and Immanuel Wallerstein, *Después del liberalismo* (Mexico: Siglo XXI, 1996).

2 Giovanni Arrighi and Beverly Silver, *Caos y orden el sistema-mundo moderno* (Madrid: Akal, 2001), 219.

3 Ruy Mauro Marini, "La acumulación capitalista mundial y el subimperialismo," 1.

4 *La Vanguardia*, Barcelona, April 24, 2011, accessed 06/17/11, http://www.lavanguardia.com/economia/20110426/54144915718/el-fmi-vaticina-que-la-economia-china-superara-a-la-de-ee-uu-en-2016.html.

5 César Benjamin et al, *A opção brasileira* (Rio de Janeiro:

Contraponto,1998), 188.

6 Ricardo Paes de Barros et al, "Desigualdade e pobreza no Brasil: retrato de uma estabilidade inaceitável," *Texto para discussâo* 800, Brasilia, IPEA, 2000, 3.

7 *O Estado de São Paulo*, May 3, 2011.

8 See Chapter 1.

9 IPEA, "O Brasil em 4 décadas" (Brasilia: IPEA, 2010), 10.

10 Banco Central do Brasil, "Nota de prensa," October 25, 2010, accessed 11/12/12, http://www.bcb.gov.br/?ecoimpext.

11 IPEA, "O Brasil em 4 décadas," 12.

12 IPEA, *Monitor da Percepção Internacional do Brasil* 5, August, 2011.

13 Revista *Fundos de Pensão* 374, Abrapp, São Paulo, October, 2011; Alexandra Cardoso, "Estudo global de ativos dos Fundos de Pensão 2011," *Towers Watson*, 2011, http://www.funcef.com.br/files/Port_TW percent20GPAS_2011_20Mai11_final.pdf.

14 "Previ é o 24º maior fundo de pensão do mundo," *IG*, September 6, 2011, accessed 01/02/12, http://colunistas.ig.com.br/guilhermebarros/2011/09/06/previ-e-o-24º-maior-fundo-de-pensao-do-mundo/.

15 Rodrigo Maschion Alves, "O investimento externo direto brasileiro: a América do Sul enquanto destino estratégico," *Meridiano 47*, Rio de Janeiro, Instituto Brasileiro de Relaçoes Internacionais, vol. 12, No. 127, September–December 2011, 28.

16 "Capitais brasileiros no exterior," Banco Central do Brasil, August 23, 2011, accessed 11/12/11, http://www4.bcb.gov.br/rex/cbe/port/ResultadoCBE2010.asp.

17 *Folha de São Paulo*, September 18, 2011.

18 "Brasil terá investimentos de R$ 3,3 trilhões," *O Globo*, February 28, 2011, accessed 01/02/12, http://oglobo.globo.com/pais/noblat/posts/2011/02/28/pais-recebera-3-3-trilhoes-em-investimentos-ate-2014-diz-bndes-366034.asp.

19 "Presenta de empreiteiras se multiplica no exterior," *Folha de São Paulo*, September 18, 2011.

20 "BNDES bate recorde de desembolsos á AL," *Folha de São Paulo*, March 8, 2010.

21 "Investimentos brasileiros na Argentina disparam nos últimos seis anos," *Portal Brasil*, August 2, 2011, accessed 11/12/11, http://www.brasil.gov.br/noticias/arquivos/2011/08/02/investimentos-brasileiros-na-argentina-disparam-nos-ultimos-seis-anos.

22 Ibid.

23 "Multiancionais brasileiras dinamizan a economia," *Valor*, October 20, 2011, accessed 01/02/12, http://www.valor.com.br/opiniao/1060138/multinacionais-brasileiras-dinamizam-economia.

24 Virginia Fontes, *O Brasil e o capital-imperialismo*, 359.

25 Mathias Seibel Luce, "O subimperialismo brasileiro revisitado: a política de integraçao regional do governo Lula (2003–2007); Virginia Fontes, *O Brasil e o capital-imperialismo*; João Bernardo "Brasil hoje e amanhã: 6) transnacionalização tardia," September 16, 2011, accessed 11/12/12, http://passapalavra.info/?p=43992.

26 Mathias Luce, "O subimperialismo brasileiro revisitado," 20.

27 Ibid., 43.

28 Ibid., 44.

29 Ibid., 37.

30 Ibid., 116.

31 Virginia Fontes, *O Brasil e o capital-imperialismo*, 149.

32 Ibid., 209.

33 O imperialismo brasileiro está nascendo?," interview with Virginia Fontes, in *IHU Online*, May 7, 2010, accessed 11/12/11, http://www.ihu.unisinos.br/index.php?option=com_noticias&Itemid=&task=detalhe&id=31982.

34 Ibid.

35 João Bernardo "Brasil hoje e amanhã."

36 João Bernardo "A viagem do Brasil da periferia para o centro: 2) o novo horizonte," May 1, 2011, accessed 11/12/11.

37 Ibid.

38 Renè Dreifuss *A conquista do Estado. Ação política, poder e golpe de classe* (Rio de Janeiro: Petrópolis, 1981), 80.

39 João Bernardo "Brasil hoje e amanhã: 5) capitalismo burocrático," September 9, 2011, accessed 11/12/11, http://passapalavra.info/?p=43953.

40 Ibid.

41 IPEA; "Sistema de indicadores de Percepção Social. Defesa Nacional," Parte I, Brasilia, February 15, 2011, 5–6.

42 Ibid., 8–9.

43 IPEA; "Sistema de indicadores de Percepção Social. Defesa Nacional," Parte II, Brasilia, January 26, 2012, 5.

44 Ibid., 15.

45 Luiz Alberto Moniz Bandeira, "A importancia Geopolítica da América do Sul na Estratégia dos Estados Unidos," *Revista da Escola Superior de Guerra* 50, Rio de Janeiro, July–December 2008, 12.

46 Ibid., 23.

47 Ibid., 28.

48 Ibid., 35.

49 Guilherme Sandoval Góes, "Por onde andará a Grande Estrategia Brasileira?," *Revista da Escola Superior de Guerra*, Rio de Janeiro, July–December 2008, 60.

50 Ibid., 61.

51 José Luis Fiori, "Brasil e América do Sul: o desafio da inserção internacional soberana."

52 Ibid., 16.

53 Ricardo Sennes, "Brasil na América do Sul: internacionalização da economia, acordos seletivos e estratégia de hub-and-spokes," revista *Tempo do Mundo* 2/3, Brasilia, IPEA, December 2010, 114.

54 Ibid., 114.

55 José Luis Fiori, "Brasil e América do Sul," 19.

56 Ricardo Sennes, "Brasil na América do Sul," 117.

57 Ibid., 132.

58 Ibid., 19.

59 Luciana Acioly, Eduardo Costa Pinto, and Marcos Antonio Macedo Cintra, "As relações bilaterais Brasil-China: a ascensão da China no sistema mundial e os desafios para o Brasil," Brasilia, Grupo de Trabalho sobre a China, IPEA, 2011, 50.

60 Ibid., 50–52.

61 José Luis Fiori, "Brasil e América do Sul," 22.

62 Ibid., 24.

63 Ibid., 32.

64 Sofía Jarrin, "Otro modelo financiero ya está en marcha en América Latina," October 14, 2011, accessed 11/24/11, http://www.bolpress. com/art.php?Cod=2011101404.

Chapter 10:

1 "Belo Monte: coerção nos canteiros de obra." Special interview with Ruy Sposato, *IHU Online*, December 5, 2011, accessed 01/02/12, http://www.ihu.unisinos.br/noticias/504572-o-clima-no-canteiro-de-obras.

2 Ibid.

3 Ibid.

4 Ibid.

5 "Sindicalistas detêm 43 percent da elite dos cargos de confiança no governo Dilma," *Folha de São Paulo*, December 27, 2010.

6 http://www.xinguvivo.org.br/participe/

7 Federico Engels, "Preface" to the Second German edition, 1892 of *La situación de la clase obrera en Inglaterra*, Obras Escogidas, volume III, Moscú, Progreso, 1974.

8 V. I. Lenin, "El imperialismo, etapa superior del capitalismo," Obras Completas, tomo XXII, Madrid, Akal, 1977, 404.

9 Ibid., 405.

10 "Estatais financiam 1º de Maio das centrais sindicais," *Folha de São Paulo*, May 24, 2011.

11 Francisco de Oliveira, "Hegemonía às avessas: descifra-me ou te devoro!," in Francisco de Oliveira, Ruy Braga and Cibele Rizek, *Hegemonia às avessas* (São Paulo: Boitempo, 2007), 21–28.

12 Marcelo Badaró Matos, "Trabalhadores e sindicatos no Brasil," Rio de Janeiro, Vicio de Leitura, 2002.

13 Roberto Leher et al, "Os rumos das lutas sociais no período 2000–2010," en *OSAL*, Buenos Aires, Clacso, No. 28, November 2010.

14 Ibid., 56.

15 CONCLAT (Conferencia Nacional de la Clase Trabajadora) was first held in 1981 during the democratization process of the country and the reorganization of the unionist movement. In 2011, both official unions and opposition to Lula's government held their meetings under this historical name.

16 Roberto Leher et al, "Projetos em disputa, eleições e dilemas da reorganização das lutas sociais," *OSAL*, Buenos Aires, Clacso, No. 29, May 2011.

17 Ibid., 65.

18 "Brasil Foods é multada em quase R$ 5 milhões por descumprir decisão da Justiça que impõe pausas," CUT, December 13, 2011 in http://www.cut.org.br/destaque-central/46884/brasil-foods-e-multada-em-quase-r-5-milhoes-por-descumprir-decisao-da-justica-que-impoe-pausas (accessed 2/01/2012).

19 Ibid.

20 "A 'moderna' industria brasileira da carne. Produção a custa da saúde e da vida dos trabalhadores," *IHU Online*, September 23, 2011 in 2/01/2012), http://www.ihu.unisinos.br/entrevistas/500466-a-moderna-industria-brasileira-da-carne-producao-a-custa-da-saude-e-da-vida-dos-trabalhadores-entrevista-especial-com-siderlei-de-oliveira.

21 Articulação Nacional dos Comités Populares da Copa, "Megaeventos e violáções de directos humanos no Brasil," 2011, 34.

22 Ibid., 98.

23 All data on the CPT can be seen in http://www.cptnacional.org.br.

24 "MST vive crise e vê cair número de acampados," *Veja*, March 28, 2011, in http://veja.abril.com.br/blog/reinaldo/geral/mst-vive-crise-e-ve-cair-numero-de-acampados/ (accessed 2/01/2012).

25 "Cidades de lona encolhem no RS," *IHU Online*, April 3, 2011, in http://www.ihu.unisinos.br/noticias/42037-cidades-de-lona-encolhem-no-rs (accessed 2/01/2012).

26 "Stédile diz que Bolsa Familia esvazia MST," *IHU Online*, April 8, 2011, in http://www.ihu.unisinos.br/noticias/42211-stedile-diz-que-bolsa-familia-esvazia-mst (accessed 2/01/2012).

27 "Renda sobe e classe média vira majoría no campo," *Valor*, December 21, 2010.

28 Bernardo Mançano Fernández, "O MST nâo está em crise, mas, sim, os pequenos agricultores," *IHU Online*, April 18, 2011, in http://www.ihu.unisinos.br/entrevistas/42460-o-mst-nao-esta-em-crise-mas-sim-os-pequenos-agricultores-entrevista-especial-com-bernardo-mancano-fernandes (accessed 2/01/2012).

29 Ibid.

30 Marcel Gomes, "MST aposta em assentados para reforçar a sua base," *ALAI*, 20 December, 2011, in http://alainet.org/active/51705&lang=es (accessed 2/01/2012).

31 Mitrsue Morissawa *A historia da luta pela terra e o MST*, São Paulo, Expressão Popular, 2001, 200.

32 Carlos Walter Porto-Gonçalves and Paulo Roberto Raposo Alentejano, "A reconfiguração da questão agrária e a questão das territorialidades," in *ALAI*, July 4, 2011, 9, in http://alainet.org/active/47807&lang=es (accessed 2/01/2012).

33 Ibid., 6.

34 Ibid., 9.

35 Ibid., 10.

36 "Carta de saída das nossas organizações (MST, MTD, Consulta Popular e Via Campesina) e do projeto estratégico defendido por elas," in http://passapalavra.info/?p=48866 (accessed 27/12/2012).

37 Discussed in Chapter 2 of *Política y Miseria*, Lavaca, Buenos Aires, 2011.

38 Francisco de Oliveira "El Brasil lulista: una hegemonía al revés," in *OSAL*, Buenos Aires, Clacso, No. 30, November, 2011, 71.

39 "MST não da trégua a Dilma e faz 70 Invasões no Abril Vermelho," *IG*, 30 April, 2011, in http://falario.com.br/2011/04/30/mst-nao-da-tregua-a-dilma-e-faz-70-invasoes-no-abril-vermelho/ (accessed 20/1/2012).

40 Marcel Gomes, "MST aposta em assentados para reforçar a sua base," cit.

Chapter 11:

1 Luiz Inácio Da Silva, "The Message of Brazil's Youth," *New York Times*, July 17, 2013.

2 Luiz Werneck Vianna, "A busca por reconhecimento e participação

política: o combutível das manifestações," *Cadernos IHU Ideias* (São Leopoldo: Instituto Humanitas Unisinos), 9.

3   Giusseppe Cocco, "Mobilização reflete nova composição técnca do trabalho imateerial das metrópoles," *Cadernos IHU Ideias* 191 (São Leopoldo: Instituto Humanitas Unisinos), 17.

4   James C. Scott, *Los dominados y el arte de la resistencia* (México DF: ERA, 2000), 264.

5   Manoel Nascimento, "Teses sobre a Revolta do Buzu," July 2009, http://tarifazero.org/wp-content/uploads/2009/07/por_QS3_RevoltaBuzu.pdf.

6   Ibid., 9.

7   Adriana Saraiva, "Movimentos em movimiento: uma visão comparativa de dos movimentos sociais juvenis no Brasil e Estados Unidos," Doctoral thesis, Brasilia, 2010, 65.

8   Manoel Nascimento, "Teses sobre a Revolta do Buzu."

9   Coletivo Maria Tonha, "Ele ajudou a fundar o Movimento Passe Livre, interview with Marcelo Pomar," accessed 08/01/13, http://tarifazero.org/tag/direito-a-cidade/.

10 Ibid.

11 Carolina Cruz and Leonardo Alves da Cunha, "Sobre o 5 anos das Revoltas da Catraca," 2009, accessed July 27, 2013, http://revoltadacatraca.wordpress.com/about/.

12 Ibid.

13 Coletivo Maria Tonha, "Ele ajudou a fundar o Movimento Passe Livre."

14 Marcelo Pomar, "Relato sobre a Plenária Nacional pelo Passe-Livre," *Centro de Midia Independente*, February 2005, accessed 07/20/13, http://www.midiaindependente.org/pt/blue/2005/02/306365.shtml.

15 Ibid.

16 Movimento pelo Passe Livre, "Resoluções tiradas na Plenária Nacional pelo Passe-Livre," February 2005, accessed 07/28/13, http://www.midiaindependente.org/pt/blue/2005/02/306116.shtml.

17 Marcelo Pomar, "Relato sobre a Plenária Nacional pelo Passe-Livre."

18 Passe Livre, "MPL reafirma seu caráter independente e horizontal,"

Centro de Midia Independente, July 2005, accessed 07/29/13, http://www.midiaindependente.org/pt/red/2005/07/324867.shtml.

19 Passe Livre, "Catracas foram queimadas no dia nacional de lutas," *Centro de Midia Independente*, October 2005, accessed 07/10/13, http://www.midiaindependente.org/pt/blue/2005/10/334402. shtml.

20 Movimento Passe Livre, "Encontro nacional amplia organização do movimiento," August 2006, accessed 07/20/13, http://www.midiaindependente.org/pt/blue/2006/08/358951.shtml.

21 Raúl Zibechi, "La lenta construcción de una nueva cultura política," *Brecha*, Montevideo, July 12, 2013.

22 Paíque Duques Lima, "A Ger´Ação Direta no DF: Reflexões sobre as lutas sociais em Brasília na primeira década dos anos 2000," Brasilia, 2013 (unpublished).

23 Adriana Saraiva, "Movimentos em movimiento," 68.

24 Ibid., 70.

25 Lucas Legume and Mariana Toledo, "O Movimento Passe Livre São Paulo e a Tarifa Zero," August 16, 2011, accessed 08/02/13, http://passapalavra.info/2011/08/44857.

26 Edemir Brasil Ferreira, "A multidão rouba a cena: O quebra-quebra em Salvador (1981)," Master's thesis, Universidade da Bahia, Salvador, 2008; Oto Filgueiras, "O quebra-quebra de Salvador" in *Caderno do Ceas* 76, November–December (Salvador: CEAS, 1981).

27 Raúl Zibechi, "La lenta construcción de una nueva cultura política."

28 Lucas Legume and Mariana Toledo, "O Movimento Passe Livre São Paulo e a Tarifa Zero."

29 Raúl Zibechi, "La lenta construcción de una nueva cultura política."

30 Adriana Saraiva, "Movimentos em movimiento," 85.

31 Paíque Duques Lima, "A Ger´Ação Direta no DF," 7.

32 James C. Scott, *Los dominados y el arte de la resistencia*, 149.

33 André Filipe De Moura Ferro, 2005 "Análise do Encontro Nacional do MPL" in <http://www.midiaindependente.org/pt/blue/2005/07/325219.shtml> accessed 25 July, 2013.

34 Paíque Duques Lima, "A Ger´Ação Direta no DF," 19.

35 Leo Vincius, *A guerra da tarifa 2005. Uma visão de dentro do*

Movimento Passe-Livre em Floripa (São Paulo: Faísca, 2005), 60–61.

36 Raúl Zibechi, "El trago amargo de la Copa," February 2012, accessed 08/02/13, http://www.cipamericas.org/es/archives/6359.

37 Comitê Popular da Copa e Olimpíadas do Rio de Janeiro, "Megaeventos e violações dos direitos humanos no Rio de Janeiro," Dossier 2012.

38 Guilherme Marques, Danielle Barros de Moura Benedicto, and Bruno Lopes, "Pan Rio 2007: manifestações e manifestantes," in Gilmar Mascharens, Glauco Bienenstein, and Fernanda Sánchez (Eds.), *O jogo continua: megaeventos esportivos e ciudades* (Rio de Janeiro: EdUERJ, 2011), 242.

39 Ibid., 245.

40 Ibid, 247.

41 *Folha de São Paulo*, "Lula vai ao Pan, Pan vaia Lula," July 14, 2007.

42 Guilherme Marques, Danielle Barros de Moura Benedicto, and Bruno Lopes, "Pan Rio 2007," 247–252.

43 Articulação Nacional dos Comitês Populares da Copa 2011, "Megaeventos e Violações de Direitos Humanos no Brasil" (Rio de Janeiro), 11.

44 Ibid., 8.

45 Comitê Popular da Copa e Olimpíadas do Rio de Janeiro, "Megaeventos e violações dos direitos humanos no Rio de Janeiro," Dossier 2012, 77.

46 *O Globo* (Rio de Janeiro), September 21, 2012, <http://oglobo.globo.com/pais/com-presenca-de-caetano-freixo-faz-comicio-na-lapa-6166441#ixzz2a69VdB3X> accessed August 3, 2013.

47 Comité Popular da Copa e Olimpíadas do Rio de Janeiro, "Megaeventos e violações dos diretos humanos no Rio de Janeiro," Dossier 2013, 54.

48 Articulação Nacional dos Comitês Populares da Copa 2011, "Megaeventos," 11–12.

49 Comité Popular da Copa e Olimpíadas do Rio de Janeiro, Dossier 2013, 59.

50 Atletas pela Cidadania, "Atletas se manifestam contra fechamento de instalações do complexo do Maracanã," accessed 08/14/13, http://www.atletas.org.br/exibe_noticia.php?id=1344.

51 Comité Popular da Copa e Olimpíadas do Rio de Janeiro, Dossier 2013, 53.

52 Ranahit Guha, *Las voces de la historia y otros estudios subalternos* (Barcelona: Crítica, 2002), 104.

53 A calculation of work minutes needed to pay for a bus ticket based on the average salary in twelve world cities places São Paulo and Rio de Janeiro as the most expensive cities for transport: 13.9 and 12 minutes of work respectively compared to 5.5 in Madrid, 6.3 in New York, 6.2 in Paris, and 1.4 in Buenos Aires (*Folha de São Paulo*, 2013).

54 Raúl Zibechi, "La lenta construcción de una nueva cultura política."

55 Raúl Zibechi, "Rio de Janeiro. De la Ciudad Maravillosa a la Ciudad Negocio" in *Brecha* (Montevideo), January 3, 2012.

56 Comité Popular da Copa e Olimpíadas do Rio de Janeiro, Dossier 2013, 113–124.

57 Guha, Ranahit, *Las voces*, 98.

58 *O Estado de São Paulo*, "Fifa não vai aceitar mudanças na Lei Geral da Copa," July 2013, accessed 08/04/13, http://www.estadao.com.br/noticias/esportes,fifa-nao-vai-aceitar-mudancas-na-lei-geral-da-copa,1052121,0.htm.

59 Lucas Legume and Mariana Toledo, "O Movimento Passe Livre São Paulo e a Tarifa Zero."

60 Coletivo Maria Tonha, "Ele ajudou a fundar o Movimento Passe Livre."

61 Adriana Saraiva, "Movimentos em movimiento," 99.

62 Raúl Zibechi, *Brasil potencia. Entre la integración regional y un nuevo imperialismo* (Bogotá: Desdeabajo, 2012).

63 Eliane Blum, "Também somos o chumbo das balas," *Época* (Rio de Janeiro), July 2013, accessed 08/30/13, http://revistaepoca.globo.com/Sociedade/eliane-brum/noticia/2013/07/tambem-somos-o-chumbo-das-balas.html.

INDEX

X

Y

Z

About AK Press

AK Press is one of the world's largest and most productive anarchist publishing houses. We're entirely worker-run and democratically managed. We operate without a corporate structure—no boss, no managers, no bullshit. We publish close to twenty books every year, and distribute thousands of other titles published by other like-minded independent presses from around the globe.

The Friends of AK program is a way that you can directly contribute to the continued existence of AK Press, and ensure that we're able to keep publishing great books just like this one! Friends pay $25 a month directly into our publishing account ($30 for Canada, $35 for international), and receive a copy of every book AK Press publishes for the duration of their membership! Friends also receive a discount on anything they order from our website or buy at a table: 50% on AK titles, and 20% on everything else. We've also added a new Friends of AK ebook program: $15 a month gets you an electronic copy of every book we publish for the duration of your membership. Combine it with a print subscription, too!

There's great stuff in the works—so sign up now to become a Friend of AK Press, and let the presses roll!

Email friendsofak@akpress.org for more info, or visit the Friends of AK Press website: www.akpress.org/programs/friendsofak